W9-CJT-006

17,50

THE ECONOMICS OF INNOVATION

The national and multinational enterprise
in technological change

The Economics of Innovation
The national and multinational enterprise in technological change

J. E. S. Parker

Longman

150731

338.06
P 241

LONGMAN GROUP LIMITED
London
*Associated companies, branches and representatives
throughout the world*

© J. E. S. Parker, 1974

All rights reserved. No part of this publication
may be reproduced, stored in a retrieval system,
or transmitted in any form or by any means, electronic,
mechanical, photocopying, recording, or otherwise,
without the prior permission of the Copyright owner.

First published 1974

ISBN 0 582 44609 0

Library of Congress Catalog
Card Number: 73–86111

*Set in I.B.M. Press Roman
by Santype Ltd. (Coldtype Division)
Salisbury, Wilts.*

*and Printed in Great Britain
by Lowe & Brydone (Printers) Ltd.,
Thetford, Norfolk*

Contents

Preface   vii

Acknowledgements   viii

1   Introduction   1

2   The competitive environment   6

3   Invention   19

4   Innovation   39

5   Management and innovation   81

6   The diffusion of innovation: the national company   99

7   Diffusion and the multinational enterprise:
    I. Technology   124

8   Diffusion and the multinational enterprise:
    II. Methodology and statistics   139

9   Diffusion and the multinational enterprise:
    III. Interpretation   176

10 Diffusion and the multinational enterprise:
    IV. The direct investment package   185

11 Patents   217

12 Conclusions   256

    Appendix 1. Classification of research intensive activities   258

    Appendix 2. Classification of the world's largest manufac-
    turing companies by their multinational
    status and their research intensity   260

    References   276

    Index   295

Preface

This study has arisen out of an interest in the economics of innovation and the stimulus of teaching final year students in the subject. The intention is to provide a survey and commentary on the process of innovation. Particular emphasis is given to the multinational enterprise as an agent in the diffusion of technology. The approach is micro in character and concentrates on the individual firm. These pages are addressed to the student of economics, but should be intelligible to the interested layman. Parts of this book have been submitted as a doctrinal dissertation to the University of Exeter.

D. G. Tucker of Extel Statistical Services, London, and Y. Schimada of Nomura Securities, London, have been very generous in providing statistics. Without this basic information, Chapters 7 and 8 would have suffered heavily. I am very grateful to them for their co-operation, and their enlightened attitude in allowing access to information which their organisations had compiled.

I would like to thank members of the Economics and Statistics Departments of the University of Exeter for their assistance with this project. Professor D. Walker, H. J. Dixon, Mrs A. C. Mayes, D. G. Mayes, F. M. M. Lewes, J. Matatko, J. F. Bradley, J. S. Chard, M. H. Cooper, and M. Macmillen have been very generous with their time and expertise.

F. V. Meyer and D. C. Corner have been exceptionally helpful and have encouraged me a great deal, and to them I owe a considerable debt of gratitude. Mrs G. M. Skinner and Miss C. Turner have been very helpful in the preparation of the statistics. Mrs H. F. Stead, Miss G. Pugh, Mrs A. B. Harris, Mrs S. Smith, Mrs A. Hill, and Mrs A. Kershaw have been very patient and tolerant of my handwriting in typing these pages; to them, thank you.

J. E. S. Parker

University of Exeter
May 1973

Acknowledgements

We are grateful to the following for permission to reproduce copyright material:
Addison-Wesley Publishing Co. Inc. for a table from *Effective Management of Research and Development* by A. Gerstenfeld, 1970, Addison-Wesley, Reading, Mass; Allen and Unwin Ltd for a table from *Economic Analysis and the Multinational Enterprise* edited by J. H. Dunning, 1973; Centre for the Study of Industrial Innovation for the table 'Summary of alleged causes of project shelving' from *On the Shelf* by the Centre for the Study of Industrial Innovation, 1971; Associated Book Publishers Ltd for the table 'Patents, Profitability, Liquidity and Firm Size' by D. J. Smith, J. M. Samuels and T. Tzoannes from *Applied Economics*, June 1972; Her Majesty's Stationery Office for the table from the *Report of the Committee of Inquiry on Small Firms (Bolten Report) Cmnd. 4811*; National Institute of Economic and Social Research for the table 'The Product Cycle' from 'United States electronics industry in international trade' by S. Hirsch from *National Institute Economic Review* No. 34, November 1965; Macmillan London and Basingstoke and W. W. Norton & Co Inc for the table 'Estimated Costs of Specific Developments' from *The Sources of Invention* by J. Jewkes, D. Sawers and R. Stillerman; Macmillan London and Basingstoke for three tables from *Wealth of Knowledge* by J. Langrish, M. Gibbons, W. G. Evans and F. R. Jevons; Organisation for Economic Co-operation and Development for tables from *Gaps in Technology — Plastics* by the O.E.C.D. Paris 1970; Princeton University Press for tables from *The Rate and Direction in Inventive Activity: Economic and Social Factors* by Richard A. Nelson, published by Princeton University Press (copyright (c) 1962 by National Bureau of Economic Research) section Table 1 p. 305 and Table 2 pp. 307-38. Reprinted by permission of Princeton University Press; Norton Bailey & Co for tables reprinted by permission from *The Economics of Technological Change* by Edwin Mansfield, published by W. W. Norton, New York, 1968 and Edwin Mansfield's *Industrial Research and Technological Innovation*, W. W. Norton, New York, 1971; The University of Sussex for a table from *Success and Failure in Industrial Innovation* by the Science Policy Research Unit of The University of Sussex; U.S. National Science Foundation for the table from *Industrial Market Structure and Economic Performance* by F. M. Scherer and in *Basic Research, Applied Research, and Development in Industry*, 1963.

We have been unable to trace the *Amer. Econ. Rev.* from which we have used material by F. M. Scherer and J. Markham. We would appreciate receiving any information that would enable us to do so.

Introduction

There is a crucial nexus between saving, investment, and innovation. Saving buys time to achieve better means of production. This is seen most clearly in a desert island economy. Robinson Crusoe may embody technological change by constructing, for example, a fishing net. This investment embodies an improved technology and enables him to improve his standard of living. One fishing trip may now provide food for a whole week. Previously, fishing by hand, most of his time was taken up in the activity. Later on Robinson Crusoe may indulge in what is known as disembodied technological change. For example, he may discover that if he casts his net in a particular fashion his catch will improve. No further investment is involved. Existing capital is used in a different way to improve efficiency. Now that Robinson Crusoe has purchased time by improving the efficiency of his fishing methods, he may apply himself to other schemes. He may improve his dwelling place, begin to till the land and so on. Thus his initial act of saving or not consuming, allows him to set in motion the investment and innovation process to improve his standard of living.

Other means of improving his material welfare may include specialisation, increases in the scale of activities, learning by experience, switching effort to more productive employment and general improvements in efficiency. By concentrating his efforts on a limited range of activities, Robinson Crusoe may enhance his skill. Specialisation normally implies a monetised economy so that particular outputs can be easily exchanged for all the other requirements of life. Enlargement of the size of operations may bring economies of scale. Increased output may be secured at lower unit costs. Familiarity with an activity may bring benefits through 'learning by doing'.[1] Switching effort to more productive employment concerns the allocation of resources. Robinson Crusoe may tend to devote more time to highly productive activities. He may also be able to attract labour by the high wage rates he is able to pay. This inflow of resources may result in increased specialisation and scale economies. General improvements in efficiency may be secured by reducing organisational slack.[2] There is probably room for improvement in any organisation. The effectiveness and quality of management is highly relevant here. Another factor relevant to efficiency is the strength of competition. Where there is a large number of producers competing in a given market, rivalry imposes a minimum standard of performance. But, as will be explained in Chapter 4 on innovation, this does not necessarily imply that a competitive market form is the most conducive to innovation.

If Robinson Crusoe is lucky he may enjoy what has been called the virtuous circle.[3] His ingenuity and inventiveness may result in the development of new products, new markets and new capital equipment. His skill as a manager may also improve the efficiency of the use of existing capital and generally raise the level of competence of factors engaged in economic activity. Achieved success may encourage further savings and investment activity. Many new techniques may be embodied in production. Increased output, higher labour productivity and higher real wages may all serve to improve aspiration levels and expectations. The general level of economic efficiency may be upgraded. Technological progress may make capital goods relatively cheap, thus encouraging the substitution of capital for labour. Wage-cost pressure may similarly encourage more intensive use of capital equipment and further increases in capital per man. International trade may be encouraged by favourable market opportunities. Worldwide trade will make resource constraints relative. Imports and exports will extend the possibilities of specialisation and make the particular resource endowment of the island less important. Prior to international trade, the economy's factor endowment was in a sense absolute. With overseas trade this becomes relative. The economy will go forward with the virtuous circle operating in its favour. Expectations, investment and standards of living will respond as success breeds success.

In contrast, the island economy may suffer from the vicious circle in operation. New products, new markets and improved methods of production may be accepted slowly. As a result the commercial rewards to the venturesome are poor. They are not encouraged to maintain high investment levels. Labour productivity thus grows slowly. International competitiveness may suffer and the balance of payments move into deficit. Action may be taken to curb the deteriorating trade position, and may include restrictions on demand, increased taxation or higher interest rates. These measures may aggravate the tendency towards low investment levels. Devaluation may also be part of the corrective package. This will improve the price competitiveness of new and old activities. But it may actually diminish the pressure to innovate by giving a new lease of commercial life to traditional goods which were previously tending to become uncompetitive on international markets. This may suggest that devaluation may be an inappropriate remedy for economies that have to rely on innovational advantage to maintain and improve their standard of living.[4]

In modern economies the link between savings, investment and innovation appears less clear. Activities tend to be highly specialised and are complicated by institutional arrangements. These may confuse the casual observer into believing that the principles which apply in a desert island economy may no longer be relevant. In practice, the primary mechanisms remain just as powerful. There is no escape from the basic rules. Savings and investment must occur and technological change remains a major determinant of productivity levels. New goods, new processes and improved services are an important source of enhanced living standards. In fact, of all the potential ways of improving the performance of modern economies, technological change is probably the most important.[5] Without invention and innovation it is highly likely than improvements in living standards would occur at a much reduced rate.

It is difficult to underestimate the importance of innovation to modern economies. In quantitative terms the development of new products and processes may be a relatively small part of current economic activity. Firms, by and large, repeat what has been done in the past. Nevertheless, innovative activity is crucially important for a number of reasons.

First, new goods tend to be growth points in companies' turnover. Innovation induces changes in production methods and output mix which may spread throughout the economy. An initial change may breed other changes, so that a relatively minor original investment in a single innovation may induce a whole series of consequential alterations. With enough time for the process to work itself through, the level of performance and growth potential of industries and economies may be upgraded. Pressures for change may come from enhanced competitive power of the innovating company, and the superior commercial performance of firms which copy quickly. They may arise from the exacting demands made on suppliers, from market opportunities in other activities where the innovation has an application, and by a strong demonstration effect where the success of a dynamic company inspires others to similar efforts. The induced or consequential effects arising from an innovation are sometimes referred to as the technological multiplier. A prime example is provided by the electronic computer. This development has had worldwide ramifications and is probably one of the most important technologies evolved during the twentieth century.

Second, innovations usually produce sophisticated goods. Their novelty and/or superior performance may have sufficient customer attraction to make the price of the article a subsidiary determinant of sales. They may thus provide a high cost economy with a means to earn an international living. They may also ease particular resource constraints. Thus, for example, where labour is scarce and costly, superior production methods may secure increased output per unit labour cost. This may be crucial to economies which have reached an advanced state of development.

Technological change involves a multilayered process. It involves a complex coupling process through a number of stages from origination to final use. Invention, innovation and diffusion are involved. The generation of a new idea is usually called invention and the coupling process innovation. Spreading of an innovation, its emulation and copying throughout firms, industries and countries, is diffusion. Intra-firm diffusion is the rate of displacement of the old by the new within companies. The conventional distinction between invention and innovation should not be slavishly maintained. The distinction turns on the origination of an idea as invention and its application as innovation.

The distinction should not be overpressed for the following reasons. The sources of invention are mixed. They may emanate from inventive effort *per se*, or from innovational effort. Individuals are probably becoming less important in the inventive process. As companies become the predominant inventors, the commercial element in the process will strengthen. This would indicate that the distinction between the origination and its application is narrowing. To adopt a strict definition of invention and innovation would obscure understanding of the process of technological change. Motives are mixed in the search for new knowledge. Profit may predominate, but the search for knowledge for its own sake may also be an important element, even in commercially orientated organisations. There is also a growing body of evidence that invention is a commercially orientated process which may be explained in terms of revenue and demand factors, rather than random and genius elements.[6]

This book will be concerned with the generation of innovations, how they spread, and what effects they have on firms, companies and commercial activity. The usual definitions of invention and innovation are merged to serve the purpose of increasing understanding of the mechanisms which generate technological change at the level of the individual firm and industry. This is a grass-roots approach which attempts to get at the sources of invention and innovations, and explain the means whereby they are spread. The approach is micro in character and will focus largely on the company as an instrument of technological change. Towards the end of the book the approach is broadened somewhat to analyse the role of the multinational producing enterprise in the diffusion of technology. Nevertheless the context of the discussion remains that of the firm, even though the scope widens to include location across many countries. Chapter 10, on Patents, is also somewhat broader in approach. This is concerned with the impact of legally enforceable periods of protection on the incentive to invent. But again the context of the discussion is that of the firm.

A major area of discussion which is not covered in this book is government intervention in research and development. The reason for this exclusion is connected with the micro approach adopted. The principles and practicalities that determine official allocation of funds to R and D are part of overall government strategy in the running of economies. This is broader in scope than the general approach adopted here. Admittedly companies are often the recipients of government funds to be spent on research. Nevertheless this aspect of the economics of innovation is not covered. The exclusion is not intended as a comment on the importance of government involvement in technological change. It merely reflects the micro approach adopted.

2

The competitive environment

In today's world companies are typically multiproduct in character. Activities are spread across many areas of commercial interest. The large single-product, highly specialised company is becoming something of a rarity. Diversified output is normal. By broadening the product base, a company should secure greater stability of results, and avoid some of the fluctuations in profitability which are a feature of small companies.[1] This greater stability of results should make for continuity of investment and allow a company to offer long-term employment prospects to its personnel. In a sense, diversified output is a reflection of the tendency towards bigness. The large company can secure all the benefits associated with specialisation and yet enjoy the commercial insurance which comes from a spread of interest. Each product line can be large enough to yield the economies associated with volume production, and the personnel involved can develop the particular skills derived from specialisation. With a multidivision form of company organisation, each division can be a specialised production unit, largely autonomous in its day-to-day affairs and yet subject to overall control from head office. In these terms, the large corporation does not sacrifice scale economies to secure the advantages of diversification. Instead it compounds its benefits by aggregation. The totality of activities covered by all of the divisions is wide, and yet each one serves a specialist function.

The range of activities covered by a large modern company can be very wide. For such companies, classification to a particular industry is likely to be misleading. Their product line may spread across many industries and defy neat summary. Conglomerate companies are examples. Their interests are so broad that classification to areas of activities rather than particular industries is more appropriate. Another interesting feature of the modern large corporation is the tendency towards multinationalism. The scope of locational options has now widened beyond the shores of the home country. Many companies now locate on a global basis and produce abroad for distribution abroad. The parent company becomes the centre of a multinational organisation where both activities and locations are diversified.

Diversified output and the multinational form of organisation make for some difficulties. Models of competition used by economists often relate to single-product companies, operating wholly within particular industries. Competitive conditions are assumed to vary with the number of competitors. Thus a large number of rivals selling a similar article, will approximate to a situation of perfect competition. Alternatively, a single producer with no rivals will act like a monopolist. Where there are fewer competitors, producing broadly similar products, inter-mediate forms of competition will apply. Oligopoly and monopolistic competition are the terms used to describe these types of rivalry. Once the complications of multiproduct organisation and transnational location are admitted, the explanatory power of single-product, single-industry models of economic behaviour becomes somewhat limited. Competitive conditions may now vary widely between differ-ent sections of a company's turnover. A company may be a sole producer of one article, and one of a thousand in another. Overseas plants may serve a monopolistic market in one country, and a severely competitive one in another. Political, tax, tariff and exchange regula-tions may be paramount influences determining the behaviour of a multinational company. In these circumstances, usage of the models of competition has to be circumspect.

The complications of product mix can to some extent be avoided by confining descriptions of the type of rivalry to specific products. Similarly, multinational organisations can to some extent be allowed for by confining observations to particular products in particular countries. However, even this procedure is likely to be unsatisfactory. The existence of an international organisation behind the particular company under scrutiny, is likely to make a considerable difference to its economic behaviour. The pretence that one branch of a multi-national will conform to the behaviour pattern that would be relevant to a comparable independent autonomous company, is unlikely to be verified. In essence, therefore, the simple head-counting procedure to classify the type of commercial environment facing today's large corporation, is likely to be highly misleading.

The complexity of modern competitive conditions is further com-pounded by innovation and differentiation. Innovative effort may create new products. Alternatively, products may be varied slightly and thus differentiated in the eyes of customers. Changed selling effort, improvement in the subjective image of the product, a new emphasis, better performance, a different location more convenient to customers, and improved service, any of these may enhance the value of the article to the buyer. Differentiation is really a minor form of innovative effort. Innovation is rather more than the development of invention. Market-ing and the general presentation to customers are part of the activity. Differentiation and innovation are distinguished, however, to emphasise a qualitative difference. Differentiation relates to small alterations which include branding, selling effort and minor changes in the physical characteristics of goods. Innovation is more fundamental and involves major changes. A significant alteration is secured in the character of the article concerned. Performance is improved, or customer appeal radically altered.

The effect of differentiation and innovation is to add a further dimension to the complexity of competition. Emphasis is now given to variation in the quality of the saleable article. Commercial rivalry takes a non-price form. Competition comes to mean product, as well as price competition. Under these conditions, customers must be informed of the superior quality of the 'new' goods. Advertising expenditure therefore becomes a significant commercial expense. Customer education and persuasion to secure volume production, becomes a part of everyday life. This type of competition may be no less dynamic than the more conventional form of price rivalry: '. . . non-price rivalry can be a dynamic, dog-eat-dog affair.'[2] Furthermore it is likely to have more relevance to the rate of technological progress than competition based on price.

The distinction between product and innovative competition is an important one. Another term sometimes used to describe innovative competition is technological competition.[3] Firms anxious to compete through innovative excellence are normally heavily committed to research and development. They are also normally involved in industries where research expenditures are high. Such companies attempt to improve their technology through 'in-house' innovative effort. Companies competing through mere differentiation need not undertake R and D. Minor alterations in the physical properties of a product, or a new selling angle, do not require the expense or expertise demanded by genuine innovational effort. This distinction is not intended to denigrate the importance of differentiation in consumer want satisfaction. It is intended to emphasise a difference in the type of effort involved in the activities. Innovative competition is usually associated with technologically advanced industries. Examples include pharmaceuticals, plastics, electronics and computers. In these industries R and D expenditure is considerable, and company participation in technological change is high. There is an active rather than passive interest in securing improved products and competition emphasises this type of rivalry. Companies are not content to adopt developments originating elsewhere. Instead they are actively engaged in adding to the impetus of technological change. The contrast with such industries as building, furniture and footwear, is considerable. Here expenditure on R and D is low and dramatic changes in the nature of products rare. Often changes are imported from other industries. In this sense, the drive to innovate is passive. Reliance is mainly on minor alterations in the products to secure competitive advantage.

The expectation that innovative competition will always be associated with R and D intensive industries should not be overstressed. The concept of innovative competition relates to particular products and not to industries. Thus it is quite possible that there will be this type of rivalry among some products in an industry which does not have a technological reputation. As will be made clear below, innovative competition may be one phase in the life cycle of a product.

Innovative competition is a concept that has yet to be absorbed into conventional theory. Models of company behaviour normally assume that the product under scrutiny has largely stabilised in its technology and production methods. Concern is to discover equilibrium levels of price and output, and then to make comment on the efficiency of the resultant allocation of resources. This approach makes the theory of limited value to those interested in innovation. Innovation results in new products and processes, and emphasises technological change. Both these characteristics are largely outside the explanatory power of most theories of the firm.[4] It may be fair comment to assert that the emphasis on the efficiency of resource allocation in these models is becoming less and less relevant to the modern world. It is probably true that the rate of technological progress is more important to the economic wellbeing of nations than the particular manner in which resources are allocated. This is certainly the view adhered to here. For example, it may be true that for a fast rate of innovation a fairly imperfect market form of a 'big firm, few firm' variety is appropriate. This is likely to clash with the requirements for efficient resource allocation when 'small firm, many firm' competition has an advantage. In the compromise that may be prescribed by legal and governmental action it is the author's bias that the emphasis should be towards securing a high rate of innovation. In other words, competition should remain 'workable', but not of such rigour that technological incentive is largely destroyed.[5]

With the process of innovation, differentiation and emulation, products are subject to economic and technical obsolescence. Their commercial life becomes limited. Any economic advantage is likely to be temporary. Once a new product or a variant of a new product is seen to be successful, rivals will begin to encroach. They will copy, modify and improve, so that they may share in the earning power of the new product. In these circumstances companies are only likely to retain a lead by continual change. A process of continuous innovation may therefore be generated by the activities of discovery, marketing and emulation. For a particular article, the type of competition will fluctuate over time. It will go through what has become known as the product cycle.[6] Early in its life it will command premium earning capacity reflecting newness and innovational edge. Gradually this economic seniority will be eroded and eventually the product will become a standard article of no novelty.

For convenience of exposition the commercial history of a particular product may be divided into three phases. These phases describe in broad fashion the major periods of the product life cycle. The basis of the classification relates to the character of competition. In Phase I the product is new. The innovating company has a marked commercial advantage. There are essentially no close substitutes. Demand for the goods tends to be high and price inelastic. It also tends to be income elastic. Such products are likely to be fairly sophisticated in character and thus find outlets where incomes are high and rising. In these early days, production runs are short and technological change rapid. Competition is likely to be of the innovative variety. Early disadvantages of the product are ironed out, guided by initial market experience and the efforts of early imitators. Scientific and technical man-power will be a high proportion of the labour input, during this introductory stage, and production will be relatively labour intensive.

Competition is clearly likely to be of a non-price variety in this early period. There are few rivals offering a substitute product. Performance characteristics and novelty allow the innovating company considerable pricing discretion. The product is sufficiently different to make the price charged merely one of a number of considerations affecting sales. How long innovative competition will persist is dependent on a number of considerations. If the technological possibilities in the field are great, competitors may respond by improvement and modification of the original product. They will go beyond emulation in their response to the initial success of the originating company. Demand prospects will also be a major determinant of the likely response. Where customers value improvements, and where companies have the knowhow to respond, conditions will favour innovative competition. The techno-logical environment and customer requirements will induce rivalry based on significant product improvement. Technological push and customer pull will operate to generate change. Under these conditions, the level of R and D may be a major indicator of the type of competition prevalent. Where R and D expenditure is considerable, management commitment to change is high. Rivalry is therefore likely to be based on product improvement. Research and development levels may not, however, be an entirely dependable indicator of the type of competition. As the technology of a particular product is exhausted, it may take progressively larger expenditures to yield even minor advances. Similarly, for a company to enter such an industry, the R and D expenditure necessary to become an effective competitor may be much higher at a later stage when development has in fact slowed down.[7]

As time passes the product moves towards Phase II. The introductory stage of the innovation is now over. Uncertainty associated with the market or technology of the new product, is largely dispelled. Knowledge and use of the article are becoming more widespread. The technology is now more stabilised and standardised production techniques become appropriate. Mass production becomes sensible. The importance of scientific and technical personnel in the labour force begins to decline. Competition becomes stronger. There are more companies in the market, and the character of rivalry may shade towards product competition. Differentiation which does not impair volume production may become common. As pointed out earlier, it is not at all clear how long innovative rivalry will postpone the onset of this phase. Some products have great development potential and may stave off this maturing process longer than others. Eventually, however, a stage is likely to be reached where producers compete on the basis of minor improvements in their version of the article.

Eventually a product may move into Phase III. Substitutes are beginning to be prevalent. Demand may even have passed its zenith and be declining. The technology is by now almost entirely stabilised. The product is fully mature. There are no longer any significant improvements coming forward. Scientific and technical manpower becomes progressively less important. Capital intensive and mass production methods are virtually obligatory for survival for companies dependent on this article. In fact, it is around Phase II/III that the multinational company may locate factories in low wage cost countries to enhance its competitive position. Production has become so cost dependent, that such a company may exercise its global locational option and produce abroad. The output may then be imported back into the originating country. However it is probably the case that cost factors may not be a predominant influence in the location pattern of multinational companies. As will be explained in some detail in the chapters on diffusion and the multinational enterprise (Chapters 7–9), the major influence is probably on the revenue and not the cost side. Such companies are likely to be anxious to exploit the commercial advantage which their innovations bring, and at the same time be ready to respond to developments secured by rivals. Multinationals may tend to be concentrated in technology-intensive activities. These involve goods in Phase I or II. These goods are not fully stabilised in their technology and may not be suitable for large scale production methods. Once a product reaches Phase III, competition may be so fierce that it is worth while seeking low labour cost locations. Mass production methods are suitable because the technology has largely stabilised and major changes in production methods are unlikely. A locational mix is therefore predicted which suggests that cost orientated locations are likely to be associated with mature or Phase III products, and market orientated locations with Phase I or II type products.

Phase III may eventually result in a monopoly or cartel type of structure. Fierce competition arising from the incursions of rivals may induce a defensive response by the major producers. If there are large companies amongst manufacturers of this hypothetical product, they may be in a position to monopolise the market. Large size may yield sufficient economies of scale to drive rivals out of business. Alternatively, such big concerns may not have a marked cost advantage. In this case, they may use other devices to crush rivals. Cross-subsidisation of this product from other more profitable areas of their turnover, may eliminate specialist rivals. Interlocking directorates, part ownership of competitors and conditional or exclusive marketing arrangements are other sorts of devices that may be used. In addition the major companies may group together to form cartels. Such joint selling ventures may be established as a result of the fierceness of competition. Companies may be driven to defend the capital invested in the product by regulating competition. This is likely to happen after a prolonged price war has convinced the survivors that joint action is appropriate. A monopoly or cartel in such circumstances is not necessarily unfavourable. Exploitation of the market is likely to be limited by memory of the conditions which gave rise to current circumstances, and by the possible entrance of new rivals.

The time taken for products to move through the various types of competition will vary widely. A major determinant of the speed at which products pass through the stages will be their economic characteristics. In the pharmaceutical industry, maturity of a product occurs pretty quickly. An innovating company will only have a relatively short time before rivals make serious inroads into the market. Substitute drugs are likely to take over the greater share of any recently established market within a period of five years.[8] In this industry innovative competition is strong. The maturity of a particular product is hastened by the development of alternatives with superior clinical properties. Rivals do not merely copy, they also tend to improve. A product suffers from technical as well as economic obsolescence. The time span of market superiority therefore tends to be severely truncated. In other industries, where the pressures to emulate are not so strong, the time scale may be much longer. In steel-making technology, the pace of change is relatively leisurely. The time scale is measured in decades rather than years.[9] The economic characteristics of innovations are such that adoption, diffusion and emulation are not swift. Technological competition is apparently not so prevalent. An innovation is perhaps subject only to economic obsolescence. Rivals merely erode the market position of the originating company by copying, not by improving. Of course, the progress of the product cycle outlined above is highly schematic. There are many possible hindrances affecting the working and time scale of the cycle. Thus, patents may debar effective rivalry until the period of protection is over. Products may not pass through all the phases. Innovative competition may not develop. The originating company may have exhausted the technological possibilities early on. Alternatively, the market may be relatively limited for the new article, so potential competitors are content to allow the innovator to continue with a virtual monopoly. These are examples of real world influences which may prevent the product cycle working out in the stylised fashion related above. Table 2.1 sets out in summary form the stages through the product cycle. Schemes put forward by various authors differ in detail, but the broad outline follows the general pattern indicated.[10]

Table 2.1 The product cycle

Characteristics	Cycle phase		
	Early	*Growth*	*Mature*
Technology	Short runs; rapidly changing techniques; dependence on external economies.	Mass production methods gradually introduced; variations in techniques still frequent	Long runs and stable technology; few innovations of importance
Capital intensity	Low	High, due to high obsolescence rate	High, due to large quantity of specialised equipment
Industry structure	Entry is knowhow determined; numerous firms providing specialised services	Growing number of firms; many casualties and mergers; growing vertical integration	Financial resources critical for entry; number of firms declining
Critical human inputs	Scientific and engineering	Management	Unskilled and semi-skilled labour
Demand structure	Sellers' market Performance and price	Individual producers face growing price elasticity; intra-industry competition reduces prices; product information spreading	Buyers' market; information easily available

Source. S. Hirsch, 'United States electronics industry in international trade', *National Institute Economic Review*, **34**, November 1965.

The pricing of a product will change in character through its life cycle. In Phase I the innovating company is likely to adopt a pricing policy based on what may be termed a cost plus, market orientated outlook. The innovational edge of the new good allows a price premium reflecting the advance over the nearest substitute product. In this sense the decision will be market orientated. There is likely to be considerable freedom in setting the price. There are no close rivals and so price will probably reflect what the market will bear. The decision will also be based on a cost plus outlook, in the sense that an important bench mark in pricing is likely to be average costs. Average costs are an important influence in pricing because the originating company is aware that as output expands, overhead costs incurred in development and production start-up are spread over a greater turnover. As a result, average costs per unit will probably decline. In these circumstances, marginal cost pricing would be wholly inappropriate. Such a procedure would not recoup total costs because when average costs fall marginal cost is less than average cost. A loss would inevitably follow such a pricing strategy. This is why average costs are referred to as a benchmark. The company concerned will be aware that full cost pricing will provide a starting point from which to add the market premium, reflecting the innovational advantage of the new product.

During Phase II the pricing freedom of the innovator becomes more constrained. There are now more competitors. Customers have the choice of substitute products which are now similar in character to the original. They will therefore tend to buy much more on price considerations. The market for this product is now moving towards a situation where the selling price is heavily influenced by rivals' prices. The distinctive properties of the original version of the good still will have some influence, but this is likely to decline as competition becomes stronger. When Phase II shades into Phase III the pricing discretion of companies will largely vanish. Output will tend to be adjusted to price. Individual companies will become price-takers and quantity makers. Product development will be largely exhausted. Production processes will have settled and economies of scale will be exploited. Pricing in these circumstances is likely to be based on marginal cost. Average cost will no longer be declining, and marginal costs are likely to be greater than average costs. The ability of a company to compete in these circumstances, will be determined largely by its capacity to organise production to minimise costs. The market form is likely to be very competitive and differentiation of a peripheral nature. If the market should move beyond competition to monopoly or cartel the character of the pricing decision is likely to change yet again. Pricing under the new conditions is likely to take on an administered flavour: concepts of fair and reasonable may creep into the negotiations between the parties concerned; the government may even act as overseer and regulate activities. Political considerations may become important.[11]

The progression through the phases of competition indicate that the 'vintage' or age of the product concerned is important. This suggests that price will start high and decline over time. In the early days, the innovating company will use its commercial advantage to secure fast recoupment of development expenses. It will also be aware that success will attract competitors, so that a high price is only likely to be possible in the early period. As time passes the technology stabilises and volume production becomes common. Costs of production fall and increased competition induces companies to pass the benefits to consumers. Later still, innovation elsewhere may force an even lower price on companies in an attempt to retain markets. As a response to technological obsolescence, they may use low prices as a trade-off for waning attraction. A price pattern over time similar to that in Fig. 2.1 is predicted.

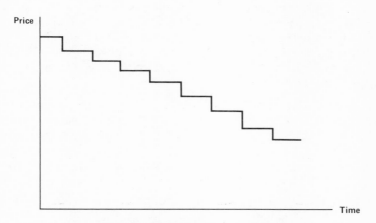

Fig. 2.1 Price pattern over time

This pattern is found with a considerable number of innovations. Table 2.2 gives some examples drawn from the plastics industry in the UK.

Table 2.2 Prices in different sectors of the UK plastics industry

	1960	*1961*	*1962*	*1963*	*1964*	*1965*
PVC granular polymer	100	90	80	80	80	80
Low density polyethylene	100	81	75	76	73	68
High density polyethylene	100	79	73	73	69	65
Polypropylene	100	89	79	70	62	62
Polystyrene GP clear	100	82	77	77	72	69
UF powder (white)	100	100	100	100	100	102
PF powder (black)	100	100	100	100	100	100

Source. OECD, *Gaps in Technology,* Paris, 1970.

Taking 1960 as the base year, Table 2.2 reveals that in the UK, high density polyethylene declined from 100 to 65 by 1965. Polypropylene shows a similar pattern, with an index number value of 62 in 1965. Data from Italy, Japan and the USA reveal a similar general pattern of price decline.[1 2]

Evidence that the product life cycle is a realistic concept is considerable.[1 3] Diffusion studies also provide confirmation. The emphasis with these studies is on the stages of demand relevant to particular innovations. Demand for a new product by users, is seen as passing through four stages: introduction, growth, maturity and decline. A fifth stage, saturation, is sometimes inserted between maturity and decline.[1 4] Demand for innovation starts in a hesitant fashion, then the product begins to catch on. Adoption by consumers accelerates through the growth stage and gradually maturity begins to set in. Eventually the market may become saturated and sales may be largely confined to replacements. Demand may then decline, accelerated perhaps by the appearance of an innovation which renders the original article technically and economically obsolescent. These stages in the demand pattern, correspond broadly to the phases of competition described above.

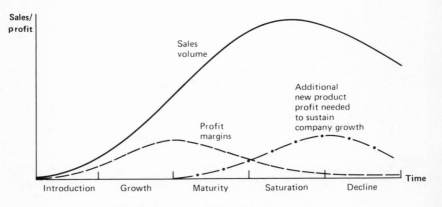

Fig. 2.2 An innovation in a company

Source. T. S. Robertson, *Innovative Behaviour and Communication* (ref. 10).

Figure 2.2 represents the commercial fortunes of an innovating company. It is an amalgam of the demand pattern for a 'representative' innovation found by diffusion studies, and the product life cycle concept. The diagram shows, in a stylised fashion, the spread of usage of an innovation and the economic consequences that follow to the innovating company. Changes in the competitive environment are reflected in the profit margin achieved over time. Thus peak profitability is not achieved when sales volume is at its highest. By this time, there are sufficient competitors to have creamed away the advantage of the innovating company. The most profitable time occurs when sales volumes are in the growth stage. Figure 2.2 also highlights the consequences of economic obsolescence for a dynamic company. The limited economic life of innovations suggests that ambitious companies will require a series of products in the pipeline, so that growth may be sustained. The quicker products succumb to obsolescence, the more vital is the need for diversification. Innovation is thus seen, not only as a means to secure technological progress, but also as a defence from the consequences of limited product life. The curve labelled 'additional new product profit needed to sustain company growth' draws attention in a blunt and almost overdramatic fashion, to the importance of a flow of new products to company growth. Innovation is a major means of providing that flow. Research and development is a company expense deliberately incurred to create innovations. The product cycle erodes economic advantage: research and development attempts to avert this by providing the next generation of novelties. One function of research and development thus becomes obvious. It provides the means and services the impetus to diversify. In fact it is not implausible to assert that companies with competent R and D teams have a built-in tendency to widen their product base.[1][5]

Under modern economic conditions the function of a research and development department becomes complex. In general terms such an organisation may be represented as an 'in-house' generator of technological change. But the motivation to carry this expenditure is likely to be mixed. Concern to maintain or improve profits is likely to be a motive common to all companies. Beyond this, R and D can serve many purposes. It can be a means to effect fast response to the innovations of rivals. This listening post function can soften the blow of competition by reducing the lead time secured by a company first in the field. R and D can provide the capability to speed the process of diversification and is also a powerful means to effect differentiation of a company's goods. The level of technological knowledge required to be an effective competitor in an industry may be a fairly strong barrier to new entrants. R and D can increase a company's stranglehold in a particular field by giving rise to a patent position. In this way a legally enforceable 'road-block' is erected against potential newcomers. The research and development department is thus seen as a many-faced creature capable of being used in a variety of ways. It can serve the process of technological change. It can also be a hindrance. Innovative competition may not arise out of research expenditure. Technological ingenuity may be used to suppress the efforts of rivals. Research effort may be devoted to achieving peripheral alterations which have consumer appeal, but little impact on technology. Research and development is a direct means to increase the pace of change. But the assumption that it will always serve this end is naive. Decision-making is complex and the competitive process sometimes obscure in its operation.

Summary

The modern corporation is typically multiproduct. It may also be multinational in character. Innovation and differentiation are important weapons of competitive strategy. Innovative competition is usually associated with technologically advanced industries. There is an active interest in technological change. This is reflected in research and development spending. The product cycle summarises the stages through which an innovation passes in the process of becoming an accepted article of no novelty. Economic and technical obsolescence eventually set in. Premium earning capacity is eroded under the pressure of competition. The time taken for this to occur varies from product to product, and reflects the economic environment relevant to the activity concerned. With limited product life, companies will take steps to ensure their commercial future. They may diversify. They may undertake R and D to provide them with a stream of innovations and to facilitate a quick response to the developments of rivals. They may also locate around the world to defer the onset of economic obsolescence of their product. The connection between research orientation and location policy is examined in the chapters on diffusion and the multinational enterprise (Chapters 7–9). The next chapter will be concerned with the economic features of invention.

Invention

Invention involves origination. It is the first stage in the process of technological innovation. 'Invention then is the act of insight by which a new and promising technical possibility is recognised and worked out (at least mentally and perhaps also physically) in its essential, most rudimentary form.'[1] Notice that in this definition no attempt is made to separate invention from the process of innovation. The Schumpeterian approach where invention is treated as a distinct activity, is not adopted.[2] Invention must precede innovation but it is not helpful to treat it as a separate process. There is not a tidy separation between the functions. The distinction should be made but not over-pressed. There is a difference in kind. Innovation is the coupling process which brings new ideas to the market place. However, it is often difficult to separate the two activities. 'Invention and innovation are to be distinguished, but they are not separate. They are often inextricably inter-linked because they stand mutually in a mixed cause relationship: each is part cause, part effect of the other.'[3] Invention can and does arise from the process of commercialisation. The inventive step can be difficult to trace. The source of ideas is often diffuse and imprecise. Individuals are becoming less important as inventors, at least in terms of patent numbers.[4] Companies are becoming predominant. Origination and application are merging as companies become more and more important in technological change.

Invention is in practice part of the process of innovation. To exclude a discussion of invention in deference to a strict definition would incur high costs. It would hamper understanding of the process whereby new knowledge is harnessed to production. In these terms invention is best treated as that subset of technical innovations which are patentable.[5] Patents are granted for tangible items which incorporate sufficient novelty to qualify. There is origination, but it typically takes the form of technology building on technology. Each patent relates to an aspect and not the whole of a product and each inventive step is really an innovative step representing an improvement of an original product. This theme will be developed during this chapter.

Theories of invention

There are three general theories of invention: the transcendentalist, the mechanistic and the cumulative synthesis.[6] The transcendentalist approach attributes invention to the inspiration of genius. Rare and infrequent flashes of insight yield brilliant ideas which become path breaking inventions. This is the traditional picture, where the individual plays a crucial role. The lone inventor makes a great impact on technology by a single creative thought. His flash of genius is largely independent of economic forces. Curiosity and fortuitous events are major elements. The mechanistic approach adopts the view that invention proceeds under the stress of necessity. Need dictates the direction of change and inventions emerge. In this approach economic forces predominate. Invention is not visualised as an autonomous process yielding to unpredictable events. Costs and revenue considerations become crucial. The individual and lone genius revolutionising technology with his curiosity orientated bent, is rejected as the typical source of invention. 'There is no indication that any individual's genius has been necessary to any invention that has had any importance. To the historian and social scientist the progress of invention appears impersonal.'[7]

The last approach sees major invention emerging from the cumulative synthesis of what has preceded. These inventions require an act of insight to overcome resistance or discontinuity. They are likely to occur to individuals who are directly concerned with the problem and its solution. The requirement of the act of insight reduces the predictability of the event. It is not certain that it will occur. Unlike the mechanistic approach, the individual is not merely an instrument in an inevitable historical process. He has an important role to play. His role is not that of the transcendentalist's genius who is struck by a brilliant idea, but rather of the mind engaged in the solution of technical problems. The act of insight will be conditioned by the specific problems encountered, and if and when it does occur will be through a synthesis of previous knowledge. This approach is probably the most realistic. Invention is not dependent on the emergence of a genius, nor is it an inevitable process dictated by the passage of time and economic pressures. Certainly, necessity will hustle invention forwards; wartime experience verifies this. Similarly great men emerge to make great inventions, but these occurrences are not the typical. Theories of invention must describe the usual not the rare. In these terms, the cumulative synthesis approach is probably the most plausible.

Sources of invention

Before unqualified support is given to cumulative synthesis, it is necessary to examine in greater detail the forces influencing invention. These will include the source of invention, the contribution of individuals and the role of economic forces.

Ideas occur in a large number of ways and come from a wide variety of sources. The most obvious source should be research and development activity. R and D is expenditure deliberately aimed at creation and improvement. Patentable ideas should be a natural product. The conventional distinction in the types of R and D is basic, applied and development. Basic research is concerned with a search for knowledge for its own sake. Fundamental principles and concepts are sought. The activity is not commercially orientated and not necessarily concerned to produce tangible outputs. The search is for understanding, not for marketable products. It is curiosity and not mission orientated. This type of research is consequently not often undertaken by companies. Universities and institutions are principally involved and typically this is financed by governments. Applied research is concerned with investigation to obtain knowledge with a commercial application. This is clearly more appropriate to company activities. Private industry accounts for approximately 65 per cent in the United States and 56 per cent for the United Kingdom.[8] Development research uses the results of basic and applied research and is directed towards the introduction of new products or applications, and may include the prototype and pilot plant stages. This is the means whereby ideas become commercial reality. Over 85 per cent in the United States and over 90 per cent in the United Kingdom is carried out by companies.

In terms of origination, basic research would appear to be the area most likely to yield invention. New principles and concepts are discovered by research at the frontiers of knowledge. Highly qualified personnel are involved in this search for improved understanding of basic principles. Discoveries of worldwide importance result. However, the relationship between basic discoveries of this character and technological change is a subject of some controversy. Views differ as to the role of basic science in the generation of inventions. Some insist that technological advance will dry up without the impetus of basic research. Others argue that technology only has an indirect connection with fundamental research and tends to have its own impetus fed from within. Certainly basic scientific research tends not to generate tangible inventions. Output typically takes the form of an increase in scientific knowhow. This is reported in learned journals and spread by contacts amongst the academic community.

The means whereby this information affects the production process is complex and not well understood. The most potent factor in spreading this understanding would appear not to be scrutiny and absorption of publications, but the movement of personnel already versed in the new knowledge.[9] Essentially the problem is to trace the contribution of basic research which is generally carried out in universities, government departments and institutions, in generating technological development. A number of studies attempt this. In

Technology in Retrospect and Critical Events in Science (TRACES), a report to the National Science Foundation in the USA,[10] it was found that non-mission orientated research was crucial in the key events leading to the development of the video-tape recorder, magnetic ferrites, the oral contraceptive pill, the electron microscope and matrix isolation. Similarly links were established between basic research by the Office of Naval Research[11] in the Navy. Project Hindsight on the other hand found little relation to basic science.[12] Critical events leading to the development of weapon systems did not reveal a close dependence. Apparently basic science was not a crucial source of ideas on which this weapon technology depended. In a study of publications in science and technology, it was found that direct interconnection between the fields are not frequent and that technology builds on technology.[13] Similarly in a study in the UK of Queen's Award winning developments the same conclusion was reached. Only a handful of direct connections was found, and the authors conclude 'that the great bulk of basic science bears only tenuously if at all on the operations of industry'.[14]

It is by no means self-evident that basic scientific research provides the discoveries which industry takes up and applies. The connections between the types of activity can be indirect and complex. Furthermore they can be two-way. Discoveries in industry can lead to basic research in an attempt to understand the processes involved. There appear to be three ways in which basic scientific research affects industry. The first is by techniques of investigation. Universities and institutions teach and develop methods and procedures of research. These techniques are passed on and become integrated into industry. The second is that trained personnel transfer from basic research institutions to industry. The third arises from the generation of a new technology or a tangible item which may be used in industry. The most important means may well be the transfer of personnel to industry. Direct benefits via the creation of usable products are probably relatively rare. Nuclear power and silicones are examples.[15] The fact that the benefits of basic scientific research may typically show themselves in an indirect and roundabout way does not of course imply that they are unimportant. It means that they are more difficult to understand and allocation of research funds should not therefore rest on a naïve model where basic scientific research is seen as the generator of discoveries, and industry as the lame recipient.

If the conclusion is accepted that industry tends to generate its own technology base, then it is to applied and development research that the investigator must turn to find the major source of inventions. Applied research is aimed at generating knowledge with commercial applications. Development research is the process which transforms technological knowledge into marketable commodities. These are the two activities which create and feed the process of technology building on technology. Companies and individuals are predominantly involved and it is from here that the majority of inventions originate. It is important to define technology before explaining how it is that industry tends to generate its own knowledge base and why science and technology appear to be parallel structures with only limited contact at the interface. Technology may be defined as the tools and techniques by which human capability is extended.[16] Alternatively, it may be defined to include concepts and knowledge which are used in the tools and techniques.[17] This wider approach puts less emphasis on tangible objects and more on knowhow. It is here that basic science may make its greatest impact. The inventions which influence wellbeing are of course those which are put to practice. It is these which are the direct concern of industry.

Industry tends to create its own knowledge base. Basic scientific research would appear to be the obvious generator of 'knowhow' for industry. 'But there are grounds for doubting whether science and technology always march together; whether science, that is to say, always carries with it an economic "pay-off".[18] The reasons are as follows: industry may create a range of problems for which basic science may not have an answer. Commerce tends to be concerned with production problems. These are often problems of practice not principle. They are often highly detailed and specific to particular organisations. The approach tends to be empirical; explanation frequently follows performance. Having found a method that works, this may lead to further development. In this sense the process of technological development may be self-feeding. Knowledge built up from experience may be sufficient. Discoveries may not occur unless those concerned are conditioned in the particular problems and subject to pressures to solve them. The knowledge required is frequently interdisciplinary. This may not fit happily within the formalised organisation of basic research institutes. Chance may be very important. Conditions for the random occurrence may not be present when theoretical understanding is being sought. Inventions do not necessarily involve fundamental principles, but frequently re-application of known ideas in new ways.

Basic scientific research may not have sufficient market orientation to perceive the need for commercial developments. It may be inefficient for this type of work to be conducted in a basic research institute. There may be too great a separation of those familiar with production requirements and those conducting the research. Industrial discoveries may be well ahead of their time and as a result lead to the foundation of a whole new field of study. In these circumstances industry will have to do its own basic research before science catches up. It may be cheaper and more convenient for industry to rediscover what is already known. The cost of information recovery can be high. It can also be time consuming. Furthermore if the scientific research is not exactly applicable it may divert rather than aid the process of development.

The environment of basic scientific research may not be conducive to invention. It is said that for an inventor to achieve recognition his commitment must be almost obsessive.[19] The security and stability offered by institutional research may not motivate an individual to such compulsive effort. Even the so-called 'science based' industries tend to generate a high proportion of their own ideas. These industries are closely associated with scientific discoveries, particularly in relation to chemistry, electronics and atomic energy. Even here the link between basic science and technology is not necessarily direct and obvious. Techniques of application can be important in themselves and amount to invention. Methods of transistorisation provide an example. Such techniques are not bequeathed to industry but are developed as part of the process of application. They represent technological knowhow which industry develops in the process of making a discovery marketable.

A few examples may help to add reality. The discovery of Nylon by Carruthers created the whole new field of polymer chemistry. This inventor could not draw on relevant knowledge available from basic scientific research. It did not exist. The famous accident which led to the discovery of the antibacterial properties of penicillin by Sir Alexander Fleming in 1928 is an example of chance in operations. The extraction of penicillin, rendering it stable and increasing yields, which was not complete until 1943, is an example of the impetus that an original discovery can give to technological development. The ingenuity required for large-scale methods of production exhibited degrees of novelty amounting to invention and illustrated the process of technology building on technology.[20] The Float-Glass process invented and developed by A. Pilkington, further illustrates the gap between a basic concept and the finished article. The British patent was sealed in 1957, and yet it was found in the USA that patents had been granted in 1902 and 1905, which incorporated the same basic idea of floating glass on molten metal to form sheets. Neither of these patents had produced an operative process, and both had joined the ranks of forgotten ingenuity. Success of the process depended on much more than the single idea of floating glass on molten metal. The actual production methods are crucial. The techniques are complex and form part of the invention. Without success in evolving methods which would transform the principle into a reality, Pilkington would have suffered a fate similar to the American inventors'. The Hovercraft provides an example of the empirical preceding the theoretical. C. Cockerell found by direct experiment that a captive air bubble would support a vehicle. A whole new field of technology has resulted. This new form of transport has established its own knowledge base and technological impetus. The problems tend to be specific. Solutions are rarely drawn all polished and complete from other fields. The impetus is from within and aimed at a particular problem.

A general picture thus emerges that technology feeds on technology and in the process provides a major source of inventions. The importance of basic science to industry is not denied. It is emphasised however that knowledge created by a study of fundamentals filters in to commerce, usually in indirect ways. Technology tends to create its own problems and solutions.

While technology may develop its own impetus, this does not mean that companies are responsible for all their own ideas. Industries and activities have a pool of knowhow which tends to be common to participating members. Stimulus to inventive activity may be generated from within a company, or may be imported. Contact with 'outsiders' may be just as important as 'in house' ideas in giving R and D direction and impetus. In a study of the origins of twenty-five important product and process innovations by du Pont, fifteen were attributable to outside sources.[21] Du Pont is a company with a high R and D commitment and a reputation as a leader in technological development. These figures are in no sense a criticism of the inventiveness of du Pont. It is one of the functions of company research to respond to ideas from wherever they originate. Without the awareness and the knowledge network which research creates, opportunities may be neglected.

Another study[22] found a similar proportion of technical ideas arising from within the firm. Fifty-six of the 158 important ideas arose internally. The authors were unable to identify a single idea as the specific origin of an innovation. Instead there were on average three useful ideas per innovation. Of the 102 ideas that originated outside firms, only ten came from universities, fifty-nine came from elsewhere in industry. Furthermore a third of the ideas came from sources outside the United Kingdom. Apparently a firm is unlikely to be self-sufficient in generating its own ideas. Typically it turns to industry for inspiration, and this source of knowledge is not necessarily confined to one country. 'And since, apart from the USA, no country can hope to produce more than 10 per cent of the world's scientific and technological knowledge, such monitoring must nearly always go beyond national boundaries to be effective.'[23] In this sense technological knowledge is international.

Table 3.1 illustrates the method of transfer of ideas from outside firms. Apparently persons joining firms are the most frequently used method. The movement of individuals is probably also the most powerful transfer agent. Certainly this is the view of a conference whose deliberations were reported in 1969.[24] An individual embodying new ideas and knowledge can synergise a firm. The employment of personnel with a particular expertise is a quick and cheap method of the company acquiring knowhow. He can pass on his knowledge and perform an educating role, while on the job. This is much more effective than retraining existing employees. As a contributor to the Conference stated the 'transfer of technology is one of agents not agencies, of moving people among establishments rather than routing through communication systems'.[25] The sources of ideas thus tend to be multiple and diffuse. Firms assess and absorb information from a wide variety of sources. They turn to industry rather than basic research institutes and do not confine themselves to their own shores.

Table 3.1 Method of transfer of 102 important ideas from outside the Award-winning firms

Transfer via person joining the firm	20½
Common knowledge via ⎰ industrial experience	15
⎱ education	9
Commercial agreement (incl. takeover and sale of knowhow)	10½
Literature (technical, scientific and patent)	9½
Personal contact in UK	8½
Collaboration with ⎰ supplier	7
⎱ customer	5
Visit overseas	6½
Passed on by government organisation	6
Conference in UK	2½
Consultancy	2
	102

Source. J. Langrish *et al* (note 6).

Technology has its own knowledge network which is international in character, and the most frequently used method of transfer is the movement of personnel.

The contribution of individual inventors

It is tempting to assert that the role of the individual inventor is declining under presentday economic conditions. Technology is becoming increasingly complex. Research and development is a costly activity.

Companies are becoming increasingly involved in innovative activity and are tending to absorb creative individuals into their organisations. These factors would appear to mitigate against the lone individual. Figures exist which illustrate the percentage of patents originating from company and individual sources. In Great Britain in 1913 patent applications from corporations were about 15 per cent of total. By 1938 this percentage was 58 per cent and by 1955 68 per cent.[26] In the USA a similar pattern emerges: corporations were responsible for approximately 18 per cent of patents at the turn of the century. By 1936 this figure was approximately 50 per cent. By 1956-60 the percentage was approximately 63.[27] The cautious conclusion to be drawn from these figures is that invention has changed from an activity overwhelmingly dominated by individuals, to one less overwhelmingly dominated by business enterprise.[28] A less cautious conclusion would take the view that if this trend of increasing company involvement continues, the day of the individual inventor is fast drawing to a close.

The cautious conclusion is more appropriate. Patent statistics are an imperfect index of invention. Furthermore the distinction between patents granted to individuals and companies is blurred. Within the individual inventor classification, there will be a number of patents which are assigned to companies. The rights may have been sold to a company before the patents were issued. Alternatively it may be a condition of employment in a company research team that individuals may take out patents but would normally assign these to the company. Patents granted to companies may also be misleading. These may include patents granted to individuals not working in research and development, but which nevertheless have to be surrendered to the company. Individuals employed in government R and D also present a problem. Patenting is not normally permitted and yet there is an inventive output. In terms of the figures, an adjustment should be made to reflect this activity. The cautious conclusion is reinforced when a closer look is taken at the figures. In some activities the individual inventor would appear to have a much better chance of making a contribution. A blanket dismissal of his efforts would be tantamount to quoting average figures without knowledge of their dispersion. The average may well disguise a wide variation, where in certain activities the role of the individual is dominant and in others insignificant. In chemicals, synthetic resins and cellulose, dyes and dyeing, distillation oils and paints, the company is dominant. The percentage of patents acquired by corporations virtually excludes the individual. In timber and furniture, scientific instruments, and textile machinery, the role of the individual is much more in evidence.[29]

When a qualitative approach is used to assess the role of the individual inventor, his significance is strengthened. A major problem with patent figures is their lack of discrimination. No indication is available of the quality of the contribution of each patent. Aggregation to establish the share of companies and individuals makes no distinction between major and trivial inventions. All have equal weight in the figures. When a case study approach is made to the problem, qualitative aspects become more important. The investigator selects significant inventions and studies their origination. The dross, the trivial and the cranky are ignored. Major steps forward are studied and a detailed picture of the process of invention emerges. In a study of sixty-one significant inventions during this century, an attempt has been made to appraise the role of the individual. During the process the authors had to evolve a definition of the 'individual inventor'. The meaning of the term is by no means obvious. A realistic definition is required which separates an individual from company activities but at the same time recognises that the line between the two is not necessarily distinct. The individual inventor is defined by three major criteria: who chooses the field of ideas in which the inventor works, who provides the resources for his work, and who stands to gain directly from his invention.[30] Notice that these criteria do not necessarily exclude an individual working in an R and D institution. If he has freedom to choose his field of interest, provides his own capital to follow his particular whim, and stands to gain from any discovery, then he would qualify as an individual inventor. To confine the definition to individuals that worked entirely on their own would be too strict. The essence of the matter is the ability to act independently.

Major inventions studied included radar, catalytic cracking of petroleum, DDT, the gyro-compass, the helicopter, insulin, the jet engine, nylon and perlon, penicillin, radio, rockets, streptomycin, television, the transistor, and xerography. In the sixty-one cases studied, more than half could be attributed to individuals.

> In the sense that much of the pioneering work was carried through by men who were working on their own behalf without the backing of research institutions and usually with limited resources and assistance, or, where the inventors were employed in institutions, these institutions were, as in the case of universities, of such a kind that the individuals were autonomous, free to follow their own ideas without hindrance.[31]

In a second edition the authors saw no reason to change their conclusions. The general picture remained the same even when ten further case studies of more recent inventions were added.[32] Other studies confirm this overall impression. In a sample of twenty-seven major inventions between 1946 and 1955, only seven came from large industrial laboratories. Twelve were traceable to independent inventors.[33] Of twenty-five important product and process innovations pioneered in the USA by du Pont between 1920 and 1950, only eleven originated from within, the remainder came from other firms and independent researchers.[34]

This general conclusion of the importance of the individual inventor needs reconciling with the impression given by the patent statistics cited earlier. On a patent numbers basis, companies would appear to predominate. In contrast, the case study approach would appear to reassert the importance of the individual as a contributor to technology. There is in fact no clash between these findings. In the case study approach, all the examples were selected because of their importance. They are what is known as primary inventions. These are discoveries which lay the basis for a new field of technology. They are brilliant discoveries which create new products and processes. Secondary inventions in contrast, are less important. They tend to build on and add to the primary inventions. These are often the product of development work. They add to existing knowledge, and supplement what has gone before. They are not spectacular breakthroughs, but more run-of-the-mill events. Studies using patent numbers will cover both sorts of invention. A comparison of these studies and those involving the more detailed case study approach will therefore only yield conclusions of a very general nature. The vast majority of patents issued both to companies and individuals are almost inevitably of a secondary character. Consequently direct comparison between the two types of studies has to be guarded. The samples are so different as to preclude anything but the most general of conclusions. A realistic summary would accept that the role of the individual has declined, but would point to some of the primary inventions which have been achieved by individuals to give a sense of balance. Company research and patenting has certainly risen dramatically during this century. If there had not been a rise in the percentage of patents to companies this would have been a cause for concern. The individual still has an important role to play. The characteristics which distinguish him are of considerable value and are unlikely to be completely swamped by organised research. He brings to a problem an uncommitted mind and unorthodox and original ideas. As an outsider he can be free of the accepted and conventional methods of thought. This may enable him to make a significant contribution to technological ideas, even when his financial resources and facilities are severely limited.

One major advantage of the case study approach is the insight it yields into invention as a creative process. It becomes clear that practically all inventors have great difficulty achieving acceptance of their ideas. An individual without the facilities to produce his invention, is essentially forced to sell his idea. In doing so he is marketing a promise, in the sense that performance is as yet unproven and the market uncertain. In attempting to persuade a company to adopt his idea he has to overcome caution generated by the character of the item he is selling. To do this requires persistence bordering on the obsessional. In this sense there are considerable 'discontinuities' in the transformation process which changes an idea into a tangible reality. Not only is he selling an unusual commodity, he is also challenging the well worn road of accepted ideas, time-polished dogmas, and the change aversion of satisficing companies. To achieve acceptance of novel ideas thus requires great efforts by the lone inventor. Furthermore this change-aversion is not aimed solely at outsiders. Companies often have to be virtually forced to adopt the ideas they generate themselves. A 'product-champion' who is prepared to stake his reputation to achieve acceptance of a new idea may be the industrial equivalent of the lone inventor. Without his backing the whole project may founder in a morass of passive resistance.[35] There are innumerable examples of frustrations encountered by inventors. 'Their laments run right through the ages for reasons which have remained strangely unchanged.'[36] It would appear that inventors must prove themselves against the complacency and inertia of accepted ideas.

In forcing their ideas on a reluctant world inventors are apparently subjected to a sociological, not an economic, test. Inertia would appear to be a costly way to weed out useless inventions. Inventors' time will be absorbed in the process of persuasion instead of further creative work, and unless they have the characteristics of persistence and drive, they are likely to fail. Fortunately for society there is rarely a single inventor of an idea. Frequently an original idea can be traced to a number of individuals. The chances of it eventually emerging are thus enhanced. There are of course other reasons explaining the phenomenon of multiple invention: poor communications between men and ideas, response to economic pressures to solve a common problem, and frustrated early application due to lack of development in parallel and supporting technologies, are all examples. However it is not unreasonable to assert that resistance to change is a major cause of multiple invention. When an idea is not adopted, it remains to be rediscovered. There are no overt applications to indicate that the principle is in operation and so another inventor may spend time and effort pursuing the same notion. The rotary piston provides a good example. Wankel, its inventor, began work in 1945 with a design invented in 1647 by an Italian scholar Cavalieri. When he finally applied for a patent it was found that many features of his engine had been anticipated by inventors in Sweden, France and Switzerland.[37] It should however be pointed out that Wankel was of the opinion that his version might have been held up had he known of these earlier ideas. Modification of these might have diverted him from the particular breakthrough which distinguished his engine.

The case study approach throws into relief the difficulties faced by individuals. A further point emerges, namely that too great an emphasis can be placed upon the individual as an inventor. In a large number of cases, companies end up shouldering the burden of developing inventions for commercial exploitation.[3,8] Without company involvement, many brilliant ideas may founder for lack of sponsorship. Invention, in the sense of origination, is the first step in bringing new products and processes into being. The individual has an important role to play, but this must be kept in perspective. The passage of an idea through to a tangible commodity on the market, can be lengthy and expensive. Companies become involved because they have the funds and the marketing organisation. Invention and development are required to achieve technological change. The individual with his uncommitted mind, and heretical approach to problems, has a significant role to play. His brilliance must not however be allowed to overshine the more routine but equally necessary task of transforming inventions into marketable commodities.

Invention and economic force

There are a great number of influences that may induce invention. These may include personal gain, curiosity, the outpourings of genius, the pressure of necessity, the type of competition, random and chance events, and economic forces in general. There is a growing consensus however that economic forces are predominant. It is believed that invention is not unlike most other goods, in that the forces of demand and supply regulate output. It is tempting to treat invention as a process outside the economic system. Creativity is such a tender plant and so susceptible to the enemies of promise that it is difficult to believe that it can be forthcoming in a predictable and ordered fashion. There is something special about the act of invention. It would seem incongruous that it should be nurtured by mundane economic forces.

The argument that economic factors predominate is backed by painstaking and exhaustive research. J. S. Schmookler has evolved techniques of investigation which make this conclusion difficult to refute. Patent numbers are used as indicators of inventive activity. Long time series are presented of patents in a number of industries including railroad, agriculture, petroleum and paper.[39] These time series are related to indicators of demand for the industries' products. A remarkably close correspondence is found between these indicators and patent numbers. 'Inventive activity tends to rise and fall with the sales of the products which they improve.'[40] There are a number of explanations for this correlation, and tests are used to establish the most plausible. Factors influencing inventive activity will include the state of perfection of the technology, chance, the cost of development of inventions, and the economic prospects in the industry concerned. Using the example of the horseshoe Schmookler shows how the annual numbers of American patents rose and then as the 'steam traction engine and later the internal combustion engine began to displace the horse, inventive interest in the field began to decline'.[41] The technical possibilities in this field for further invention were by no means exhausted. The explanation for the decline thus lay with the economic payoff. Apparently inventors were not prepared to waste their ingenuity in an area with such poor prospects. Competition for superior technologies had made invention unattractive, and so patenting responded in a predictable manner. The economic payoff, however, is not just determined by demand. Cost considerations are relevant. An industry may have a high level and rising demand, but if invention becomes increasingly expensive as the technology approaches perfection, patenting may well decline. In these circumstances the expenditure involved may regulate inventive effort, and not demand prospects. Further tests are therefore necessary to discriminate between these components in the motivation to invent. Accordingly the patent statistics within an industry are segregated into different categories. These categories represent separate technologies, each with its own distinct body of knowledge. For example in the railroad industry, inventions are separated into track and non-track patents, or in shoemaking into leather-sewing and sole-making techniques. Even when these adjustments are made the time series of segregated patent numbers still exhibits a close association. Apparently there is an overriding force in action which induces a correspondence in the various technologies. If two key assumptions are accepted, then this force is seen to be demand. The assumptions necessary for this conclusion are:

1. that the cost of a given advance varies between technologies used within an industry.
2. that the different technologies adopted by an industry do not approach perfection together and thus exhaust the need for further invention at the same time.

These assumptions are entirely plausible. It is unlikely that different technologies used within a given industry will approach perfection together. Similarly it is unlikely that the costs of a given advance will be the same between technologies, linked by usage in the same industry. If inventive activity were to continue independently of demand conditions, techniques would be developed until they reached their own state of perfection. The series of patent numbers would illustrate no correspondence. If costs of achieving a given advance are different, again there would be no close relationship between inventive activity in the technologies. There would be a different amount of interest according to the costs involved, and thus a differential pace of development. When the time series do in fact show a close degree of parallelism the conclusion of the supremacy of demand as a determinant of technological activity is difficult to resist. Economic prospects would appear to overrule differences in the cost of development as well as the state of perfection of the various techniques. Apparently even inventive activity is governed by the extent of the market. The decision to invent is primarily an economic one. The primacy of value over cost is established. 'In short, the output of technological advances is sensitive to the same economic factors that influence the output of more pedestrian products and services'.[42]

The conclusion that economic prospects regulate technological activity is important. It means that 'demand induces the inventions that satisfy it',[43] and that progress in an industry slows down because it becomes less valuable, not because it becomes more costly. Economic prospects shown through realised and expected sales, regulate inventive activity and thus establish the predominant motive. Apparently invention is susceptible to and regulated by economic forces. The prospect of higher profits will induce effort. There is at any time a stock of unfinished inventions which are brought to fruition by the inducement of higher profits in expanding industries, or as a response for additional output when capacity is at a premium.[44] Invention is not outside the economic system. Creativity and ingenuity respond to the stimulus of attractive prospects. They are demand orientated phenomena serving the interests of technological progress.

Before proceeding further it is necessary to point out some of the problems associated with Schmookler's approach. Patent numbers are used as indicators of inventive activity. These suffer from a variety of limitations. Not all inventions are patented. Patents vary greatly in their importance. Some are trivial, others are path-breaking. The standards applied by the authorities to acquire a patent may change over time. Companies may have a high propensity to patents. This may represent their desire to deter the entry of rivals, or to use patents as negotiating counters in company diplomacy. The most serious objection, however, relates to the inability of patent statistics to separate origination from development. A brilliant idea embodied in a single patent may represent a much higher level of inventive output, than all the subsequent patents which reflect later modification and improvements. Invention has been defined earlier as that subset of technical innovations which are patentable. Furthermore the argument has been put forward that invention is inextricably linked with the later process of coupling new ideas to the market place. In a later chapter it will be argued that the most realistic model of patents shows them arising from the process of technology building on technology. They are a product of the development of knowhow in industries and as such reflect efforts to improve existing technologies. If, however, patents are supposed to segregate inventive from innovative activity, that is to distinguish origination from development, then there may be real problems. In the sense of the strict definition, primary and secondary invention would have to be separated. Primary inventions lay the foundations for new products and processes and open up new areas of technology. Secondary inventions arise as a result of development of the original invention and are really the process of technology building on technology. Clearly this activity will be market orientated. Effort is unlikely to be forthcoming unless commercial prospects are attractive. If patents are typically generated by secondary invention, then their economic motivation is obvious.

As pointed out earlier, the case study approach concentrates on primary inventions. If economic motivation is shown to be relevant here also, then Schmookler's general conclusion will indeed be hard to refute. The joint authors of *The Sources of Invention*, which adopts the case study approach, are however of the opinion that non-economic factors should not be underestimated. 'The motives of the inventor are not wholly economic. We think that Schmookler tends to over-emphasise the importance of economic demand.'[4 5] They cite examples of inventions arising as a result of technology for technology's sake, and of important inventions which had no immediately obvious final use. In addition they give examples of inventions 'produced before their time'. In some cases it was not indifferent commercial judgment, but an illustration of the secondary importance of economic motivation. These observations on Schmookler's work are valid. Non-economic factors clearly have some importance. They are however not sufficiently forceful to cause a reappraisal of the general findings. It is the predominant motive which is of interest to the investigator. The conclusion that invention is largely guided by economic forces is not intended to exclude other motives. It is intended to put them in perspective. They are likely to play a subordinate role in the majority of cases. The typical invention will be guided not by chance or intellectual curiosity, but by the economic prospects anticipated in meeting a market need. The findings in *The Sources of Invention* do in fact add weight to Schmookler's general conclusion. Of all the inventions, primary inventions are likely to be the least susceptible to economic forces. Such path-breaking discoveries often involve entirely new principles. They are acts of creation whose outcome is frequently unpredictable. Likely markets for such inventions are unknown and economic prospects therefore hazy. Even so, twenty-six of the inventions studied came from the research laboratories of manufacturing companies.[46] It is fair to assume that these inventions all had a strong economic orientation. They resulted from corporate research effort and presumably were guided by profit criteria. In addition, if the time period covered by *The Sources of Invention* is confined to a more recent era, the role of large companies appears more significant.[47]

Of those inventions attributable to individuals the strands of commercial orientation can be traced in quite a number of cases. Another less direct indicator of motivation is the tendency for multiple invention. Frequently an inventor's basic idea is anticipated. Multiple invention may represent the effects of poor communication. Knowledge of a previous patent may not reach the current inventor. Alternatively it may represent the pressure of economic forces inducing effort in similar worthwhile directions. A surprising number of the case histories revealed multiple inventions. Some of the explanation lies with the allocative effects of economic forces. Schmookler's general conclusion is therefore accepted. The major inducement to invention is economic. Furthermore it is demand rather than cost which predominates as an allocator of inventive resources.

Conclusion

Inventions typically involve minor improvements in technology. The major breakthrough is important but rare. Individuals are still significant despite the rise in corporate R and D. Basic scientific research has important but indirect links with technology. The sources of invention are wide and diffuse. Economic factors are predominant in the motivation to invent. The primacy of economic forces carries with it no implication as to how research should be organised. It does not imply that resources should be diverted to commercially orientated institutions. To concentrate effort in one particular form of organisation may stifle inventive output. There are clearly virtues in keeping the potential sources of invention as wide as possible. 'The conditions under which inventions have arisen up to the present day are so diverse that safety would seem to lie in numbers and in variety of attack.'[48]

Of the theories of invention, cumulative synthesis would appear the most plausible. The transcendentalist approach is rejected. Innovation is not a random and chance phenomenon. There is too much evidence of economic motivation and too many examples of multiple invention, to make this convincing. The mechanistic approach has more realism. This is consistent with economic motivation and multiple invention. It lacks persuasion, however, in its assumption that invention will proceed smoothly from a given set of circumstances. Insufficient emphasis is given to overcoming 'discontinuities' in the economic system in bringing an idea to fruition. The cumulative synthesis approach would therefore appear the most realistic. It recognises the resistance to change which has to be overcome in introducing an invention. It squares with the concept of technology building on technology, in that progress represents a synthesis of what has gone before, and is not a random and unpredictable process. The role of the individual remains important, and it is consistent with the increasing involvement of companies.

Summary

Invention is the first stage in the process of technological innovation. Little is gained by separating invention from innovation. There is no tidy distinction, although there is a qualitative difference in the activities. They are often inextricably linked. The source of ideas behind an inventive step is often diffuse and imprecise. Individuals are becoming less important as inventors, and companies more predominant. Invention is best treated as that subset of technical innovations which are patentable. The origination involved typically takes the form of technology building on technology.

There are three general theories of invention: the transcendentalist, the mechanistic, and the cumulative synthesis. The transcendentalist approach gives pride of place to the individual genius. The lone inventor makes a great impact on technology with a single creative thought. The mechanistic approach adopts the view that invention proceeds under the stress of necessity, where need dictates and technology complies. Economic forces predominate and the role of the individual genius is rejected. The third approach sees invention arising from a cumulative synthesis of what has preceded. An act of insight is required and the individual may play an important role in the solution of technical problems. His role is not that of a genius, nor is he pushed aside by the onrush of an inevitable historical process. By a synthesis of previous knowledge and an act of insight he may overcome a discontinuity. Cumulative synthesis is probably the most realistic theory of invention. Necessity is the mother of invention in times of national crisis, and there are great men of genius. But the typical is more prosaic and suggests that invention arises out of past technological activity.

Basic scientific research would appear the activity most likely to yield inventions. But the relationship between basic discoveries and technological change is an area of some controversy. There are findings which appear to conflict. Some indicate a strong link between basic research and invention, others suggest only limited contact at the interface between basic science and technology. There is considerable evidence that industry tends to generate its own technology base. Applied and development research are the activities which create and feed the process of technology building on technology. It may well be that basic science and technology are parallel activities with indirect links, with the major source of invention arising from the process of technology building on technology. This does not deny the importance of basic scientific research, it merely indicates the typical. Industry generates its own knowledge base through production and selling experience, and even the science-based companies generate a high proportion of their own knowhow. Firms are, however, unlikely to be self-sufficient in generating ideas. Outside sources are likely to be responsible for a significant proportion of research ideas, but these are likely to be drawn not from science but from industry. Personnel movements are considered the most potent form of transfer agent.

The role of the individual inventor would appear to be declining. However, his contribution is by no means insignificant, especially in certain activities. Patent statistics may be misleading as indicators of the importance of the individual. A qualitative approach may be more revealing. In a study based on sixty major inventions, over half were attributable to individuals. The criteria defining the individual inventor, are based on an ability to act independently. The impression of the continuing importance of the individual is confirmed by other studies. The apparent clash between studies based on patent statistics and those adopting a case study approach, is probably related to the character of the samples concerned. A comparison is being made between primary and secondary inventions. This can be misleading. A realistic conclusion accepts that the role of the individual is declining, but that he has an important role to play.

Individuals have considerable difficulty in persuading industry to adopt their inventions. Similarly, industry would appear almost equally reluctant to adopt its own ideas. A 'product champion' is a significant factor in persuading a company to adopt its own projects. This resistance to change may be a costly attitude. Fortunately there is rarely a single inventor of an idea. Multiple invention is not uncommon. It may also be possible to overstress the role of the individual inventor and forget the crucial importance of the development function. Frequently companies end up shoulderir.g the burden of making an invention commercial.

There is a growing consensus that economic forces predominate in invention. The painstaking work of J. S. Schmookler has made this conclusion difficult to resist. The major motivation to invent would appear to be commercial. In a broad sense, demand induces the inventions that satisfy it, and inventive interest in an industry slows down because it becomes less valuable, not because it becomes more costly. Invention is thus not outside the reach of economic forces. Even primary inventions may be susceptible to economic forces. The frequency of multiple invention may be indirect evidence of such an allocation effect.

The typical invention involves a minor improvement in technology. The transcendentalist approach is rejected because of the evidence of economic motivation and the occurrence of multiple invention. The cumulative synthesis approach is accepted as the most realistic. There are discontinuities in the system which have to be overcome, and it squares with the concept of technology building on technology. The role of the individual remains important, and it is consistent with the increasing involvement of companies.

Innovation

The previous chapter emphasised that invention was an early part of the process of innovation. This chapter will concentrate on the stages which transform a promising technical possibility into a marketable reality. The innovative process can be divided into four functions: invention, entrepreneurship, investment and development. The entrepreneurial function involves deciding to go forward with the effort, organising it and obtaining financial support. Investment is the act of risking funds for the venture. Development is the lengthy sequence of detail-orientated technical activities, including trial and error testing, through which the original concept is modified and perfected until it is ready for commercial utilisation.[1] Innovation thus covers all the activities in bringing a new product or process to the market. It is the pre-imitation stage. The term diffusion is reserved to describe what occurs later, and includes the spread of an innovation and its adoption by rivals.

Innovation produces technological goods. Such goods have economic characteristics which induce an ambivalent attitude in those involved in their creation. This ambivalence arises from an awareness of the nature of the benefits arising from innovation and the costs involved. Innovation may be a lengthy process. It involves team work and facing relatively high levels of risk. It is an expensive, time-consuming transformation process, which is management and resource intensive. Goods produced as a result of innovation have an element of novelty. They are new and advanced. Price elasticity tends to be low and income elasticity high. A price premium may be charged which represents the innovational edge over the nearest substitute products. They are likely to be readily exportable to advanced economies with high standards of living and thus offer the firm concerned a market which is worldwide in potential.[2] A company which innovates successfully is likely to enjoy a much enhanced economic performance. Its growth rate is likely to increase and also its profitability.[3] The economic life of an innovation is, however, limited. New goods will be copied and eventually become accepted and traditional products. The premium will be eroded as competitors appear and the character of the pricing decision shifts from what the market will bear, to what rivals will allow. The upheaval involved in introducing a new product may be considerable. The resistance to change mentioned in the previous chapter may have some economic rationale. If an innovation attracts a large number of rivals quickly, the resultant profit may not justify the investment effort. It is a paradox of the process of innovation that the greater the success of a product, the faster its novelty is likely to be eroded. Thus unless a company has the prospect of an adequate recoupment period it may be deterred from the effort. Patents have been evolved as a legal device to damp the encroachment of rivals. There are other means of defending an innovational lead. These include sheer size, monopoly and multi-national status. But none of these other defences will be available to small companies and the private individual. Patents therefore not only attempt to raise the incentive to invent, but also widen the potential source to the weaker units in an economy.[4] The ambivalent attitude of innovators thus arises from an awareness that successful innovation can synergise economic performance, but that the process is inherently risky. Investment in innovation is thus likely to carry a fairly heavy cautionary discount, and tend to be the prerogative of thrusting companies. What induces companies to become involved in R and D, the optimum size of company, the factors determining success or failure, and the general nature of the process of innovation will be discussed in this chapter.

Economic characteristics of development

Development tends to be a much more expensive activity than invention. 'Some companies have a working rule that the cost of development is approximately ten times the cost of the basic invention.'[5] Because of the cost involved companies often end up shouldering the burden of developing invention originating from

Table 4.1 Division of costs incurred in bringing an invention to the market

Stage	Average % of total cost arising at each stage	
	A	B
1 Applied research	9.5 ⎫	5–10
2 Specifications	7.6 ⎭	
3 Prototype or pilot plant	29.1	10–20
4 Tooling and manufacturing facilities	36.9	40–60
5 Manufacturing start-up	9.1	5–15
6 Marketing start-up	7.7	10–25

Sources. A. Mansfield *et al.*, 1971 (note 10); B. US Department of Commerce, *Technological Innovation*, 1967, quoted in E. Mansfield, *Economics of Technological Change*, Norton, 1968.

individuals. It is therefore sensible to discuss innovation in terms of companies rather than private individuals. It is not intended to give the impression that this is exclusively the preserve of companies, but the figures that follow will make it clear that the private individual is likely to be at a considerable disadvantage. Invention is relatively cheap, development on the other hand is typically much more expensive. Companies have access to funds on a scale which is normally beyond the pocket of the ordinary individual, and so are financially better placed to become involved in expenditure of this kind.

Table 4.1 illustrates the division of costs incurred through the stages in bringing an invention to the market. The invention stage is seen to involve only between 5 and 10 per cent of the total costs. The remainder, which represents the commercialisation sequence, is at least

Table 4.2 Estimated costs of specific developments

	Period	*Cost*	*Comments*
Float glass			
Pilkingtons	1952–7	£500,000	Including pilot plant
	1952–67	£7,000,000	Including first float line
Surface modified			
float process	1963–7	Nearly £1,000,000	
Hovercraft			
SRN1		£120,000	For design, construction and early testing
SRN1		£350,000	Whole programme including early tests on flexible skirts
Transistor			
Bell Labs.	1946–50	$140,000	Up to patenting of the process of producing transistors
	1950–61	$28,000,000	
	1961–5	$28,000,000	
Computers			
ASCC	1937–44	$400,000	
ENIAC	1942–6	$500,000	
LEO	1947–53	£129,000	
Missiles		Over	
Atlas		$3,000,000,000	
Atom Bomb			
Electro-magnetic separation plant	Up to 1946	$304,000,000	
Gaseous diffusion plant	Up to 1946	$253,000,000	

Source. Based on J. Jewkes, D. Sawers and R. Stillerman in *The Sources of Invention*, 2nd edition, Macmillan, 1969.

ten times as expensive as the initial inventive step. The figures represent average costs through the stages. There is in fact considerable variation in the distribution of costs for individual products. Particular projects do have cost patterns which vary widely from the average.[6] Time taken to complete the stages also varies considerably. The prototype or pilot plant work typically takes up about 50 per cent of the time taken to achieve the whole innovation process. Stages 1 and 4 also take up a considerable proportion of the time, together accounting for about 30 per cent.[7]

Table 4.2 gives some examples of the cost of specific development. Direct comparison of individual figures should be avoided. The figures are merely intended to give an impression of the scale of expenditures involved. The costs of specific developments are not easy to define. In some cases they include the cost of pilot plants and in others the long-term costs of improving a product which already has a substantial market. The reader should also avoid the impression that all developments involve expenditure on this sort of scale. The determinants of the costs of development include the size and complexity of the advance being sought, the time taken to achieve this, and the means by which the process is being organised. If the basic knowledge already exists and the step forward aimed for is modest, then with appropriate management skill the costs involved may be relatively low. The examples given in Table 4.2 are drawn from some of the really significant technological advances achieved during this century. These are innovations which have created their own industries or revolutionised existing ones. Less spectacular and more ordinary achievements will probably involve commensurately smaller sums. The run of the mill invention is not likely to involve a major departure from existing technologies. It will be a modification, improvement or new application. Development costs will be more modest. A frequency distribution of development costs representing technological possibilities open to a given firm, will probably be highly skewed. At the one extreme will be the few spectacular and costly innovations, and at the other will be the more numerous mundane and ordinary developments involving much lower costs. The mode of the distribution may be in the range of $50,000 to $30,000.[8] The small firm is not therefore necessarily excluded by the costs involved. The less spectacular development offers such a company a foothold in the process of technological development. It is still likely, however, that development costs will be considerably greater than those involved in the inventive step. The 'ten times' rule above probably has generality in the ordinal sense, that development is typically more costly than invention. However, the precise degree by which development exceeds invention will probably vary from project to project.

Table 4.3 Estimated time interval between invention and innovation, forty-six inventions, selected industries

Invention*	Interval (years)	Invention	Interval (years)
Distillation of hydrocarbons with heat and pressure (Burton)	24	Steam engine (Watt)	11
		Ball-point pen	6
Distillation of gas oil with heat and pressure (Burton)	3	DDT	3
		Electric precipitation	25
Continuous cracking (Holmes-Manley)	11	Freon refrigerants	1
		Gyro-compass	56
Continuous cracking (Dubbs)	13	Hardening of fats	8
'Clean circulation' (Dubbs)	3	Jet engine	14
Tube and Tank process	13	Turbo-jet engine	10
Cross process	5	Long playing record	3
Houdry catalytic cracking	9	Magnetic recording	5
Fluid catalytic cracking	13	Plexiglas, lucite	3
Catalytic cracking (moving bed)	8	Nylon	11
Gas lift for catalyst pellets	13	Cotton picker	53
Safety razor	9	Crease-resistant fabrics	14
Fluorescent lamp	79	Power steering	6
Television	22	Radar	13
Wireless telegraph	8	Self-winding watch	6
Wireless telephone	8	Shell molding	3
Triode vacuum tube	7	Streptomycin	5
Radio (oscillator)	8	Terylene, dacron	12
Spinning jenny	5	Titanium reduction	7
Spinning machine (water frame)	6	Xerography	13
Spinning mule	4	Zipper	27
Steam engine (Newcomen)	6		

Source. Enos, 'Invention and innovation in the petroleum refining industry', (ref. 25), pp. 307−8.
*The first eleven inventions were those that occurred in petroleum refining.

Table 4.3 illustrates the estimated time interval between invention and innovation. The average time interval for the petroleum industry is eleven years, and in others fourteen years. Mechanical innovations appear to require the shortest interval, followed by those in the chemical and pharmaceutical industries.[9] The time taken to achieve an innovation is part cause part effect of the cost involved. To some extent fast development can be purchased through high R and D spending. The classic examples are the atom bomb and the expenditure involved in getting man to the moon. The paramount demand for speedy results combined with the enormous depth of pocket of the United States government enabled these startling technological breakthroughs to be achieved in a fraction of the expected time. In more normal circumstances, an innovation that comes readily to fruition over a short time period, is likely to be cheaper than one which is technologically complicated and yields only grudgingly. For a given innovation a relationship between development time and expenditure involved probably exists, suggesting that the trade-off for quicker development is higher cost.[10] The generality of this relationship should not be overworked. Development is essentially a knowledge building process, where mastery is dependent on understandings. The quality of personnel involved in the R and D effort will be crucial. The way in which it is managed will also have an important bearing on the cost of a development.

In bringing an invention to the market a sequence of steps is involved where earlier knowledge feeds what follows. If speed is paramount this sequential knowledge building process may be sidestepped in the sense that tasks which would normally be carried out in order may be performed concurrently. This raises the risk of duplication and wasted effort, and may incur diminishing returns as more and more personnel become involved. The costs of shortening development time therefore may be high. Given the technological capability, the time taken to develop an invention becomes a management problem where the trade-off between the time taken and the costs involved must be

Table 4.4 Average rate of development of selected technological innovations*

	Average time interval (years)		
Factors influencing the rate of technological development	Incubation period†	Commercial development‡	Total
Time Period			
Early twentieth century (1885—1919)	30	7	37
Post-World War I (1920—1944)	16	8	24
Post-World War II (1945—1964)	9	5	14
Type of market application			
Consumer	13	7	20
Industrial	28	6	34
Source of development			
Private industry	24	7	31
Federal government	12	7	19

Source. Frank Lynn, 'An investigation of the rate of development and diffusion of technology in our modern industrial society', *Report of the National Commission on Technology, Automation, and Economic Progress*, Washington, D.C., 1966.
*Based on study of twenty major innovations whose commercial development started in the period 1885—1950.
†Incubation period—begins with basic discovery and establishment of technological feasibility, and ends when commercial development begins.
‡Commercial development—begins with recognition of commercial potential and the commitment of development funds to reach a reasonably well-defined commercial objective, and ends when the innovation is introduced as a commercial product or process.
See also E. Mansfield in the *Economics of Technological Change*, Norton, 1968.

balanced to achieve the desired solution. More will be said on this in Chapter 5, on the management of innovation.

There is evidence which suggests that the average time taken to develop inventions is shortening. Intuitively this would appear likely as more and more is being spent on R and D and more companies are becoming involved. Government commitment to technological change is increasing, and as a result so is funding to achieve this purpose. The technological capability of developed economies is presumably increasing along with this expenditure and therefore ought to show in a reduction in the average lag between invention and marketing.

Table 4.4 shows the average rate of development of twenty major inventions whose commercial development started in the period 1885–1950. The results seem to indicate a considerable decline in the timelag and also that consumer products typically take less time to develop than their industrial counterparts.[11] In addition, where innovations are developed with government funds the period is shorter than when private means are used. All these findings accord with expectations. The government's purse is deep, consumer goods are probably less complex than industrial innovations, and technological orientation of developed economies is increasing. One of these findings, namely that the development timelag is decreasing, should be treated with caution. There is considerable difficulty in identifying with satisfactory accuracy the starting point of an innovation. Thus, for example, in a well-known chart[12] the starting point chosen for photography is 1725 and spans a period of 112 years from 'discovery' to practical adoption. Equally plausible dates could have been 1822 with the first permanent photograph, or with the earliest demonstration of the darkening of silver salts in 1565. The starting point for atomic weapons is chosen at the beginning of the Manhattan Project which took six years to complete. The antecedents of the atomic bomb can, however, be traced back to 1905 to the demonstration of the equivalence of mass and energy. A further difficulty associated with such an exercise is that discoveries that have yet to be applied will not be included. This means that it is inherently impossible to observe anything other than a short timelag for recent discoveries.[13] The idea that the development lag is decreasing over time has gained considerable credence, but it is not satisfactorily established.[14] It remains a possibility that requires further elucidation.

Technical risk

In developing an invention, companies commit funds in the hope of future benefit. They deliberately carry risks. These take the form of technical and market risks. Technical risk reflects the likelihood of being thwarted, in the sense that no saleable output will result. Market risk relates to the likelihood of commercial success of a given technological development. The size and complexity of the advance sought will be a major determinant of the technical risk involved in converting a promising concept into a marketable reality. Where a company attempts a large step forward technical risk is likely to be high. Existing knowledge of the invention is by definition small. A firm will be involved in establishing the technological parameters and also in the creation of a high proportion of the knowledge required for successful application. If the research personnel are not of sufficient quality such an ambitious project is likely to founder. The novelty of the techniques required and the complexity of application will increase the probability of failure. A less ambitious project well within the technological capability of a firm is likely to have a much lower level of risk. Knowledge and application will be within the main stream of the company's experience. The costs and time to fruition are likely to be subject to much less deviation.

Technical risk is not an independent variable outside the control of a company. A company is in a position to have a considerable influence over the level of risk it faces. Development activities can be hedged by spreading projects, so that if one should prove technologically cussed this will not be disastrous. By adopting a large numbers approach a company can take on individual projects with very high technical risk, and yet enjoy an average level of risk which is still relatively low. There are a number of risk-shifting devices which enable a company to become involved only when the probability of success has been narrowed to an acceptable limit. Contract research allows a fixed sum commitment, without tying up company research and development resources. It also permits a company access to scientific knowledge which may be beyond its normal ambit. If the contracted project shows promise then the company may become involved at an appropriate stage. If risks are considered high a firm may adopt parallel research efforts to improve the likelihood of technical success. Where there is no consensus indicating the most promising alternatives, by organising separate approaches to a common problem both the time taken to achieve success and the total cost may be reduced. Too early a commitment to one approach can be avoided, and knowledge from the other parallel research efforts may contribute significantly to success with the method finally adopted.

The fact that companies can influence the level of technical risk by the way in which projects are organised raises problems for the investigator. Companies' assessment of risk levels will be subjective.

Additional factors such as their past record of success, their general level of competence, their size, profits, and economic stability, will also colour judgment. One company may view a particular project as highly risky, and another consider it a safe bet. Figures for the expected probability of success of projects must therefore be treated with due caution. Those drawn from a single company are most likely to have a common thread of judgment. Others from a number of companies are unlikely to have uniform criteria.

In a study of seventy projects in one leading USA company it has been found that expected probability of technical success in about threequarters of the cases exceeded 0.80.[15] Only seven projects had probabilities of success of below 0.6. When these expectations were compared with results achieved, it transpired that 44 per cent of the projects were successful. Only 16 per cent failed because of unforeseen technical difficulties. A high proportion of the remaining failures could be ascribed to deliberate company policies. In 9 per cent the objectives of a project were changed and in 18 per cent manpower was diverted to higher priority usage. If only the projects which were carried out as planned are included the chances of success average 0.75. The study also revealed that the company concentrated on short-reach projects. Most projects were expected to be completed in less than four years. Among those that were delayed the average slippage factor (the revised time to completion divided by the original estimated time) was about 1.30. Deviation in costs from estimated expenditure was such that in about half of the cases, actual costs were more than 20 per cent below the budget. In about 15 per cent actual expenditure was 20 per cent or more above the planned amount. The major reasons for deviation were changes in project objective or lack of suitable manpower. In over 200 R and D projects in the USA in chemicals and pharmaceuticals about 60 per cent of each laboratory's projects were technically completed. In addition the figures suggest that small advances in familiar areas of technology yielded higher probabilities of completion.[16] Another study based on a sample of 170 companies drawn from the 1968 *Fortune's* 500 and Moody's Industrials not listed in the 500[17] finds that average estimated probability of technical success before a company would become committed to an R and D project was 0.71. Average project time was again less than four years. The *Fortune's* 500 companies had an average project time of 3.3 years and the others 2.1 years. Project failure in a study of ninety-one R and D projects in a Government and Metallurgical laboratory revealed that only 15 per cent of failures could be ascribed to technical reasons.[18] The majority of failures were not due to the cussedness of technology but to other factors.

Market risk

Market risk relates to the likelihood of commercial success. This is much more difficult to assess than technical risk. There are a great many factors which will influence the commercial outcome of a given innovation. Unlike technical risk, market risk is to a much greater extent beyond the control of a company. Technical risk is largely determined by the competence of R and D teams. Market risk, on the other hand, is more susceptible to outside influences. If a company develops an innovation, commercial success will depend on generating an adequate market for the new product. A high proportion of the non-technical failures are found to be due to lack of interaction between the marketing and the R and D functions.[19] In the Queen's Award for industry study, of the factors causing delay in innovation over 20 per cent was attributable to 'no market or need'.[20] In a study based on American experience 45 per cent of failures could be linked with inadequate market analysis and weakness in marketing effort.[21] Assessment of market potential is a crucial function in the innovation process. Unless this is part of the selection procedure, money is likely to be spent on projects which are successful in a technical sense, but which fail because of lack of market outlets. Even where market potential has been assessed and outlets developed quickly there is no assurance that sales will be longlived. Rivals may copy and encroach.

Table 4.5 Years elapsed between first use and introduction by 30 per cent or 60 per cent of major producers

Innovation	30%	60%
Packaging beer in tin cans	.75	1
High speed beer bottle filler	5	7
Continuous wide-strip steel mill	5	9
Byproduct coke oven for steel mill	11	18
Continuous annealing of tin-plated steel	14	20
Continuous coal-mining machinery	2	4
Diesel locomotives	4	11

Source. Based on Mansfield, *Industrial Research and Technological Innovation* (ref. 15).

Table 4.5 shows the time taken for 30 per cent and 60 per cent of major producers to introduce the process innovations. The percentages are chosen to illustrate in an impressionistic fashion the period over which the inventing company will have a cost advantage. By the time 60 per cent of the major producers have introduced the relevant innovation, the process will have become an accepted part of the industry's technology. At the 30 per cent level, the innovating company will be amongst a minority and presumably have a fairly marked cost advantage over most of its rivals. The innovations in the table are drawn from the bituminous coal, iron and steel, brewing, and railroad industries, but have not been chosen because of their outstanding importance. Patents did not impede the imitation process and so the adoption lags represent the market response to the advantages which these processes offered. Whether these figures are typical of imitation rates is not known. However, it is plausible to argue that at least in one respect the figures are representative. They indicate a wide range of response rates. This is likely to be the case because imitation is determined by the economic characteristics of the innovations concerned. These are likely to vary considerably. Essentially the speed of response is determined by the profitability of adoption and the size of the investment required.[22] Innovations that require relatively small investment and are highly profitable tend to be copied fast. Those which are not so profitable and require relatively high investment tend to be copied slowly. Unless a company is a monopolist, or has a watertight patent position, the imitation rate is a factor outside its control. This will be a significant influence in its assessment of market risk.

If rival companies imitate extremely fast, recoupment of development costs may not be possible. If on the other hand rivals' reaction is slow, a handsome profit which extends over a considerable period of time may await the innovator. Unfortunately there is limited direct evidence on market or commercial risk. What evidence there is suggests that if a project is commercialised the probability of market success, defined in terms of profits earned, is about 40 per cent.[23] For the most part however assessment of commercial risk has to be inferred from the planning decisions taken by companies in their allocation to R and D, the payback period required and the expected rate of return. The criterion applied by companies will yield considerable insight into their assessment of market risk. For example, if companies require a short payback period, expect high average rates of return, allocate a small percentage of funds to R and D, and favour particular types of projects, then this will imply that managements assume market risk to be high.

Table 4.6 Comparison of R and D policy in *Fortune's* 500 and others

	% of sales spent on company financed R and D	Average expected payback time in years	Estimated probability of technical success	Average project time in years
Fortune's '500'	3.1	4.26	0.71	3.3
Others	3.1	3.50	0.71	2.1

Source. Gerstenfeld, *Effective Management of Research and Development* (ref. 17), p. 22.

Table 4.6 summarises the position well. Average project time is below four years. Average expected payback time even for the largest companies represented by the *Fortune's* 500, is 4.26 years. There is a suggestion that the largest companies are prepared to take a longer view. Both average project times and average expected payback times are longer than those required by the other category, which is composed of smaller companies drawn from Moody's list of smaller industrials not in the larger 500. However, both groups of companies require a payback period of less than five years. Managements assume that on average a rate of return that will support a recoupment of the original cost of a project in under five years, is acceptable given typical rates of imitation. In terms of Table 4.5, perhaps 30 per cent of rivals may have adopted the innovation, by the time the originating company has recouped its capital investment. Generally rates of return on successful projects are thought to be very high. Certainly studies in agriculture,[24] petroleum refining,[25] and electrical equipment and appliance manufacture indicate that this is the case.[26] Managements apparently require a high inducement to compensate for the risks involved, and apply a heavy cautionary discount before accepting projects.

Table 4.3, showing the timelag between invention and innovation, gives the impression that development is essentially a long-term process, yet Table 4.6 shows that companies select projects which on average have a completion time of less than four years. In these terms only seven of the forty-six primary inventions in Table 4.3 would come to fruition within the average completion time. There would thus appear to be a clash between the findings. The explanation probably lies in the character of the innovations concerned. Table 4.3 represents a selection of primary inventions, whereas the typical project undertaken by companies is probably of a secondary character. As a risk-minimising device companies tend to emphasise short-reach projects which seek relatively minor advances in technology. Essentially Table 4.3 should not be used to illustrate the characteristics of the run of the mill innovation. The examples given there have been selected because of their importance. If the survival of patents is any guide, the normal invention is relatively unimportant. It is secondary in character and of itself makes only a minor contribution to technology. In these terms, the development time for average projects is relatively short, but if significant advances of a primary character are sought, these are likely to involve a longer time span. The typical attitude of companies does not mean that they will necessarily shun the longer term development, but does imply that they will tend to be in a numerical minority.

Another interesting general attitude of management towards research and development is the preference for particular types of projects. Companies prefer product to process innovation.[27] Management clearly believe that greater market impact is secured by launching new products rather than existing products at a cheaper price or at the same price but with an enhanced margin. This attitude is probably a reflection of an aversion to price competition, and the desire of companies to insulate themselves from rivals' encroachment by product differentiation. The distinction between product and process innovation is not clear, and perhaps the best interpretation of the apparent preference for product innovation is a general management predilection for sales security rather than cost advantage.

Table 4.7 R and D expenditure in 1968/9 as a percentage of net output in 1968; UK industries

Industry	%
Aerospace	39.1
Electronics and telecommunications	19.6
Mineral oil refining	12.2
Plastics	7.9
Pharmaceuticals and toiletries	7.0
Scientific instruments	5.5
Electrical machinery	5.3
Chemicals and coal products	4.6
Motor vehicles	4.2
Mechanical engineering	2.5
Textiles and manmade fibres	1.1
Food, drink and tobacco	0.9
Clothing and footwear	0.2

Sources. Economic Trends, Nov. 1970; *Board of Trade Journal*, 31 Dec. 1969.

Table 4.7 illustrates the allocation to R and D as a percentage of net output by industry in the UK. Net output is defined as in the Census of Production and represents the value added to materials by the process of production. It is the fund from which such items as wages, salaries and other costs, including depreciation and profits, are paid. Industries at the top of the list would appear to spend an impressively high percentage on R and D. However, the figures include money provided from government sources. When the percentages are calculated showing the amount of R and D financed from companies' own funds, the allocations appear much more modest. Thus, for example, Aerospace becomes 6.8 per cent, Electronics 10.1 per cent and Pharmaceuticals 6.4 per cent. Apparently even though expected rates of return to innovation are high, technical risk low and average project and pay-back periods are short, managements adopt a cautious attitude towards research and development. Their behaviour indicates that they believe market risk is high. In spite of selection procedures which insure a fairly high probability of technical success, a high rate of return is required either as a cautionary discount or as a compensatory inducement to face the market risks involved. The typical allocation to R and D is kept relatively modest, commensurate with general management attitudes to this expenditure.

The separation of technical and market risk into distinct categories is a somewhat artificial procedure. In practice both types of risk have a bearing on each other. A really significant invention is likely to involve a relatively high level of technical and market risk. The degree of novelty will have a direct bearing on the marketing function. If the product is genuinely new then a market will have to be created. The parameters of demand potential cannot be easily inferred, because previous experience is not there as a guide. Concorde is an interesting example. In developing supersonic passenger travel the British and French Governments face a high level of both technical and market risk. The development costs to date are approximately £1000 million, over four times the original estimate. Marketing difficulties involve persuading customers of the advantages of swift travel as a compensation for the high selling price and also overcoming a strong environmental and pollution lobby. The aircraft is so far advanced that a considerable market reluctance has to be overcome to achieve acceptance. Of course this is an extreme example, nevertheless the general point emerges, namely that technical and market risk are related and the more advanced an innovation is the higher these risks are likely to be. Reasonable data exist indicating that technical risk, in so far as it may be separated, is relatively low. Information on market risk is more limited. The evidence in one study suggests the following progression: of 100 projects, 57 may be completed technically, 31 may be made commercial, and 12 are likely to be a success. Thus the odds on success would appear to be approximately one in eight. These findings are based on 220 projects in three research and development laboratories in the USA in chemicals and drugs.[28] The general behaviour of companies implies that they believe market risk to be high. However, the data of the allocation to R and D by industry also indicates that some industries take a less jaundiced view than others. The reasons for this are explained below.

Company research and development commitment will be determined partly by industrial factors and partly by the attitude of individual managements. In general, allocation to research and development will be influenced by consumer priority for technological change, the ease of obtaining advances, the market structure and nature of competition, and managements' risk preference. Research and development within a firm serves a number of purposes. It confers on a company an 'in house' technological capability to generate innovations, and permits swift response to those developed by rivals. As a result the product potential of a company is widened. Research activity can smooth the path of diversification. It is a major influence making for non price competition. R and D can soften the blow of competition by permitting skilful differentiation of products. Alternatively it can service innovative competition, where companies vie with each other in the technological excellence of their products and the speed at which these can be improved.

Research and development tends to be expensive and in the nature of a fixed cost. There are three major reasons why R and D tends to be a fixed cost. First, research is normally financed by a lump sum rather than a proportionate allocation from profit. Second, there are probably minimum levels of expenditure below which a company is unlikely to achieve results. Third, there are persuasive reasons making for stability and continuity in research and development allocations. Continuity of employment is important. Personnel leaving a company will take expertise with them. A rival company acquiring such individuals will immediately have access to such knowledge at very low cost. It takes a number of years before a newly formed research and development team becomes productive. As a consequence companies tend to gear research and development expenditure to a level which is maintainable over all likely profit fluctuations. In this way they should avoid the necessity of having to dismiss R and D personnel and thus maintain continuity. It would be a most unwise concern that varied its research commitment with immediate commercial results. The prudent company will adopt a lagged partial adaptation procedure, where R and D allocation is geared to profits but responds in such a fashion that the allocation is maintainable.

Minimum levels of research and development have been estimated for the electronic capital goods industry. The figures relate to 'threshold' levels of research expenditure. These represent sufficient expenditure to keep abreast of technological change, to keep a flow of improvements, and where necessary to launch new models. The threshold figures are absolute values. When these are divided by the lead time, then approximate annual figures are derived. Lead time is the period between project preparation and the launch of full scale production. Derived annual figures range from £40,000 p.a. for radio communication receivers to £8 million p.a. for a communications satellite.[29] Other industries may be less daunting in the minimum sums required. A low figure may make a significant impact in mechanical engineering or furniture, where the character and complexity of typical products is perhaps not so great. Table 4.7 makes it clear that R and D commitments do vary by industry. It is fair to label computers, electrical equipment, aircraft, and pharmaceuticals, as research intensive; furniture, footwear, and food, by contrast are the least involved.

Presumably the minimum level in an R and D intensive industry will tend to be higher than in less technologically orientated activities. Explanations for this varying commitment to research tend to centre on the nature of the product and the industrial environment. Technological push or customer pull are descriptive labels for the type of pressures to which companies respond.

Table 4.8 Technological environment

Industries	r^2, *patents on sales*
Food and tobacco products	0.52
Paper and allied products	0.07
General chemicals	0.73
Petroleum	0.68
Fabricated metal products and miscellaneous	0.32
electrical equipment and communications	0.90
All industries	0.42

Source. Scherer, *American Economic Review*, 1965 (ref. 46).

Table 4.8 provides examples to show interindustry differences in the pressure of the technological environment. Where the correlation between patents and sales is high, this indicates that there is a strong pressure for technological change. Where the relationship is low, the pressure is assumed to be correspondingly low. If this table is compared with Table 4.7 it becomes clear that industries with a high R and D sales ratio also tend to have a high patent sales correlation. It has also been found elsewhere that there is a fairly close relationship between input measures (research and development expenditure and R and D employees), and output measures (patents acquired and value of new product sales).[30] In effect the indicators of technological orientation are good substitutes one for the other. Either input or output measures may be used with reasonable confidence.

Technological push is a descriptive term for the impetus to change which tradition and the type of activity generate. It represents the commitment to change and opportunities for technological activity arising from within an industry. Suppliers may undertake a whole series of innovations and thus force consequential changes along the chain of production. The major product of the industry may be relatively new and undergoing rapid change as modifications and improvements are incorporated. An industry may be 'science based' and able to draw freely from discoveries originating in universities, government and basic research institutes. An industry may be hustled forward by its own technological impetus. The type of competition and the structure of the industry may encourage this form of innovative rivalry.

Customer pull is the pressure exerted by purchasers of the industry's products. The consumer may supply a considerable incentive by choosing the most advanced products. By opting for these and against companies with the least technological advantage, customers exert economic pressure. Companies with up-to-date products are seen to be profitable, and those with old fashioned goods suffer. Resources shift towards the change-oriented companies and firms with obsolete products either go out of existence or make efforts to change. A potent customer pull effect can be exerted by governments and nationalised industries. The United States government-sponsored space effort had a dynamising effect on all the companies involved. This effect spun off throughout the chain of contractors and subcontractors, and galvanised economic and technological performances. Similar effects can be traced in the Concorde and the Advanced Passenger Train project in the United Kingdom.[31] These are examples of monopsonistic buying power where governments acting through publicly controlled bodies can exert tremendous customer pull.

The 'push and pull' models of innovation can be subdivided as follows:[32] 'Science discovers, technology applies' (DS), and the technological discovery model (DT). DS is used to describe scientific discoveries which are applied by industry; DT represents the process of technology building on technology, where the impetus is not based on a scientific discovery but on a technological development. Technological or need pull, is similarly divided into customer need (NC), and management by objectives (NX). NC refers to need pull of a sort where market research or customer requirements indicate a market; NX refers to a need identified by management rather than customers. For example, the need to reduce costs or produce a new product as a defence against takeover.[33]

Table 4.9 shows a classification of the character of stimulant present in the case of eighty-four successful innovations. The innovations were successful in that they were all developed by British companies who

Table 4.9 Stimulant to successful innovation: comparison of large technological change innovations with others

Innovation model	Large technological change	Smaller technological change
Not known	1	7
DT	3	2
NC	1	17
NX	2	16
Dual	4	31
Total	11	73

Source. J. Langrish *et al., Wealth from Knowledge* (ref. 13), p. 77.

subsequently won the Queen's Award for industry. A large technological change refers to innovations which have a considerable impact on existing technology. If the innovation induces a significant alteration in teaching at university level then this is classed as large. For example, a new textbook or a considerable revision of existing textbooks may be necessary. Smaller technological changes refer to innovations which cause at most revision of one or two chapters or the addition of new chapters. Dual refers to innovations which cannot be clearly classified to a single type of model. The table indicates that the need or customer pull model is the most frequent stimulant. The run of the mill minor innovation, arises not from the application of basic discoveries but is need and technology orientated. In contrast, major innovations perhaps indicate a greater leaning towards the discovery push type of model although there were no DS observations. This would accord with expectations. Major innovations are likely to involve new principles. More modest developments are likely to represent improvements on current technology and be more market or customer orientated.

The major attraction of innovation as an industrial activity is the economic potential. Company performance will be greatly enhanced by successful innovation. In a study of a sample of companies from the American steel and petroleum industries it has been found that in companies with comparable initial size successful innovation had considerable economic payoff. A comparison with companies' growth rate before innovation and the performance of other non-innovating companies indicates, in every time interval and in both industries, that the successful innovators grew much faster. This tendency was not exhibited before the innovations. The average effect of a successful innovation was to raise a firm's annual growth rate by 4 to 13 per cent.[34] However, as already indicated, other economic characteristics tend to reduce the attraction of innovation. Judgment of technical and market risk will influence companies' allocation of funds to R and D, so also will the industrial environment. For some industries innovative activity is part of their way of life, for others it is an optional extra. Particular companies in given industries can of course behave as deviants and a company in a research intensive industry can express its own management preference by not being involved in R and D. Similarly, another company in a low technology activity may in fact be research intensive. Company involvement tends to be a reflection of management preference, industrial environment and structural influences. These influences will be discussed below.

Innovation and the size of companies

Company expenditure on R and D is an expression of a desire to be involved in the process of technological change. The large company should have a marked advantage in technological activity. Size confers a number of benefits which have a direct bearing on R and D. The shares of a large company tend to be highly marketable. The valuation ratio (value of the ordinary shares divided by the book value of the assets) tends to be greater than that of a small company.[35] Because the shares are so marketable raising additional capital is relatively cheap. In addition the proportion of cash required to take over another company is relatively small. This can make the large company an effective predator in takeover battles. There are also indications that the likelihood of takeover is reduced by size. The larger a company is the lower tends to be the probability of takeover.[36] This is not a strong relationship but there is sufficient evidence to suggest that it does exist and to some extent therefore the large company is lifted from the threat of takeover. Financial results also indicate that the large company tends to have a lower level of deviation in average profitability. There are also signs that this stability may represent a form of trade off where lower deviation is purchased at the expense of lower than average profitability.[37] The power of the large company to effect takeovers and also to resist them, and their financial stability amount to important influences making for continuity in any research and development programme. Such companies are able to isolate their research and development departments from the threats which may prevail in smaller companies. As has been argued earlier, continuity and stability may be significant factors in productive research effort. Large companies are more likely to be able to provide these conditions. Companies with high turnover are better able to carry the fixed costs involved with R and D and reduce these to a relatively small percentage claim on total resources. They have the economic power to bring new discoveries to the market quickly. They are able to adopt risk-shifting devices in the organisation of their research and can adopt a large number approach. Failures can be carried by successes so that the overall level of uncertainty incurred in research programmes becomes acceptable. Market power should allow large firms to secure high returns on innovations and to recoup expenses fast. Furthermore innovational edge should not be eroded too fast by the encroachment of rivals. If large companies are diversified, this should confer yet another advantage. It should permit them to produce and market a high proportion of the unexpected inventions which are the almost inevitable outcome of research.[38]

Large size may not be without its disadvantages. There may be a temptation to substitute numbers for quality in research personnel. The propensity to 'empire build' will have much more scope in the sizeable corporation. Reins of control are difficult to keep taut. The chain of command through from senior management to the level at which orders are executed may be long. Personal involvement and intensity of motivation may suffer in a bureaucratic atmosphere. Small autonomous research departments which compete with each other within the company may even be set up to combat lethargy. On balance, however, the specific financial advantages of large companies would appear powerful. As long as managements are aware of the disadvantages of size, action can be taken to safeguard against these. This ought to leave the large corporation with a marked advantage in R and D. The advantages of the large company in research and development would appear overwhelming. Nevertheless empirical evidence of the importance of firm size in relation to R and D yields mixed results. It has been found that the percentage of companies undertaking research increases steadily with the size of the firm.[39] In effect the larger the firm the greater the likelihood of its carrying out some research and development. But when evidence is collected of relative efforts, the picture becomes less clear.

Table 4.10 Privately financed research and development expenditures as a percentage of sales, USA, 1963

| Industry group | *Companies with total employment of* | | |
	less than 1000	*1000 to 4999*	*5000 or more*
All industries combined	1.5	1.4	2.1
Chemicals and drugs	2.7	3.3	3.7
Petroleum refining and extraction	n.a.	1.0	0.9
Machinery	1.5	2.0	4.0
Electrical equipment and communications	3.2	2.5	3.8
Motor vehicles and other transportation equipment	0.8	0.7	2.6
Aircraft and missiles	2.0	2.0	2.6
Professional and scientific instruments	3.1	3.4	5.5

Source. Scherer, *Industrial Market Structure and Economic Performance* (ref. 1).

Table 4.10 shows that in each and every industry group except petroleum refining, research activity increases with size. However, when larger companies are taken, with employment of more than 5000 personnel, there is a broad tendency for R and D not to rise in proportion. Amongst the largest 500 companies in the USA there is a tendency in the majority of cases for increases in size to have a stultifying effect on R and D intensity.[40] A summary of these findings would indicate that 'up to a certain size, innovational effort increases more than proportional to size: at that size, which varies from industry to industry, a fitted curve has an inflection point and among the largest few firms innovational effort generally does not increase and may decline with size'.[41] There would thus appear to be a relationship between size and willingness to put resources at risk in search of new products and processes. The relationship is not simple, nor likely to have an unambiguous meaning. There may be an optimum size of company, but this will probably be specific to particular industries. This is hardly surprising because technological pressure varies between activities and also with the level of effort required to make an impact. Furthermore the overall pattern is consistent with a wide variety of individual findings. For example, an investigation which only includes the largest companies, may reveal a negative relationship between size and R and D. The sample may cover only that section where research declines as size increases. Alternatively a sample that spans the middle range may reveal a low or zero correlation, and one which covers only relatively small companies may reveal a strong and positive association. All these findings are consistent with the overall pattern. In broad terms there would appear to be a tendency for R and D inputs to rise until a size level of approximately 5000 employees is reached. Beyond this size there is a tendency for there not to be a proportionate rise, and amongst the largest companies R and D allocations may decline.

When the relationship between firms' size and research is examined, not from a research expenditure point of view but in terms of innovations actually introduced, there is broad confirmation of the general pattern that it is possible for companies to be too large. In a study of the United States iron and steel, petroleum refining, and bituminous coal industries, important processes and products introduced since 1918 were examined to determine whether the four largest firms in each sector were responsible for a disproportionately large share.[42] A disproportionate share is assumed to exist where a firm's share of innovations is greater than its market share. It transpired that the largest companies did not always introduce a disproportionate share of innovations. In petroleum and coal, the four largest companies introduced more than their market share. In steel they did not. General factors which worked in favour of large size included: innovations which required large investment relative to the size of the potential user; a minimum size of firm for effective commercial use of the innovation which was large compared to the average firm; and an average size of the four firms under investigation which was much larger than the average size of potential users.

A similar conclusion emerges on the effects of size when scale effects are examined in the organisation of research. There may be considerable economies of scale in R and D. The largest firms may have a marked advantage in the productivity of their innovative effort. The output of research departments organised within large companies may be demonstrably superior to that of smaller concerns. Alternatively diseconomies may arise and output per unit expenditure may decline as the scale of spending increases. Examination of the influence of scale can be resolved into two issues. First, is a unit of research effort more productive when carried out in a large or small firm? Second, in firms of a given size, is a greater research effort associated with greater research output? These are organisational questions which attempt to establish the effectiveness of a unit of research expenditure in terms of innovative output, in firms of varying size and the effects of varying R and D expenditure in firms of a similar size.

In a study based on major firms in the USA in chemicals, petroleum and steel, an attempt is made to investigate these scale effects.[43] On the first issue relating to the influence of varying firm size on a unit of research expenditure, the inventive output seemed to be lower per unit expenditure in the largest firms compared with the medium and large ones. Apparently a given sum spent on research is not necessarily more effectively employed in the largest companies. There were indications problems arose with control and organisation. On the second issue, which attempts to determine the influence of greater research expenditure in firms of a given size, the indications were that holding firm size constant, the number of inventions seemed strongly influenced by the amount of R and D expenditure in all of the industries. But there appeared to be a more than proportional increase in inventive output only in chemicals. In the other industries there was no evidence of economies of scale in research expenditure. This perhaps indicates that there are no marked advantages of the largest scale research activities over the medium and large ones. There would appear to be conflicting forces in action. These are the disadvantages in terms of average productivity per unit of expenditure of organising research within the largest firms, and the influence of more expenditure within firms of a given size. Perhaps it is possible to be too large for effective organisation of research. The largest companies may risk passing the optimum.

There is also weak evidence that the quality of innovation among the largest companies is lower than those achieved by less sizeable concerns. The largest companies appear to spend more on R and D per patent pending, and they tend to use a lower proportion of their patents for commercial exploitation.[44] Apparently smaller concerns secure patents for a lower R and D cost and utilise a higher proportion. This, of course, is only broad evidence and will not stand much generalisation, nevertheless it is perhaps indicative.

The reader should remember that these figures relate to the USA, and also that the indicators of size are really a catch-all for a wide variety of other influences which need separating. In effect it may not be size, as such, which is important, but the consequences of size. The character of the general arguments on the advantages of size only indicate potential benefits. The nature of the arguments makes it clear that size is really being used as a proxy for a large number of influences that may be conducive to technological commitment. For example, the following may be relevant to a company's R and D expenditure: management motivation and skill, industrial and technological environment, past success in innovation, the type of research involved, profit earning power, the efficiency of research departments, and the company's product mix. These are the type of factors which make size such a catch-all and an unsatisfactory indicator. Essentially there is a considerable identification problem and the investigator has to probe deeper for improved understanding.

Diversified output

Arguments favouring size usually assume that large companies are likely to be multiproduct in character. This may be a significant factor inducing increased research and development commitment. Diversified output may mean that the unexpected findings which are almost inevitable from research may be utilised. The probability that the findings are compatible with existing output is enhanced when a company has a wide variety of products. The knowledge generated by R and D may also be relevant for more than one product. Furthermore the effect of diversified output may be earlier utilisation of an innovation. Such companies enjoy a form of commercial insurance in that their success is not dependent on a specialised output, but on a wide variety of products. This may induce a bolder approach to development and thus an earlier introduction of innovations. A firm which has a diversified output is also likely to operate in one or more progressive industries. Its knowledge network, and thus the potential source of ideas, is likely to be wide. This should improve the flow of commercially useful ideas. A company is unlikely to become technologically stagnant. The impetus from activities in the newer and dynamic parts of turnover should prevent this form of relaxation. The profit performance of diversified companies should be relatively stable and the R and D commitment commensurably higher. Basic research which is likely to yield the most unexpected results, should benefit most from this profit stability and widespread range of products.[4][5]

There is as yet insufficient evidence to establish the proposition that diversified companies are more involved in basic research. On the general effect of diversified companies and research and development there are conflicting findings. One study concludes that 'diversification is not per se a structural condition necessarily favourable to patentable invention'.[4][6] The author calculates a diversification index to measure the number of technologically distinct manufacturing lines. He uses this in regression equations of patenting on sales, and R and D employment on sales, in seventy-one firms in fourteen broad industry groups. In the two most research intensive groups, chemicals and drugs, and electrical equipment, the partial correlations relating to diversification were negative and statistically insignificant. In the other groups which did little R and D there were positive and significant relationships with the index of diversification. In essence the findings were the opposite to those expected. Apparently diversification was not a stimulus to R and D. Instead the data illustrated the favourable effect of operating in dynamic industries, by firms whose base was not conducive to patenting and research and development. Another study of forty-one firms in chemical, drug and petroleum industries finds that R and D as a percentage of sales in companies rises with the amount of diversification.[47] In this study the findings are in line with expectations.

With the conflict in the evidence, the appropriate conclusion on the effects of diversification may be as follows. There are a number of arguments which suggest that diversification should be favourable to R and D. It may not, however, be a primary variable in the determination of the level of research spending. Potentially, diversification may have favourable effects on R and D. It may also be a structural means to gain a foothold in more progressive industries without committing companies to the level of research expenditure typical in these activities.

Market form

Arguments indicating the advantage of large companies in the R and D process tend to include a degree of market power as a beneficial influence. It is implied that large companies are likely to have a considerable degree of market power. This should ensure considerable consumer goodwill when a new product is launched and also wide market coverage. Large companies probably enjoy a degree of monopoly and therefore may have a profitability and liquidity advantage which should be propitious to research orientation. But the particular market form most conducive to R and D is by no means clear. In order to encourage innovative competition, companies require sufficient market power to recoup the costs involved and provide an adequate reward to encourage a continuing and high level involvement with R and D. The degree of market power must not be so great as to induce economic lethargy or allow too much economic slack to develop. There must be sufficient threat from rivals to keep a company on its toes and at the same time competition must not be so fierce that the incentive to innovate is destroyed. This type of argument tends to narrow the market forms suitable for innovative competition to those lying between the extremes of perfect competition and monopoly. The intermediate market forms become candidates, by a process of elimination. Under perfect competition a firm has no incentive to generate new products or processes. There is unlikely to be enough priority in time for an innovator to recoup his research costs. There are no entry barriers or restrictions preventing copying. Any company innovating in these circumstances will benefit competitors and not itself. They will be able to adopt the new technology, incurring only the costs involved with copying. The price will inevitably drop to a level where the imitators are earning normal profits and so the initiating company incurs losses. Thus under perfect competition there is an extreme appropriation problem, which makes this type of market form inimical to research and development. In order to accommodate technological change arising from research efforts of member firms, the perfectly competitive model has to be modified. Entry restrictions, licensing or tax arrangements to make imitators contribute towards the original research costs, patent protection, collective research, these are the types of alterations which would be required. All these modifications amount to a curb on the rigour of the competitive process to generate an incentive to invent.

At the other extreme, monopoly may not be conducive to research. Two types of arguments should be distinguished. First is the expectation of becoming a monopolist, and the second is the performance of a company which already is a monopolist. The first argument stresses the motivation to become a monopolist and emphasises the attractions of achieving supernormal profits. The second argument, relating to companies which are already monopolists, stresses that market power and financial stability may be conducive to innovative activity. The expectational arguments can apply to any type of company. There is always the possibility that a firm may become a monopolist by the sheer brilliance of its performance. In practice this expectation is reinforced deliberately by the legal device of a patent. Discussion on whether patents are successful in this role, is deferred until Chapter 10. The conclusions from the arguments relating to established monopolies are less clearcut than those applying to perfect competition. A company can earn long-run supernormal profits. Therefore it is in a position to devote funds to R and D and will have little fear of rivals' encroachment when new products are launched. It may even undertake long-run research of a basic character as well as the more usual type of innovative activity. Recoupment of costs is unlikely to be a problem. Appropriation of the benefits of innovative activity is not in question, nor is the financial means to generate new goods.

The case against monopoly is essentially behavioural. The incentive for continuous improvement of product or process range may be damped by the commercial success which monopolies have already achieved. A monopolist has a large amount of discretion in its operating criterion. It may be a profit maximiser, a sales maximiser, a quiet lifer or a satisficer. Unlike perfect competition, profit maximisation is not a prerequisite for survival. A monopolist may choose the desired level of performance. Lack of pressure from rivals and the optional character of the required economic performance are likely to generate managerial slack. Profits may be too permanent to provide an adequate stimulus for continuing effort. Motivation for high level performance is not imposed by outside economic pressure but has to be generated from within. As a result there is a presumption that monopolies are likely to become lethargic and turn away from innovative activity. Investment in R and D is only one of many possible ways in which company funds can be spent. With so many potential outlets why should effort be devoted to this management intensive, risky and costly activity? Economic affluence may not breed the conditions propitious to innovative activity. The stress of a less well established market position may be much more appropriate. Managerial slack and economic complacency generated by the absence of competition may thus reduce the case for monopoly as the market form most likely to encourage innovation.

When monopolistic competition is under review as a candidate for innovative excellence the process of elimination continues. Monopolistic competition is rivalry between many companies, but where each has just sufficient market influence to make product differentiation a worthwhile economic strategy. There is an economic incentive to distinguish goods from those of rivals. This has the effect of creating an element of protection from rivals' encroachments because consumer loyalty is generated. At the same time products are deliberately not made too different from those typical in the industry, so that new customers will be attracted. There is a degree of differentiation, but this is hedged by the practical requirement that products should not be too unlike those of rivals. The pricing discretion of an individual company is therefore fairly limited. The incentive to invent is presumed to be low. With many firms in the industry, the relative market share of one company is likely to be small. The immediate impact secured by an innovation is likely to be minor and with rapid imitation by rivals, the recoupment period is likely to be short. On cost grounds, minor improvements rather than radical innovations are therefore likely to be typical. Companies are probably small and thus incapable of carrying large R and D programmes. In essence monopolistic competition can be plausibly represented as 'small firm, many firm competition', with a low propensity to generate technological change.

The remaining market form of an intermediate character is oligopoly. This is competition between a few companies. The emphasis on non-price rivalry is likely to be high. Companies are closely interrelated in that what one achieves has an immediate and obvious effect on the others. Competition in this sense becomes highly personal and directed. Companies assess their rivals' reactions before adopting a particular policy. A move elicits a response, and the whole commercial process takes on a strategic flavour, where rivals' reactions become a major parameter in decision-making. In these circumstances companies tend to be highly averse to price competition. There is a quiescent situation where a power struggle is always a possibility. The sharpest and most feared weapon in the competitive armoury is the price cut. This is so because short-term operating criteria dictate that only prime costs need be covered. A price war may therefore become destructive in character where the stakes are survival or bankruptcy. Less fraught means of competition therefore tend to be preferred. Product competition does not present an immediate threat to other companies in the industry. Companies can weigh customer reaction to a new variation. If it proves successful they can adopt the change. They can afford to play the waiting game because copying is usually cheaper than initiation. Admittedly they may lose the goodwill which may reward the innovating company, and the earnings premium available to the company first in the field, but at least their livelihood is not immediately threatened. In addition product competition has the attraction that it can soften the blow of rivals' price cuts. Products are not exactly similar so the attraction of a lower price is not immediately obvious to the customer. Non-price competition is therefore a favoured form of commercial rivalry. It can to some extent inure customers to the blandishment of rivals' products and mitigate the effects of price competition.

Under oligopoly, companies are likely to be big. Each one will control a significant proportion of the market. Size should confer a degree of earning power and profit stability, and also a turnover of sufficient magnitude to carry a viable R and D programme. The incentive to carry out research will be present because non-price competition is the preferred type of rivalry. At the same time motivation for continuing effort should remain high because unlike monopoly there is sufficient rivalry to reduce complacency. A compromise is achieved whereby the disadvantages of fierce competition are avoided, and also the enervating effects of monopoly. Companies under oligopoly should have sufficient financial power to institute and maintain a continuous R and D effort. In addition they should have enough power to launch innovations quickly and effectively. Recoupment of expenses should be fast enough to sustain managements' confidence in the competitive benefits of research. This does not mean that every project has to be highly profitable, but that the balance of success and failure indicates research expenditure to be worth while. Rivals' reactions have to be muted in the sense that they must not be so prompt as to destroy the incentive to innovate, yet they must be sufficiently vigorous to prevent the onset of complacency. The number of companies in the oligopolist market structure should be sufficient to prevent collusion and should not be so large that the benefits of size are lost. Collusive oligopoly will approximate to monopoly in its behaviour, and large number oligopoly will tend to the behaviour pattern associated with monopolistic competition. A loose rather than tight market pattern is prescribed where there is 'few firm, big firm' competition, with an active level of commercial rivalry and a strong bias towards R and D. This is sometimes called competitive oligopoly. The word competitive is included to stress that rivalry must be active and that there must be no collusion.[48]

The general character of the arguments supporting an intermediate market form as that most propitious to innovative activity turns on the benefits of size, market influence, the availability of finance and the incentive to undertake research and development. Passing support for the contention that an intermediate market form is likely to be propitious to research comes from studies investigating the relationship between the financial position of companies and their allocation to research. It has been argued that large companies should be in a favourable position to undertake R and D. Their powerful financial position should sustain a considerable research effort. Spread across a sizeable turnover an effective research and development programme should not be too great a surcharge on current activities. Although management will be aware of the dangers of too great an R and D commitment, the profit stability of major companies should engender confidence. Because profits do not fluctuate as widely as in small companies, expenditure can be planned on a longer term basis and more closely geared to current earning power. A reasonably close correspondence between current financial results and subsequent R and D output is therefore a plausible expectation. However, in a study of over 400 companies drawn from *Fortune's* 1955 list, no significant correlation was found between profits as a percentage of sales, to patents per unit sales, even when plausible lags were introduced. When liquid assets to total assets is used as a measure of the financial health of companies, there is still no significant relationship with patents per unit sales. Apparently current liquidity and profits are not useful predictors of subsequent research performance.[49]

In a study of UK companies in four technologically orientated industries, chemicals, electrical engineering, electronics, and machine tools, innovative activity measured by patent numbers is apparently not influenced by prior profitability. Prior profitability is the average return on capital in the five years before the period covered by the patent. No significant correlations were found.[50] When prior cash flow (undistributed profits plus depreciation) is used as a liquidity measure mixed results emerge. Absolute cash flow figures are used. The influence of firm size is not removed by dividing by a measure of capital employed. This measure of liquidity proved to be a significant influence on patenting in chemicals and machine tools but not in electrical engineering and electronics firms.[51] However, if the hypothesis is reversed from a presumption that financial strength is a determinant of innovative activity, to an assertion that good profits are the results of past technological success, more interesting results emerge.

If patenting is assumed to lead to sales and then profits, and data lagged in appropriate fashion, significant relationships are found. Apparently patenting has an impact on sales and then profits, with a timelag of approximately four years.[52] Similarly in an analysis of eighteen chemical and five pharmaceutical companies in the USA it has been found that 'causality runs from R and D to productivity and finally to profitability'.[53] In other words present profitability is a result of past R and D activity, rather than the other way round. Apparently profitability does not determine R and D and thus changes in productivity. The link is not the expected one. Current profitability is not a good index of future research expenditure. It is more likely to reflect past research effort. This conclusion is not unchallenged, but the weight of evidence suggests that on balance this may turn out to be the predominant causal relationship.[54]

If it is accepted that causality runs from research to patents via productivity, then some insight into the nature of R and D decision-making process may emerge. Current research allocation becomes not merely a reflection of a company's financial strength to carry this expenditure, but an expression of a desire to enhance future profits. The motivation for research may come not from the existence of high profits, but from a desire to improve the present level of profits. High level current profits may therefore act as a disincentive. A stronger management motive to research may be generated by a level of profits adequate to carry viable research but not so large as to induce economic lethargy. In terms of the preconditions suitable to high level R and D commitment, stress may be more effective as a management motivator than an economic environment where rivals' encroachments are muzzled by the monopoly power of market leaders. The market form likely to confer sufficient stress and yet allow adequate profits, is unlikely to be monopoly.

Figure 4.1 summarises the type of considerations relevant to a

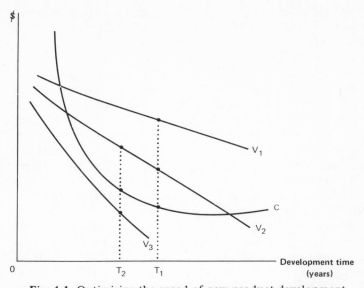

Fig. 4.1 Optimising the speed of new product development

Source. Scherer, *Industrial Market Structure and Economic Performance* (ref. 1).

particular company which already undertakes R and D, in assessing a particular development. It also helps to make plain the general arguments supporting particular market forms, by drawing out the assumptions which lie behind the discussions. Curve C summarises the expected cost/time tradeoff, where fast development of the project incurs high cost and a more leisurely approach lower cost. The curves labelled V1, 2 or 3 represent the benefits functions and indicate the expected discounted surplus of sales revenue over production and distribution costs, from the new product at varying introduction dates. Earlier introduction is assumed to yield higher benefits because a firm has more time to exploit profit potential and also its market share may be enhanced by the innovative reputation which it creates. On a profit maximising assumption, the firm will apply the familiar marginal criteria. The position of optimum new product development will occur where the slope of the time/cost function equals the slope of the relevant benefits function. The marginal cost of accelerating development will equal the marginal discounted surplus as a result of the shortened development period. Assume that V1 represents the benefits function of a monopolist. The slope of V1 is relatively flat. This implies that for such a company there is little to gain by speeding up the introduction of an innovation. There are no rivals of significance, so the monopolist is in a position to appropriate the majority of the expected revenues. Assume also that V2 represents a company under oligopoly, and V3 a company under monopolistic competition. Under V2 there are say four to six companies and under V3 say fifteen to twenty. V2 is below V1 because the market is shared between more rivals. V2 has also swung in a clockwise direction. There is now more pressure to introduce products earlier. The innovator will gain markets from competitors during his period of leadership. The innovator will often be anxious about the activities of rivals and these fears may spur him on. The result is an optimum development time, T2, which is appreciably faster than under monopoly. In addition more is spent on the venture. Apparently with more companies development time is speeded up.

Generalising is hazardous because the diagram represents decisions relating to individual products, but it does suggest in broad terms that oligopoly may be superior to monopoly. Companies with significant but not dominant market shares will feel impelled to earlier development. Their market shares are worth acquiring by rivals, and by the same token the benefits to a company of increasing its sales at the expense of fellow companies is considerable. If yet more firms are competing for a market, the incentive to innovate may be completely destroyed. In Fig. 4.1 V3 is below C, so there is no incentive to develop. The benefits function has been compressed so far to the left that pioneering of new products is no longer an economic proposition. The slope of the benefits function has increased, but the whole function has moved downwards and to the left, in line with the reduced profit potential expected from sharing the market with many imitators. This may actually be a situation where the pioneer may lose and all imitators gain. Companies may then deliberately hang back to avoid introducing new products. The market form will induce imitative competition and any company which is bold enough to pioneer an innovation may benefit rivals and not itself. The structural requirements for optimum development would thus appear to need a balance between the number of companies to provide a stimulus, and sufficient market influence to make R and D profitable. Too many companies may put a great emphasis on speed of development but not provide the market and profit prospects to support the high R and D costs that have to be incurred to bring a project to quick fruition. Too few companies may provide the market potential for an innovation but not the incentive for prompt development. A compromise is required which makes R and D profitable but also applies pressure for speedy fruition. An oligopolistic type of market would thus appear to be the best candidate for consideration.

Before this conclusion is accepted, a number of possible qualifications need to be noted. A dominant company may not be a vigorous innovator, but once challenged may respond extremely quickly. The large market share of a monopolist may be a deep temptation to the potential investor, and because there is so much to lose a challenge can have a galvanising effect on the industrial effort of the leading firm. In an attempt to reinstate its lost portion of the market it may respond by imitation with almost destructive force. This tendency for fast imitation by a dominant company may make a powerful case for a highly concentrated market form. It may be that imitation is more important to the economic wellbeing of a nation, than the initiation of technological change. No country except the USA and the USSR can hope to generate more than a small proportion of its own technological knowledge. In these terms it may be important to establish market conditions which are more conducive to copying than initiation. The role of waking the sleeping giant may fall to the small company. A monopoly may tolerate a few such companies in the interstices of the market. It may pay for its complacency by being prodded into action. The concern that small companies may warrant special treatment arises, not from a sentimental attachment to them, but from a realisation that technological ingenuity is by no means confined to large and well established firms. It also arises from an awareness that small companies may have a radical effect on the performance of a monopoly by providing a challenge.

The model used above assumes that each company carries out its own research and development and analyses the nature of the decision process relating to specific projects. Companies are assumed to have a commitment to research and development. Figure 4.1 is not concerned to illuminate which type of company will be the first to be involved in research and development. The arguments can however be recast. For example, assume that research is currently unprofitable for all types of companies whatever their market structure. V3 would be such a position. If all projects appear to have these characteristics then no company will be involved in development. The criterion for the earliest involvement would be tangency between C and V3. Assume that the passage of time will bring C and V3 closer together. Increasing wealth of consumers, shifts in factor costs and advances in knowledge are examples of forces which will influence the cost and benefits functions. If the convergence of the functions occurs smoothly, where C and V3 gradually move towards each other, then in these circumstances a monopolist will be the first type of company where the criteria for earliest possible involvement will apply. There will be no rivals to share the market, so the benefits schedule will be higher and further to the north-east than those of oligopoly and monopolistic competition. The tangency position will therefore be reached before any other market form, and monopoly would appear the most propitious in terms of the earliest involvement in R and D. The fact that the criteria are met does not mean however that a monopoly will necessarily be the first involved. It may choose to defer in the knowledge that later development may be more profitable. Given time, the benefits function may not merely be tangential to the cost function but well above it. Thus there may be a contrast between the theoretical conditions for earliest possible involvement and the actual time of involvement. On theoretical grounds, assuming a smooth convergence of the relevant schedules, the monopolist would appear the most favourable market form for this type of decision. On the practical grounds of the actual time of involvement, the monopolist may not be first in the field. It may defer R and D so long, that the situation becomes sufficiently profitable to support an oligopolistic market. With the incentive effect spurring them on, oligopolistic companies may thus become involved before the monopolist.

Where the cost and benefit schedules move together, not smoothly but discontinuously, following in the wake of a technological breakthrough, the conclusions are even less clear. As argued in Chapter 3, on invention, technological advance probably does not proceed in an orderly and smooth fashion. There are discontinuities which have to be overcome. The process of invention is characterised by spurts of progress where discoveries are made and applied. Involvement in these innovations can be highly profitable. In terms of Fig. 4.1, V3 may shift extremely rapidly, from below to well above the C schedule. With ample profits and prospects the market form which will induce the most rapid development will be that where the stimulus effect is the greatest. Under these conditions companies which are most on their toes and quickest to recognise the potential of an invention, and have the greatest incentive, will be the first to be involved in R and D. If the project is sufficiently profitable, companies under monopolistic competition may be the first to undertake development. In essence then, the size and speed of the shift in the V function will determine the market form most likely to be first involved. As this will vary in practice with the type and character of innovations, no firm conclusions can be drawn on this issue.

The character of development undertaken may vary between market forms. It was argued earlier that monopolies can earn long-run supernormal profits. Management can thus afford to undertake investment projects with long-time horizons. In terms of R and D involvement, monopolies are therefore more likely to undertake basic research than most other companies. They can undertake higher levels of technological risk and countenance a longer period to fruition. Alternatively, where they undertake normal applied research the cautionary discount applied in assessing the returns may be lower than companies in more competitive situations. Because their potential developments are unlikely to be encroached on their allowance for market risk may be relatively low. In terms of Fig. 4.1, it is now being argued that there may be little comparability between the type of research undertaken in different market forms or in the criterion applied in their assessment. Monopoly may reach for really significant developments, oligopoly may pursue less ambitious projects, and monopolistic competition may undertake mere differentiation. To compare the speed of development of a given project whose time/cost trade off is represented by a single schedule common to all types of market structure, may thus be superimposing too great a degree of comparability into the situation. Companies in differing market positions may adopt development projects appropriate to their financial and market status. A comparison of a single project which is a practical possibility for all types of market structures, may thus be an interesting theoretical exercise, but may have the effect of focusing attention on an area empty of empirical content. There is some evidence to indicate a degree of specialisation in innovation. Table 4.11 shows the involvement of small firms by the type of industrial effort. Small firms are defined as those with a labour force of 200 or less. The small firm typically avoids involvement in aerospace, glass, shipbuilding, motor vehicles and public utilities. The capital intensive nature of production processes make these an inappropriate area for research activity by the small firm. Their particular forte lies in areas which are not so demanding in resources. Timber and furniture, scientific instruments, textile machinery and leather and footwear are examples. In these areas the contribution of the small firm is marked.

There has been a considerable academic effort to determine the economic environment most conducive to research and development. A major problem has been that of identification. Real world situations make it difficult to establish for certainty the type of competition prevailing. The normal measures of the type of competition are the numbers of companies operating in an industry or the concentration ratio. The concentration ratio is a measure of the percentage of sales accounted for by the leading companies. The higher the percentage of sales accounted for by the major companies, the closer the situation approximates to monopoly. In the same way the fewer the companies there are in a given industry the less competitive a situation is assumed to be. But these head countings and percentage calculation procedures are subject to a number of major difficulties. These include the practical problems of defining an industry, the independence of companies and the difficulties associated with multinational companies.

Today big companies tend to be multiproduct in character. They have a diversified output as a form of commercial insurance. They are aware that particular products only have a limited economic life, so a strategy is adopted to give a product mix which avoids the perils of

Table 4.11 Share of innovations in the UK since 1945 by large, medium and small enterprises and capital-intensity of branch of industry

Industry 1958 SIC	Capital expenditure as a percentage of net output, 1963	Percentage share of innovations: large firms (1000+ employed)	Percentage share of innovations: medium firms (200–999 employed)	Percentage share of innovations: small firms (1–199 employed)
Gas	41	93	7	0
Cement	27	100	0	0
Steel	19	96	4	0
Dyes	14	86	14	0
Aluminium	14	100	0	0
Paper and board	13	50	30	20
Motor vehicles	12	89	7	4
Food	12	75	17	8
Coal	12	100	0	0
Plastics	11	94	2	4
Glass	10	100	0	0
Textiles	9	79	11	10
Shipbuilding	8	96	2	2
Machine tools	7	86	3	11
Scientific instruments	7	60	12	28
Electronics	6	86	6	8
Aerospace	6	98	2	0
General machinery	6	67	16	17
Textile machinery	6	42	35	23
Construction	6	55	33	12
Timber and furniture	6	22	39	39
Leather and footwear	5	54	20	26
Pharmaceuticals	5	98	2	0

Source. SPRU Survey prepared for the Bolton Committee of Enquiry on Small Firms. Cmnd 4811, 1971.

dependence on specialist output and gives the advantage of a large numbers approach. They do not necessarily sacrifice the advantages associated with specialisation. Such companies are generally big enough to enjoy scale economies with each of their product lines. With multiproduct companies the concept of an industry becomes difficult to apply. Allocation of companies to particular industries becomes dependent on the definitions adopted and misleading interpretations can result.

The independence of companies relates to the likelihood of collusion and/or arrangements between companies which may frustrate competition. Examples include interlocking directories, trade investments, part ownership of competitors, conditional purchase arrangements involving for example full-line selling and tie-in sales, and conditional or exclusive marketing arrangements. Such devices may make an assessment of the competitive environment difficult. A low concentration ratio or a large number of companies within a particular activity, may indicate strong commercial rivalry. Reality may be different: the true situation could approximate to the most grinding form of monopoly.

Subsidiary companies raise similar problems in assessing the character of the economic environment. Such companies are offshoots from other companies. They may be owned by foreign-based concerns or backed by home companies. In either case they are difficult to assess because their economic power is not well summarised by normal performance data. The competitive threat of a subsidiary is probably much greater than that presented by a similar sized independent and autonomous company. Parent company knowhow, availability of group capital, and the protection which a subsidiary may enjoy from the full rigour of the competitive process, suggest that even a small subsidiary could exercise a degree of commercial influence out of all proportion to its size. There is evidence that subsidiaries are peculiar in the sense that they appear less constrained by normal commercial criteria. They can achieve spectacular growth rates even with unpromising profit figures. Parent company funds can sustain operation and subsidise activities until they reach a viable size. The normal association between growth and profit rates which govern autonomous companies may not operate.[55] The competitive environment of an industry which has a significant proportion of subsidiary companies is therefore likely to be particularly difficult to assess. The normal indicators are likely to be misleading.

The problems raised by subsidiaries are closely linked with those created by multinational companies. Multinationals are firms which locate production facilities in more than one country. It is these companies which are responsible for a significant proportion of subsidiaries throughout the world. The effect of the multinational is to make the concept of an industry or market look even more ragged. Such companies effectively destroy the usefulness of any simple means for judging the economic climate prevalent in a particular activity. Company attitudes will be worldwide in scope. No longer can local economic conditions prevalent in a particular country be expected to have a great influence on companies whose turnover is global in scope. This objection cannot be sidestepped on the grounds that these companies are numerically unimportant. Multinationals are fast growing in number and are prevalent in high technology activities. For example, the greatest concentration of foreign owned subsidiaries in the United Kingdom is to be found in those industries with the highest growth rate and with the greatest research and development orientation.[56] A similar pattern may apply in the majority of Western European nations. Thus the real world problems involved in assessing the character of the economic environment tend to put the theoretical discussion into perspective. The difficulties associated with defining an industry and assessing the competitive environment make for results which require great care in interpretation.

Studies of the relationship between market form and the level of innovative activity yield mixed results. Where the growth of productivity is used as an index of technological progress, the results are not particularly illuminating. One study indicates a positive correlation between increases in productivity and concentration,[57] another indicates that productivity increases more in low concentration industries.[58] Both studies have a considerable overlap in the data and time period covered, though there are differences in the measures of concentration used. Nevertheless they appear to yield diametrically opposed results. Reasons for this clash probably turn on varying opportunities for technological involvement in the industries concerned and the difference in the economic environment in activities with the same concentration ratio. For example, an industry with bright future prospects is likely to have a completely different attitude to investment from that of one where the concentration ratio may be the same but where the future is gloomy. However, the most fundamental reason for the apparent contradiction in the results probably turns on the use of increases in productivity as a proxy for technological progressiveness. Improvements in output per man reflect a large number of factors. These include changes in capital intensity, improved management, a higher rate of adoption of improved techniques, and a new range of products. In essence increases in productivity as a measure for technological progressiveness does not separate the two distinct activities; the internal generation of innovations and the adoption of those which have been developed elsewhere. Thus the findings of the studies can be consistent with one another. As argued in relation to Fig. 4.1 low concentration industries are likely to be fast adopters, but may be hesitant as initiators. High concentration industries, on the other hand, may have sufficient profit potential to be innovators but lack the incentive to hasten development. Thus low concentration industries may improve their productivity fast on borrowed technology, and appear more progressive than their highly concentrated counterparts. Alternatively the monopolistic industry may appear more progressive as a result of the fruits of its own innovation. Because the measures make no distinction between 'in house' and borrowed technology, but merely reflect the results of all influences making for improvements in productivity, it is not surprising that clearcut results do not emerge.

Some examples may help. The textile industry is an illustration of change occurring as a result of borrowed technology. A whole range of manmade fibres have been evolved to revolutionise the raw material base and output range of the industry.[59] A high proportion of this change has not been developed within the textile industry but has come from basic discoveries in chemicals. A similar effect can be observed in machine tools. Numerically controlled machines are an application of computer technology. The control function of an operator is replaced by coded instructions fed to the machine. The technology was evolved not in the machine tool industry but outside. The construction industry is a further example. Prefabrication, plastic based raw materials, and instant adhesives, are illustrations of processes and products which enhance productivity, which have not been developed by the industry itself. All the examples given here come from older industries. They tend to have low concentration, fragmented structures, and low R and D spending. The character of competition and a commitment to traditional production methods probably inhibit internal innovation. The industries do respond to technological change, but this tends to come from outside. New methods and products are grafted on to existing activities. The industries could appear highly innovative when changes in productivity are used as an indicator. But to conclude that they are amongst the technological peers would of course be highly misleading.

Where indices are used which are closer to a direct measure of innovative orientation, more consensus emerges. Studies using R and D to sales ratios find a significant relation. The correlations range between 0.29 to 0.54.[60] Apparently there is a relationship between concentration and R and D commitment, which varies from weak to fairly strong. This should not be used however as an argument to support industrial concentration as an innovative stimulant. This would be too naïve. The expectation that the market form is a key factor in the decision to innovate is probably overoptimistic. Policy makers would be delighted if a simple and unambiguous relationship existed. This would mean that in order to induce a high level R and D effort all that would be required would be a series of mergers or disentanglements to achieve the required market form. Unfortunately the complexities of the real world do not support the wisdom of such rules of thumb. When studies take account of the technological opportunities available to industries the apparent influence of the market form declines considerably. Some industries tend to have considerable technological push and pull. They tend to be new, and have a product base which is not yet standardised. They are able to dip into rich veins of unexplored technology to improve their products. They may be science based in the sense that they may be closely connected to scientific discoveries and thus enjoy a wider range of research options than other industries which do not have such contacts.

Obvious examples of these industries are chemicals, electronics, aircraft and electrical engineering. When the industry data is sophisticated to make some allowance for the potential to make innovations, the influence of concentration declines. In effect technological opportunity emerges as a more important influence on R and D than concentration. In a study using data from the 1960 Census of Population in USA of natural scientists and engineers to total employment in fifty-six industries, a simple correlation of 0.46 was found between the ratio of technical personnel to total employment, and the concentration index. When differences in product technology were allowed for, the partial correlation between the technical personnel index, and concentration fell to 0.20.[61] This finding is confirmed by the experience of others.[62]

Interpretation of the finding that technological opportunity is an important influence on the strength of the correlation between R and D commitment and industrial concentration is not easy. It is eminently plausible that in their outlook towards research spending companies should be influenced by the opportunities available. Unfortunately the concept of technological opportunity is difficult. Just what does it mean? Does it mean a high probability of technical success, a low R and D cost per unit discovery, or a high profitability of differentiation? In terms of Fig. 4.1 the problem is to identify the effects on the C and V functions. Customer pull presumably influences the V function. There is such market pressure for improved products and processes that a company is motivated towards innovation by the attraction of high returns. Technological push presumably influences the C function. The knowledge base of the industry may be expanding so fast that the probability of achieving a given step forward is increased and the cost of doing so reduced. More specifically the time/cost function may shift towards the origin and thus make R and D profitable even for companies with little market influence. If technological opportunity is defined by the gap between the C and V functions, then it may be possible to identify the circumstances where high concentration is crucial to research orientation. In terms of Fig. 4.1, high concentration is likely to be important where there is a small gap between the C and V function. In these circumstances if the market for the innovation is shared between more than a few companies, research would be unprofitable. Where the gap is wide, high concentration may not be a prerequisite and thus high research and development may be positively associated with low concentration. This pattern would predict that high concentration is an important causative influence on the level of R and D where technological opportunity is low. Similarly it would predict that high concentration would be unimportant where technological opportunity is high. These predictions are confirmed by the evidence. Reasonably strong correlations are found between R and D intensity and concentration in industries with low innovative opportunities.[63] Also a negative relationship is found for five industries in the chemicals class where the innovative opportunities are relatively high.[64] Apparently the relationship between concentration and research intensity is not a simple two-way affair. A third factor intervenes, namely technological opportunity. The influence of concentration on R and D is modified according to the ethos in the industry favouring product and process change. Where this is favourable, high concentration may discourage research orientation. There may be sufficient profit potential to make a fragmented industrial structure more appropriate. Alternatively, where profit potential for innovation is low, high concentration may be crucial to research and development. The effect of concentration thus becomes specific to industrial circumstances and therefore should not form the basis of broad and generalised policy recommendations.

Conclusions

In spite of the shortcomings of the evidence, it seems clear that the largest companies do not emerge with a striking advantage. In terms of expenditure on R and D, productivity of research spending, and the quality of their inventions, the largest companies do not appear as the unchallenged technological leaders. It seems that large firms come up with proportionally the same number of inventions, and in a number of industries actually achieve less than medium sized firms.[65] In terms of major inventions, one observer is of the opinion that small companies and lone inventors may have a comparative advantage, and the large company's forte may lie in development and follow-up improvements.[66] There does not seem to be a simple and unambiguous relationship between size and technological capability. The same appears to be true of the influence of specific market structures. There are many reasons why size and market structures do not exhibit a clearcut influence on innovation. Included among these will be patenting, which may confer a degree of protection upon holders, licensing arrangements whereby the economically weak may ally themselves with those with resources and influence, sponsored research, industrial cooperative research, government influence and the widespread source of ideas. In the final analysis, the most crucial factor in the organisation of R and D may actually relate to the number of independent centres of initiative. By having a large number of potentially creative units an economy may improve its option on further developments.[67]

Summary

The term innovation covers all the activities in bringing a new product or process to the market. It tends to be an expensive, time-consuming transformation process, which is management and resource intensive. The benefits to a firm can be important. But there are risks which tend to make for a cautious attitude.

Development tends to be a more expensive activity than invention. The time interval between invention and innovation is considerable. There is weak evidence that this time interval is shortening. The risks involved in development can be divided into technical and market risk. Major determinants of technical risk are the size and complexity of the advance sought. A company may, however, influence the average level of technical risk it carries by the mix of projects which it undertakes. There are also risk-shifting and risk-reducing devices which may be employed. These include contract research and parallel research effort. Figures indicate that companies are unlikely to become involved in a project unless the average estimated probability of technical success is in the region of 0.7. The majority of failures are not attributable to drawbacks of technology but to other reasons. Market or commercial risk is, to a much greater extent, beyond the control of a company and is highly dependent on the achievement of an adequate market. Rivals' reactions are crucial here and are largely determined by the profitability of adoption and the size of the investment required. The criteria applied by management in the selection of projects suggests that they believe market risk to be high. Allocations to research are typically modest, and payback periods required are short.

Research and development tends to be expensive and in the nature of a fixed cost. Commitment to research varies by industry and reflects technological push and customer pull. Successful innovation has a notable impact on the economic performance of companies. Growth and profit rates are enhanced. Large companies appear to have marked advantages in the conduct of research, but in terms of relative expenditure, the very largest companies may carry out proportionately less research than the not so large. Size is, however, an unsatisfactory measure because it is serving as a proxy for a large number of influences which may be relevant to R and D. These include diversified output and the market form. Evidence on the effect of diversified output is inconclusive and therefore perhaps suggests that it is a secondary influence on research intensity. The market form most likely to be conducive to research is competitive oligopoly. Innovative competition may be stimulated by 'big firm, few firm' rivalry. These structural conditions are most likely to occur under oligopoly. Firm conclusions are difficult to draw because there are so many issues involved. Studies yield mixed results. This suggests that the market form may not be a key factor in the decision to commit funds to R and D. When technological opportunity is allowed for, the influence of the market form as indicated by the degree of concentration is considerably reduced. Furthermore, the effect of concentration becomes specific to industrial circumstances. Ultimately the most important single influence on innovative output may be the number of independent centres of creative initiative.

5
Management and innovation

Innovation is management intensive. Companies which undertake R and D have deliberately shunned the quiet life. They have undertaken an activity whose express function is to alter settled products and processes. Innovation is aimed at achieving competitive advantage through change. A company will no longer rely on emulation to keep up with progress. It has made an explicit commitment to add to the impetus of technology. The result is a considerable drain on managerial resources. Innovation is prodigal in its use of managerial talent for a number of reasons. The risks involved with pioneering are normally greater than those associated with conventional investment. Assessment and appraisal of the whole decision-taking process will absorb significant amounts of time and resources. The redisposition of productive capacity to accommodate a new product or process will involve considerable upheaval. Planning, supervision and control all must be undertaken. The R and D department itself must be managed. Considerations of profit and loss must impinge on research budgets and personnel. Project selection, timing decisions of a stop-start, accelerate, defer, character must be made. The actual size of the overall allocation must be decided. All these activities absorb managerial resources. The quality of management will have a crucial influence on the innovational success achieved by a company. The supervision and control of R and D is a management problem of considerable difficulty. Creative personnel cannot just be left to follow their research hunches. The whole process of innovation requires management of a high calibre. The preconditions for success are not just brilliant research personnel.

Success/Failure

The last chapter went some way in identifying general factors important to innovation. Nothing was said about the particular circumstances within companies which influence success or failure. Detailed discussion of this has been reserved because of its importance to the management of innovation. When the characteristics associated with successful innovation are examined a number of important guiding principles emerge.

Table 5.1 gives the relative occurrence of factors in success. The

Table 5.1 Factors in success

Factors of importance in success of firm	Relative occurrence of factors (%)				
	Chemical $n = 12$	Mech. Eng. $n = 40$	Electrical $n = 23$	'Craft' $n = 9$	All $n = 84$
Top person	22.2	27.1	25.7	18.5	25.1
Other person	5.6	14.4	21.4	11.1	14.7
Clear identification of a need	19.4	18.8	14.5	9.3	16.7
Realisation of potential usefulness of a discovery	2.8	7.5	6.5	3.7	6.2
Good co-operation	8.3	3.1	5.1	7.4	4.9
Availability of resources	8.3	12.1	2.5	5.6	8.2
Help from government sources	8.3	4.6	2.5	11.1	5.3
Not classified	25.0	12.5	21.7	33.3	19.0

Source. Langrish *et al., Wealth from Knowledge* (ref. 1).

study relates to companies which have won the Queen's Award for Technological Innovation between 1966 and 1967. The 'top person' emerges as the major factor in all the groupings. A top person is 'an outstanding person in a position of authority'.[1] The contribution of an influential person appeared to show itself in two main ways. First, in the initiation of a project as a result of identifying the area to be worked in; second, by the generation of enthusiasm, by ensuring that funds are available by taking a personal interest in the project and by acting as spokesman. The 'other person' category relates to a specific individual who may be crucial to a project. Without his unique knowledge, a project may well fail to come to anything. Such an individual may be labelled by his colleagues as a genius. Dependence on this type of individual appeared less often than the championing of a project by an individual in a position of authority. Clear identification of need emerged as the second major influence in success. This was generally more often of greater importance than the realisation of the potential usefulness of a discovery. However, when the innovations are subdivided into the categories of small and large technological change, it becomes clear that for large technological change realisation of potential usefulness of a discovery becomes important more often than clear identification of need.[2] When a small firm category is added, another possibility emerges. In autonomous companies employing less than 1000 persons it appeared that for such firms, innovations tended to depend more often on a discovery, and for identification of a need to be important less often. The top person phenomena also appeared more prominent.[3]

Confirmation of the general tendency of these findings comes from another study based on fifty-eight innovations.[4] The innovations are arranged into twenty-nine pairs, seventeen in chemicals and twelve in instruments. Each pair consists of one commercially successful innovation and one which is less successful. The less successful innovation is a 'failure' in the sense that a worthwhile market share and/or profit does not result. It is not a failure in the technical sense. The product works and carries out its required function. The failure occurs when sales hopes are not realised after commercial launch. The other feature of a pair is that both innovations are aimed at the same market. The innovations are not grouped by their technology but by their market orientation. Two firms may adopt very different solutions to a common technical problem. The qualifying feature is their interest in the same market. Arranging innovation in pairs highlights the reasons for success or failure. The difference becomes clear by contrast. The pairing technique is somewhat like using a control in biological experiments. Confidence in explanations is improved by reference to a standard. In this instance the common feature between the companies concerned, is the desire to capture a given market. The difference is the degree of success achieved with their innovations. The study is confined to two industrial sectors, chemicals and instruments, and to innovations occurring since World War II. All the chemical innovations are classed as process innovations and the instrument innovations as product innovations.

The greater part of the statistical analysis is based on 122 variables. These were used to throw light on theories relating to innovative success. The probabilities that the observed differences between the successful and failed innovation on the variables, are calculated. The results indicate that no single factor can by itself explain the success/failure difference. Innovation involves a complex sequence of events through from discovery up to selling. A one variable explanation does not provide an adequate description of the process. Five statements summarise the influences which best distinguish success. These are:

1. successful companies have a much better understanding of user needs;
2. they pay much more attention to marketing;
3. development work is performed more efficiently but not necessarily more quickly;
4. more effective use is made of outside technology and scientific advice, even though successful firms perform more of their own R and D;
5. responsible individuals in successful innovations are usually more senior and have greater authority than their counterparts who fail.

In essence failures reveal themselves by an ignorance of users' requirements; by a neglect of market research publicity and user education; elimination of technical faults after launch; poor contacts with the scientific community relating to their specific area of technology; and a lower company rank of the individuals responsible for the innovation concerned.

Further tests are applied to distinguish success/failure differences. Index variables of linear combinations of some of the 122 variables are calculated, scaled to the range −1 +1. All variables have equal weighting, but account is taken of the expected sign. The efficiency of each index variable in support of the various hypotheses, is gauged by the per cent of success points achieved. Success points relate to observations with a positive sign.

Table 5.2 Classification of success points by index variables

Index variable	% of points correctly classified: both industries	% of points correctly classified: chemicals	% of points correctly classified: instruments
Risk	48.3	64.7	25.0
Management techniques	58.6	70.6	41.7
Management strength	62.1	70.6	50.0
Organisational structure	37.9	35.3	41.7
User needs	75.9	76.5	75.0
Familiarity	48.3	52.9	41.7
R and D strength	75.9	82.4	66.7
Communication	69.0	64.7	75.0
Pressure	48.3	52.9	41.7
Marketing	82.8	76.5	92.2

Source. Science Policy Research Unit, University of Sussex, *Success and Failure in Industrial Innovation* (ref. 4).

Table 5.2 shows the results. There are differences between the industries but these are largely of emphasis. The same index variables feature amongst those with the highest success points. The best description of success/failure for both of the industries is achieved by: marketing, user needs, R and D strength, communications, and management strength. It becomes clear that successful innovation in a firm is associated with good marketing and a clear understanding of user requirements. Good external communication is found to be important. Efficient use of outside information and good coupling of scientific and technological knowledge are characteristic of successful firms. There is also a suggestion that proximity aided communication and successful innovation. Successful companies appeared to be less scattered geographically than others. On the R and D side, the successful firms made sure that technical problems were solved before commercial sales were made, and also that management was strong and efficient. Complexity of technological problems for users was not in itself a barrier to success, but the company that neglected user education or did not foresee their problems was more likely to fail. Within management the concept of the key individual or top person, received some support. The study attempted to identify four key roles in the conduct of innovation. These were the technical innovator, business innovator, chief executive, and the product champion. The technical innovator is the individual who has made the major contribution to the technical side of a development or design of the innovation. He is not necessarily in the innovating firm, nor is he always the inventor. The business innovator is the individual who takes managerial responsibility for progress achieved on the project. He may be the research director or technical director, and can also be the same man as the technical innovator. In a smaller firm he may be the chief executive for the organisation as a whole. The chief executive is the head of the executive structure of the innovating organisation. A usual title is managing director. The product champion is any individual who makes a decisive contribution to the innovation by actively and enthusiastically promoting its progress through the critical stages.[5] In each project there was an identifiable chief executive and almost always a business innovator. Technical innovators and product champions were not always identifiable. The most important result concerned the business innovator. The individual responsible for the outcome of the project in the chemical industry where average firms size was larger, was not often the chief executive. In the instrument industry this was not the case. He was more frequently the chief executive. Significantly, in both industries the business innovator had greater power, carried more responsibility and had higher formal status in successful firms. The role of the product champion was also confirmed in the sense that an enthusiastic and powerful protagonist was closely linked with innovative success. A key decision maker with high rank and personal involvement is apparently an important ingredient in success.

Some hypotheses found no support in this detailed study. The size of firms did not emerge as a good discriminator of success. Even within the same branch of industry, size did not correlate systematically with success. This does not of course deny the importance of size, but may help to stress that bigness may be one of a number of preconditions which have a propitious general influence on innovation, but cannot be described as a primary cause. One size measure was, however, of some importance, namely the size of the project team at the peak of effort. This was a critical factor in discriminating between categories of success. In chemicals the size of the team at the beginning of a project was also important. The level of effort on a particular innovation as measured by the numbers of personnel involved is apparently an important factor distinguishing successful innovations. As a measure of commitment to a project, numbers involved is presumably an index of management confidence in the outcome. It may also reflect the powers of persuasion and authority of the key management personnel involved.

Questions were included in the investigation relating to the use of management techniques and planning. Most of the companies under-took some kind of systematic forecasting and planning, but in the analysis no evidence supported the view that the use of such techniques was crucial. Their use did not distinguish success from failure. This finding does not deny the importance of a serious and systematic approach to the planning of innovations, it merely indicates that, in the observations concerned, the use of management and planning tech-niques was not a factor which distinguished successful innovations. Discriminating power was also not revealed by the number of QSEs in the R and D department, nor the number on the Board of Directors.

Various other hypotheses relating to the organisation of R and D were tested. The presence of a formal R and D group was not a factor differentiating between success and failure, but usually a necessary condition for attempting innovation. The majority of innovations were developed within companies. However the 'in house' versus the outside or 'not invented here' arguments did not yield a significant differen-tiation. There was some evidence, however, that subcontracting particu-larly at the prototype/pilot plant stage is associated more with failure than with success.

In a study confined to innovations which have failed, the importance of market orientation is again stressed. Development projects tend to fail not for technical but commercial reasons.[6] The study attempted to discover the reasons for abandonment of technically satisfactory developments. Case studies were drawn from twenty companies in the electrical, electronic, chemical and engineering industries and covered fifty-three abandoned projects. The projects were all shelved before market launch. Unlike the previous study, failure in this case is a deliberate decision by a company to abandon a development before it reaches its customers. The most common reason given explaining shelving decisions related to the size and character of the market, and to limited production and marketing resources within the firm. Of these factors 'unattractively small market' was the most frequently given reason.

Table 5.3 gives a summary of related causes of project shelving. The environmental causes can be considered as factors outside the control of a particular firm. Organisational causes are those internal to the firm. Shelving decisions of an organisational or internal character are a direct

Table 5.3 Summary of alleged causes of project shelving

	Total	Electrical	Mechanical	Chemical
Environmental				
Unattractively small market	19	10	2	7
Uncertainty with monopsonistic buyers	12	4	6	2
Unattractive level of competition	11	4	3	4
Uncertainty with suppliers	6	2	3	1
Obsolescence	3	2	1	0
	51	22	15	14
Organisational				
Lack of marketing capacity or expertise	14	4	6	4
Lack of production capacity or expertise	13	5	6	2
Faulty communications with associated firms	7	4	3	0
R and D cost escalation	6	4	1	1
Shortage of R and D resources	4	0	4	0
	44	17	20	7
Total	95	39	35	21

Source. Centre for the Study of Industrial Innovation, *On the Shelf* (ref. 6).

reflection of the quality of management. These factors are within the control of companies and therefore are eminently avoidable reasons for failure. It should however be pointed out that a shelve decision may be less costly than to await the verdict of the market after an innovation has been launched. It is true that an R and D project that fails represents a poor allocation of resources and a waste, but given that a proportion of failures is inevitable it is probably cheaper to withdraw support for a project earlier rather than later. To incur all the expenses associated with marketing and suffer all the damaging effects to goodwill, is probably the most expensive type of failure. Management that abandons an innovation at the prelaunch stage may therefore be exercising high quality control. The authors of the study indicate however that a large proportion of the projects should have been shelved earlier before so much had been spent on them. Furthermore some of them should not have been commenced at all. Fourteen projects were resurrected and put to some later commercial use; eight resulted from unexpected market changes or an alternative use, and were subsequently put to work in the originating firm. Six were exploited by licensing for use by other firms. These six were examples of shelved technology which did not fit in to the pattern of operations of the companies concerned. They were however put to advantage by external transfer to other concerns. The high proportion of resurrections (26 per cent) suggests that project reappraisals should be a standard part of company procedures. Circumstances relevant to the original shelve decision clearly do change, and with them the possibility to capitalise on the idle technology. Companies neglecting this function are forgetting an important commercial truth. Use and application rather than discovery may be the key to success. A significant proportion of innovations are reapplications of old ideas. For example, of 102 technical ideas made use of by Queen's Award winning firms, twenty-four could be described as originating from common knowledge. Effectively these were old ideas available for use by anyone. The feature that distinguished the innovating company in these circumstances was the realisation that they might have a use. In this sense 'it may be that detecting the change in the market circumstances is more important than the production of the idea'.[7] Companies neglecting the reappraisal function are thus asserting the sanctity of past decisions. This may be a costly attitude.

The arguments so far have made it clear that the chain of events leading to a successful innovation extends well beyond the R and D function. It extends beyond the discovery and development of a technically acceptable article, right up to the marketing function. Without sales an innovation cannot be a success, and without R and D there can be no 'in house' technological change. Somehow R and D and marketing activities must be sufficiently fused so that there is enough interaction to avoid projects being shelved for lack of commercial appeal. This is a major function of the management of R and D. Research must be commercially orientated and therefore there must be adequate feedback from sales. Market research should be continuous so that progress in the development of a project may be monitored against current judgment of market potential. In this way management decisions to expand, contract or shelve current research projects can be improved.

The efficiency of this type of decision will turn on this process of continual assessment. With a typical project in its early phase of development there is an act of faith by management. They know that there will be a considerable timelag before a commercial product will result. As a consequence market assessment is bound to be subject to a fairly high level of uncertainty. As time passes and the project nears technical fruition demand potential becomes more firm. The properties of the new product are now known and the characteristics of the market are more concrete simply because launch is not far in the future. If assessment is discontinuous and confined to the start decision and the launch decision then management is taking an unnecessarily high risk. By not having a routine process of appraisal throughout the development phase, control opportunities are lost. This may be costly especially where a 'discontinue' or 'shelve' decision would be appropriate. As with all economic decisions, timing is important. If a project is shelved late in its development then this is more costly than necessary. Similarly if market omens are particularly good it may be appropriate to speed up development. Again this signal will be ignored and an opportunity to improve the efficiency of project management will have been lost.

The ground rules for successful management of innovation which emerge from the detailed case studies indicate that user needs, marketing, efficiency of development work, communications and seniority of management, are crucial differentiating influences. Companies which neglect these factors do so at their own risk. The rules do not of course provide an automatic recipe for success, but they do perhaps help to avoid the more obvious routes to failure. Certain recommendations emerge. An influential manager of high rank should be made personally responsible for particular projects. Project selection should exhibit a strong bias towards user needs. Company organisation should ensure excellent interaction between marketing and R and D; and project reappraisal should be a routine and continuous process. Companies which take steps along these lines are less likely to fail. They will have gone a considerable way towards establishing conditions which are propitious for innovative success.

Project selection

In the last chapter some time was spent in describing the nature of the time/cost tradeoff function in developing a particular innovation. Further discussion is now appropriate as part of the general problems associated with managing R and D. Funds have to be allocated to particular projects. General strategic guidelines have to be established. The functions of research and development may have to be separated. Decisions have to be made on the timing of development. The speed of development has a considerable bearing on how the process is organised and the cost involved. In practice little is known about how projects are selected for development. The quantitative techniques most frequently used are probably adaptations of methods of capital budgeting. These include the pay-out period, the rate of return or discounted cash flow and a composite index for project ranking. Of these a calculation of estimated rate of return is probably the most popular.[8] A positive influence on the use of quantitative selection techniques appears to be the size of the research laboratory involved. A sizeable research unit will have more projects and personnel to collate and process data. There is some evidence that the larger the laboratory the greater the probability that some quantitative selection method is used.[9] Hunch or intuition is not however replaced. Quantitative techniques are only part of the selection procedure. This is probably a justifiable attitude. Quantitative techniques can do much to make assumptions explicit and also force management to identify relevant factors. But the accuracy of project selection techniques is limited. The estimates involved are subject to errors which are large, and are likely to lead to predictions which are poor. Unfortunately the limitations of the quantitative techniques would not appear to be fully appreciated. Only about 10 to 20 per cent of laboratory directors regarded such estimates as poor or untrustworthy.[10] This degree of faith in the usefulness of the techniques could be harmful. A proper attitude is one of scepticism, biased towards an appreciation that quantitative techniques are no more than an aid.

Projects for consideration can arise from internal or external sources. A study of nineteen laboratories in chemicals, drugs, electronics and petroleum, indicates that the majority of accepted projects were suggested by R and D staff and these, together with other sources internal to the firm, accounted for practically all suggestions that were accepted.[11] On average 62 per cent of projects originated from R and D staff, 27 per cent from marketing and other sources within the firm, and 11 per cent from groups outside the firm. These results should not, however, mislead the reader into believing that firms make the majority of their own discoveries. The findings only related to scientific research projects, not to the discoveries or ideas on which they are based. As already pointed out, a significant proportion of technical ideas embodied in innovations can be described as common knowledge.[12] Or in terms of discoveries on which projects are based, approximately half of sixty-eight pharmaceutical innovations are traceable to sources external to the firms concerned. When account is taken of the medical and economic significance this proportion rises to about 70 per cent.[13] The findings thus carry no implication as to the source of the idea or discovery. They only indicate where the initiative to implement a project comes from. It is hardly surprising that firms display a preference for projects suggested within their own organisation. Projects initiated by company personnel are more likely to be compatible with existing activities, and the management are more likely to take notice of suggestions from individuals among their ranks. But the importance of external sources of ideas and discoveries should warn companies against the dangers of being too introverted.

The screening process applied by management in the selection of projects, even where it is based on intuition, will turn on considerations of the likelihood of success and the likely cost and revenues involved. A major influence in acceptance will be the prospects of a high rate of return. A model which performs reasonably well as a predictor, has as a central assumption of a form of profit maximising procedure. In selecting projects put up for consideration by R and D, management operate within an overall budget constraint. Within this constraint which is the total allocation of funds to research, projects appear to be selected on a profit maximising basis. The allocation to a particular budget can be explained fairly well by a model which assumes that spending is increased to the point where the increase in the probability of success is no longer worth its cost. Within the R and D budget projects compete for acceptance on a basis of their profit expectations, and the expenditure on each reflects a balance of cost and probability of success.[14] The explanatory power of a model of this character is considerable. About half of the observed allocation of funds can be explained by profit expectations. The unexplained portion is probably accounted for by a number of factors which include a preference for safe over risky projects given profit expectations, intrafirm politics, effectiveness of particular individuals in making a case for projects they are sponsoring, and an attempt to satisfy scientific interests as well as commercial objectives.

Cost of development

Knowledge of the factors that influence the cost of development will be crucial to the quality of R and D management. Academic knowledge of the determinants of development cost is rudimentary. Managements' grasp of the subject may be equally weak. They will have an understanding based on experience, but this may not be sufficient to permit a firm statement of the major influences, with an indication of their importance. This is not meant to imply that management proceed in the dark, but rather that the aggregated knowledge available from collective business experience is in a form which has not yet been processed into a series of hypotheses backed by appropriate testing procedures. In effect, there is plenty of conventional wisdom of an intuitive kind, but little of an econometric variety.

The types of influences which management will gauge in predicting development costs are likely to include familiarity with the product area, the complexity of the development, the extent of the advance sought, the existing knowledge of the potential development, the strategy used, and the time to completion.[15] A study which attempts to add precision to the debate concentrates on seven variables. The data is drawn from one large ethical drug company in the USA. Seventy-five development projects are involved and all of them have been marketed.[16] The variables covered are the nature of the new drug sought, the extent of the technological advance, the use of parallel development efforts, the priority of the particular project, and time. Development projects are classified into three categories; new chemical entities, compounded products, and alternative dosage forms. This is done because of the different nature of the development work involved. The nature of the drug sought relates to the type of dosage form, product category, and spectrum of activity. These factors have an influence on the type of development work involved. Dosage form is a term describing the method by which a drug is taken. Tablets, injection, sprays and suppositories are examples. Product category essentially describes the relevant area of medical interest. Thus a preparation may act on the respiratory or central nervous system, or be concerned with parasitic and infectious diseases. The spectrum of activity measures the range of a drug's biological activity. A broad spectrum product will cover a large number of therapeutic markets. The extent of the technological advance sought is based on subjective assessment by project administrators of the step forward involved. Technological advance scores are compiled for each project and used in the regression procedures. The variable parallel development effort is included wherever a project is organised along these lines. Parallel research efforts are most likely to be used where there is considerable uncertainty about the outcome of a project. Consequently where a new chemical entity is sought and/or considerable technological advance is involved, this method of approach is likely to be adopted. Project priority relates to the importance attached to the specific development concerned. Two priority ratings are used, A and B. Category A indicates that all efforts are devoted towards marketing as early as possible. Category B indicates a lower level of importance. These projects are assumed to be interruptable and usually represent developments whose market potential is thought to be of a lower order. Plausibly, category A projects are likely to be more costly than those in category B. They probably involve more complex and significant developments, and may well have shorter development time. The last variable time does not, however, relate to the planned time to completion which is relevant to the time/cost tradeoff function, but to changes in development costs over time, due to inflationary and other influences. The seven variables achieved considerable explanatory power. Superior results are, however, achieved with the model when less ambitious development projects are under consideration. Innovations which involve considerable technological advance are not so well explained. An important point also emerges. When forecasts from the model are compared with those prepared by the firm at the beginning of the development of projects, it was found that the econometric forecasts tended to be superior to those used by the firm. It hardly needs pointing out, that this emphasises the importance of this type of study as a management aid.

An important influence on the cost of a particular project is the time taken for development. The time/cost tradeoff function mentioned in the last chapter indicated that in order to speed up the fruition of a project there may be cost penalties. An earlier fruition date would normally imply higher costs. The tradeoff function represents particular approaches to a project which yield minimum expected costs for a given expected time. An innovation is only carried out once so there will be only one time/cost point. This point cannot lie below the function. It may lie above if the minimum expected costs are not achieved. Because innovation involves uncertainty the variables time and cost are expressed in terms of expectations. At the planning or *ex ante* stage they represent the range of expected options open to management before any work is begun. At the realisation or *ex post* stage they represent what might have happened if a different time/cost point had been chosen. At the *ex post* stage management 'job backwards' and review the cost of completion that might have been incurred at different and alternative times. At the *ex ante* stage, management look forward at the full range of options in deciding the appropriate cost or time to completion before committing themselves. Strictly a different time/cost tradeoff function exists at each point in time, because management's subjective probability distributions will change over time with the process of learning and re-evaluation. But for purposes of exposition the *ex ante, ex post* distinction is useful. It oversimplifies the decision taking process, but nevertheless reveals its essence.

There is considerable agreement among economists that the slope of the time/cost tradeoff function is probably negative.[17] There is less consensus about the shape of the function. It is plausible to assume convexity. There may be diminishing returns, in the sense that to secure a given decrease in completion time may require a relatively increased cost. Put another way, increases in the research budget allocated to the particular project may bring the expected completion time forward but only by successively decreasing amounts. In a study of twenty-nine commercialised innovations in eleven firms, interviews were conducted to establish some insight into the cost tradeoff functions. The data collected refer to chemical, machinery, and electronics innovations which were actually completed, and thus relates to the *ex post* function.[18] The respondents in the interviews were managers principally responsible for the innovations, who were senior enough to have an overall view of the entire process. They were in a position to provide reasonably accurate answers to the questions concerned. The approach used in the interviews was based on obtaining estimates of various points on the tradeoff function using actual time and costs of a particular innovation as a starting point. Included in the questions was one relating to the expected cost that would have been involved if the project had received top priority and no expense been spared to achieve fast results. Between six and ten estimates of points on the time/cost function were obtained for each innovation. The data yielded results which indicate that the functions are likely to be negatively sloped. There is also some support for the diminishing returns hypothesis. When observations are confined to the particular range likely to be chosen by a firm interested in keeping expected time and expected cost to a minimum, then a large proportion of the sample exhibit convexity. The relevance of confining observations to a particular range covers the possibility that observations outside the range offer management choices which would never be knowingly accepted. Thus point A in Fig. 5.1 would never be chosen when B is available at a shorter time for the same expected development cost.

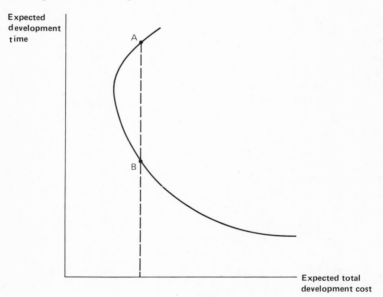

Fig. 5.1 Development possibility curve

Observations of a character similar to A are of course a possibility. They may be low priority projects which receive a small budget allocation and are expected to take second place to more urgent developments. They may be carried out so slowly that continuity is lost and important economies forfeited. There is limited evidence that a greater number of R and D projects may operate in the A range than would be expected.[19] If such observations are common it perhaps emphasises that management is not aware of the favourable alternatives and does not appreciate the nature of the trade off between time and cost.

The slope of the time/cost function indicates that fast development is probably associated with high costs. If the shape of the function is convex then there will be an increasing relative cost penalty for a given percentage reduction in time. General reasons were given in the last chapter to explain why costs are likely to be higher with faster development time. It was argued that crash programmes are likely to involve considerable duplication of effort. In attempting to concentrate development time a firm raises the likelihood of wasted effort. Project stages will exhibit a high degree of overlap and the normal sequential knowledge building process will be truncated. Experience will have to be generated independently within each stage because what would normally occur in order, is now executed concurrently.

A development project is deemed to pass through five stages on its way to the market: (1) applied research, (2) specifications, (3) prototype or pilot plant, (4) tooling and manufacturing facilities, (5) manufacturing start up. Overlap occurs when adjacent stages are carried out simultaneously. The overlap structure is a percentage measure of the overlap between one stage and the next, relating the ratio of the length of time the two stages go on simultaneously to the sum of the duration of the two stages.[20] Plausibly enough, the closer projects are to their minimum expected duration the more the amount of overlap increases. Furthermore, the size of firms is related to the overlap structure. A large firm is likely to have sufficient personnel and facilities to enable simultaneous execution of adjacent stages. The smaller company with fewer specialised employees may not be able to achieve such a degree of overlap. This impression would appear to be confirmed by the data. Firm size would appear to be a significant influence on the strategy of development. The larger company appears to be able to adopt development procedures involving more overlap. When the influence of overlap on the cost of development is examined in terms of the relative cost of stage (4) a significant relationship emerges. There is a positive relationship between the proportion of total costs incurred in this stage, and the degree of overlap between adjacent stages. The more stages (3) and (5) overlap stage (4), the more the proportion of total costs incurred in stage (4) increases. The particular test used does not show overlap increases total cost, but rather that the cost of stage (4) tends to increase, relative to the adjacent stages the more these overlap. Apparently the effect of shortening development time by increasing overlap, is to raise the proportion of total costs incurred at the relevant stage. In this instance the costs incurred at tooling and manufacturing facilities (Stage (4)) tend to rise. Although the tests do not show increased overlap raises total costs of development, management are of the opinion that this is likely to be an important source of higher costs with shorter development time. They believe that simultaneous execution of adjacent stages is likely to be a significant cause of rising total costs.

Details of the cost penalties associated with shortening development time reveal that a project which involves a significant addition to technology is likely to be more costly to speed up than a less ambitious development. Furthermore, innovations within large firms tend to be more expensive to speed up than those undertaken in smaller concerns.[21] With ambitious projects each stage in the development process is very dependent on what has gone before. There is more learning to do and therefore anticipation of results of an earlier stage is likely to be less accurate. More run of the mill projects will not involve such a big departure from common experience and so, for example, retooling can be undertaken with greater confidence prior to completion of the earlier stages. The speeding up of innovations within large firms is probably more expensive because of administrative problems. The chain of command will be longer than in smaller companies. The process of decision-making may well be more protracted and flexibility of approach may suffer.

The cost penalties associated with speeding up development time can be expressed in elasticity terms. The elasticity of cost with respect to time is the relative expected extra cost of reducing the expected duration of a project by 1 per cent. Results based on calculations relating to twenty-nine innovations indicate the costs of reducing expected durations by 1 per cent. When the expected time is very close to the minimum possible time (t/α = 1.3 or less where t = expected time and α can be considered as the minimum expected time to complete the project), in over one-third of the cases the expected cost increased by 2 per cent or more. When expected development time is more leisurely, i.e. t/α is between 1.3 and 1.8, the median elasticity is 0.5 per cent. This indicates that a 1 per cent decrease in expected project time incurs a 0.5 per cent increase in expected cost. When t/α is between 1.8 and 2.5 the median value of elasticity is 0.25. In over three-quarters of the cases, a 1 per cent time saving can be 'purchased' at a cost increase of less than 1 per cent.

The authors of the study are careful to point out that the elasticity values may not represent true options for management. It may not be possible to vary the cost to achieve the desired time. Once a start has been made on a project, an alternative development strategy may no longer be feasible. The particular approach adopted may rule out any other offering a different time to completion. When elasticities of cost with respect to time are calculated relevant to the t/α points actually realised, then over half of the elasticities are less than 1 at these points. Thus the cost of saving time relative to the times actually realised, indicates that the expected extra cost of reducing completion time by 1 per cent would be less than 1 per cent.[22] Apparently management achieve development times which lie in the relatively flat portion of the *ex post* time/cost function.

There may be grounds for arguing that achieved development times are too leisurely. In an attempt to test whether companies achieve development times which maximise expected profits, managers were asked to make estimates of the effects of various development times on the discounted value of expected profits.[2 3] In terms of Fig. 4.1 (p. 68), an attempt is being made to discover the shape of the benefits function for particular innovations. This is then compared with the relevant time/cost tradeoff functions. The optimum is defined by the development time which maximises expected discounted profits, i.e. where the slopes of the benefits function and time/cost function are equal. This optimum is then compared with the actual development time achieved for particular projects, to assess how closely companies are to the 'best' solution. Of course this procedure is very dependent on the quality of the estimates received from project managers and further-more represents an exercise in normative economics. An attempt is being made to determine how companies measure up to a standard. This standard may, in fact, not be relevant to the firms concerned. They may not be interested in maximising profits on particular projects, but may have other selection criteria.

Accepting all of these qualifications, the findings are most interest-ing. They reveal that in every case, the development time exceeds the optimum. In all sixteen projects, the time to fruition took longer than the standard established by the testing procedure. Interpretation of this result requires caution. A conclusion that management consciously reject a profit maximising approach in deciding on a development period for projects would not be appropriate. This would be too sweeping a deduction. More persuasive explanations would include, the contrast between the initial start or *ex ante* decision, and the completion or *ex post* situation. The practicalities involved with continuous reappraisal of the time scheduling of projects are also likely to be relevant. Early decisions establish priorities. These may be difficult to dislodge in midstream. Circumstances warranting a change in the time-scale of development may not be easy to detect. In a continuing business situation, perception of change is difficult. Without routine appraisal procedures, small changes may go unnoticed. These may accumulate over time and add up to circumstances radically different from those envisaged at the start. Where review is not routine and is widely spaced, altered circumstances may be readily detected but control may therefore be somewhat heavyhanded. Management time is always limited, and faster development is likely to absorb more of this valuable commodity. There may therefore be an unconscious prefer-ence for slower development times. Awareness of the optimism of research personnel may result in management overcompensating and applying heavy cautionary discounts both to market prospects and likely development time. The result may be a scheduled development period greater than the optimum. Reasons of this character are likely to be included among the explanations for the less than optimum development times achieved. Certainly the conclusion that management deliberately satisfice and reject profit maximisation for individual projects should be treated with great caution. It may be appropriate to conclude, however, that managements may be unaware that the consequences of slippage and extended development times, are that profit potential is directly eroded. If there is a general and common tendency for development times to be longer than optimum, this may reflect a lack of management awareness.

Summary

Innovation is a management intensive activity. Studies of success/failure in projects development indicate 'ground rules' to avoid the more obvious mistakes. User needs, marketing, efficiency of development work, communications and seniority of management would appear to be important discriminating influences. Project selection can be explained reasonably well by a profit maximisation model. Major influences on the cost of developments include the nature of the product, the extent of the advance sought, the priority of the project, the use of parallel research effort and time. At the planning stage knowledge of the time/cost tradeoff may be important as a management aid. Quicker development may be 'purchased' by increased costs. Management would appear to achieve development times which are somewhat leisurely. In terms of maximising expected discounted profits, achieved development times tend to be sub-optimum. This may reflect a lack of management awareness of the importance of time or the practicalities of continuous reappraisal of project schedules.

The diffusion of innovation: the national company

This chapter provides background discussion of diffusion as a company process. Chapter 7 broadens the approach and deals specifically with the spread of technology and the multinational enterprise.

Diffusion is defined as the 'process by which the use of an innovation spreads and grows'.[1] The transfer of technology is involved. 'Technology may be defined as the means or capacity to perform a particular activity. The transfer of technology must then mean the utilisation of an existing technology in an instance where it has not previously been used.'[2] Diffusion is the means whereby innovations become part of the production function or product range of economic units which are not the originators. Without diffusion innovations would remain localised and in the hands of their original sponsors. Imitation and adoption are equally good synonyms for the process which broadens usage from source. Innovation is the activity which applies inventions and brings them into the production process. Diffusion is the later stage where the benefits of innovation are generalised. From source, an innovation passes to other users until it finally becomes a commonplace and accepted part of productive activity. Notice that the definition of diffusion is concerned with the spread of the physical thing, the innovation, and is not concerned with its effects. An innovation will influence the production function of companies that adopt it. If, as a result, their output is more effective or cheaper this will induce changes among users. Companies later in the chain of production will rearrange their input in response, or final consumers will alter purchasing patterns. These induced changes represent the spreading of the effects of an innovation. Diffusion as defined here is not concerned with effects but rather with the spread of an innovation. For example, Concorde may make supersonic passenger traffic a reality in the next decade. Diffusion in this context would be concerned with the rate of adoption of Concorde by airlines. It would not be concerned with the wider effects induced by faster air travel. The distinction between effects and usage is drawn for practical reasons. Adoption of a particular innovation is relatively easy to trace. Effects are not.

Figure 6.1 will help consolidate understanding, and emphasise a

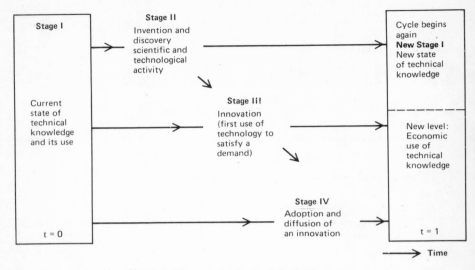

Fig. 6.1 Four stages in technical advance

Source. Gruber and Marquis, 'Research on the human factor in the transfer of technology', in *Factors in the Transfer of Technology* (ref. 2).

number of points from the previous chapter. It shows in schematic fashion a four stage process of technical advance. At a given point of time represented by stage I ($t=0$) there is an inventory of technical knowledge. A high proportion of this knowledge will be embodied in current production functions. The remainder which is not in use will represent technologies which have been superseded, technical knowledge which has yet to be adopted, and information which may be in the nature of a catalyst inducing further developments but which may not of itself make a direct economic contribution. Stage II represents activity deliberately aimed at adding to knowledge. This is indicated by the arrow pointing to the extreme righthand block. It is also an activity which services innovation, as indicated by the arrow to stage III. 'Scientific and technological activity' have been deliberately grouped together in order to stress that innovation can arise from scientific discovery, or from the process of technology building on technology. Stage III, Innovation, represents the first stage at which the technological transfer achieves an economic value. The knowledge is utilised to produce a marketable output. It becomes an innovation. If it is a failure, use is likely to be confined to the originator. The arrow indicating progression through the stages will then bypass stage IV and go straight to the righthand block. Where the innovation is profitable, multiple use will occur. Rivals will adopt and diffusion will take place. It is at stage IV that the economic impact of an innovation really begins to be felt.

By spreading among users the innovation eventually becomes an accepted part of everyday technology.

A number of cautionary points need to be made about Fig. 6.1. First, the time scale is not intended to give the impression that technical advance proceeds in a smooth and orderly fashion. In practice the period to economic acceptance varies widely with particular circumstances. The stages in Fig. 6.1 are evenly spaced for clarity of presentation, not for economic inference. Second, the stages would appear to be self-contained and easily identifiable. Each has its own distinct label and would appear to represent a distinct function. Again this impression should be avoided. In practice the distinction between invention, innovation and scientific and technological activity may not be at all clear. In fact, the general approach has been adopted here that invention is an early part of the process of innovation. No attempt has been made to stress the distinction between the activities. The labels should therefore be treated in an appropriate fashion. Third, the figure shows that technical advance is possible without economic use. The dotted line in the righthand block should convey the impression that there can be a new state of technical knowledge which has no current bearing on the 'new level economic use of technical knowledge'. In jargon terms, scientific and innovative activities can proceed along parallel courses with limited contact at the interface. This can mean that the new knowledge has no economic application, or is as yet insufficiently developed to warrant application, or it may mean that supporting and complementary technologies are so far insufficiently advanced to warrant innovation. Or again it can mean that there is a communication or managerial gap. In this last instance managerial appreciation of potential economic application is lacking or communication so poor that little is known of the idea. It is not intended to give the impression that the separation is necessarily complete, but rather that in this particular round of the cycle, the knowledge has not been embodied in economic usage. With these reservations the most significant message from the Fig. 6.1 is that the economic impact of an innovation really begins to be felt once stage IV is underway. It is the diffusion process that broadens the economic use of technical knowledge, and spreads the benefits through firms, industries and economies.

The importance of diffusion in the process of technological change is difficult to underestimate. By assimilation of new products and processes performance disparities between economic units may be narrowed. Technological gaps may be closed. Firms may upgrade the quality of output or reduce costs by imitation. Countries may catch up in the growth rate race by technological borrowing. They may sift the best and disregard the worst in the process of industrial adjustment. Diffusion allows specialisation in inventive effort. A firm or country does not have to be expert in all fields of technology. Because developments may be copied, effort may be concentrated in particular areas in the knowledge that the deficiencies elsewhere may be rectified by appropriate 'borrowing'. In essence, diffusion services competition between economic units. Successful innovation confers to the originator a marked competitive edge. Adoption by rivals provides the means to erode this advantage. Diffusion is thus the means whereby innovations are generalised and is also an important part of the competitive process. Consequently it is no surprise to find it stated that 'in principle, a country has a much greater opportunity to gain an advantage in the growth rate race by reducing the gap between average and best practice than by advancing the frontiers of knowledge'.[3]

This chapter will be concerned with the major factors affecting diffusion. It will deal with the identity of adopters, the economic characteristics of innovation, the means and methods of transfer and the influences which may hinder diffusion. There is now a very considerable literature on the subject of diffusion. A bibliography involving more than a thousand works exists on this subject alone.[4] Not all of these have an economic content. They cover subjects which include anthropology, sociology, medicine, agriculture and education. One common feature among the studies is their concern with communications. Diffusion involves knowledge flows. The stages preceding consumer acceptance are essentially concerned with information exchange. A potential adopter becomes aware of the existence of an innovation. The means whereby his perception is made aware may include contact with users, the influence of opinion leaders, marketing, advertising and chance. Reaction to knowledge of an innovation will be determined in part by the behavioural characteristics of the recipient and in part by the features of the innovation. Product or process acceptance is essentially a communication process. This is the backcloth to all diffusion studies. A second common feature among the studies is a degree of consensus on the pattern of acceptance. The pattern of adoption by users generally exhibits a rising trend which eventually slows as the innovation becomes an accepted part of technology.

Figure 6.2 shows a logistic or S-shaped pattern of adoption. This form receives the most support in the literature. Evidence from agricultural technology,[5] medicine,[6] manufacturing technology,[7] nuclear power, computers, plastics, manmade fibres,[8] and the spread of quantitative project selection techniques in laboratories,[9] are examples where investigators find this type of pattern. A generalised picture emerges of the diffusion process showing a series of fairly distinct stages in the life cycle of innovations. These stages have been labelled Introduction, Growth, Maturity and Decline.[10] Adoption by consumers exhibits an

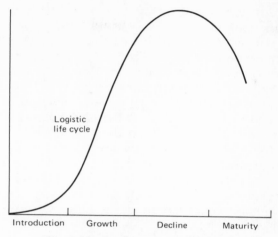

Logistic
life cycle

Introduction   Growth   Decline   Maturity

Fig. 6.2 Logistic pattern of adoption

early hesitancy. This slow rate of acceptance characterises the introduction stage. Early reluctance gives way to a quickening adoption
through the growth part of the cycle. As maturity is reached the rate of
adoption slows and the cumulative proportion of users reaches its peak.
Finally in decline, sufficient users are switching to alternatives, that the
curve falls away below the level reached in the previous stage.

The pattern of market acceptance exhibited by the S-shaped curve is
found surprisingly often. As a result it has become part of marketing
lore. The reason why diffusion patterns generally exhibit this form is
not well understood. It is one of those cases where an observed
empirical phenomenon awaits a satisfactory theoretical explanation.
There are a number of theories which rest on arguments demonstrating
the cumulative effect of opinion leaders, 'band-wagon' or contagion
effects. In spite of these there remain a number of open questions.
These include the extent to which this is a 'natural' or induced
phenomenon, and the particular influence of sales effort in modifying
and adjusting responses. Furthermore the particular shape of the curve
is not unchallenged. There are studies which have found an exponential
form more appropriate. With this pattern of consumer demand the
initial period of slow growth is not present and customer acceptance is
rapid. Unlike the S-shaped pattern, market response is virtually
immediate. This type of demand pattern is probably appropriate for
minor improvements and modifications of existing well-known products. The new version of the accepted product is sufficiently like its
predecessors to avoid the hesitant market phase. It will not have to
await the verdict of the adventurous minority who are pioneers, but
will achieve immediate recognition from the majority of buyers.[11]

A number of diffusion studies have found it helpful to classify adopters by the time of first use. Various labels have been used. One which has become standard nomenclature divides users into innovators, early adopters, early majority, late majority, and laggards.[1][2] Categories of adopters are arranged in order of their speed of reaction. Thus the innovators are the fastest to adopt and laggards the slowest. Note that the term 'innovator' is being used in a special sense. It describes the earliest users and is not confined to the developers and originators of the innovation. In a diffusion context the pioneer consumers are classed as the innovators. When adopters are arranged in categories according to their speed of response the distributions tend to approximate to the normal. This is convenient. Categories of adopters may now be defined in terms of deviations from the mean. Thus the early majority is defined within one standard deviation to the left of the mean, and the late majority within one standard deviation to the right. Similarly the laggards are defined as those beyond one standard deviation to the right, and the early adopters between one and two to the left. The innovators are defined as lying beyond two standard deviations to the left. Percentage fugures can be apportioned to each category. Thus, for example, the early majority will account for 34 per cent of the distribution, while the innovators will only be responsible for 2.5 per cent. The classification system is, of course, arbitrary and reflects the degree of normality of the distribution. Within these limitations the scheme is useful. It permits a standardised description of the diffusion of innovations as illustrated in Fig. 6.3.

The purpose of distinguishing categories of adopters by the speed of their response is essentially practical. Investigators are anxious to discover the special characteristics relevant to each group, in the hope that useful guides to future behaviour will emerge. For example, income, occupation, age and educational status may give considerable

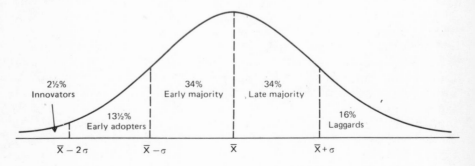

Time of adoption of innovation

Fig. 6.3 Diffusion of innovations

clues to likely future behaviour. This may aid a company in launching a new product. Customer acceptance and market penetration may be affected more rapidly if sales effort is directed at those who are likely to respond early in the life of a product. By stratifying potential customers by their likely response, the efficiency of marketing may improve. Volume production may be reached earlier and company and customers benefit alike. Innovators in farming may be profiled as follows. They are venturesome, young, high in social status, wealthy, cosmopolitan and in close contact with the scientific community. In contrast, laggards tend to be tradition orientated, older, semi-isolated and low in social status and income.[13] Among companies, quick adopters are likely to have excellent communications both inside and outside the firm, are likely to use relatively advanced management techniques, and adopt a positive attitude to science and technology.[14] The skill in marketing lies in identifying potential customers and employing the most effective means to awaken perception and effective demand. Diffusion studies aid in this process by yielding insight into the behavioural characteristics of customers.

Reactions to innovation will be determined in part by the behavioural characteristics of the potential customers, and in part by the features of the product concerned. The S-shaped or logistic curve has become accepted as a generalised pattern of customer response. For most innovations, the market profile is likely to be of this typical form. The characteristics of a given innovation are unlikely to alter the shape of this acceptance pattern. They may, however, have a major influence over the time scale during which the particular pattern evolves. Some innovations may diffuse in months, others in years and yet others in generations. With products and processes, the major influence on the time to diffuse will be their economic characteristics. These will be the concern of the following pages.

General influences which affect the rate of diffusion of innovations include, business secrecy and patents, labour fears, poor communications, management attitudes and longlived fixed capital equipment. The spread of a new process may be frustrated by a patent position, or by a deliberately secretive attitude on the part of the pioneering company. Labour may resist change in fear of redundancy. Improved machinery may present a threat to those likely to be displaced. Reaction to modernisation may defer adoption or limit its scale. Companies may be slow to hear of innovations. Communications may be poor and thus knowledge of new products and techniques take a considerable time to spread from source. Management may resist change. Resistance may arise from a quiet life attitude, from sheer inertia, from a reluctance to abandon well-worn methods and practices, and from an overcautious investment attitude. This caution may show itself in a reluctance to part with capital equipment which has been fully depreciated. In these circumstances machines may continue in use to the end of their physical lives. They may remain in use despite their technical obsolescence, because there are only variable costs to meet. Longlived and with few alternative uses, such equipment may be an important factor inhibiting the adoption of newer and more productive methods. They are likely to remain employed so long as they cover the supply price of the transferable factors which are involved in their operation. These are usually labour and raw material inputs.[15]

More specific influences affecting the rate of adoption of innovations will include the intensity of competition, the elasticity of substitution of new for old capital and capital for labour, relative price movements and the expected value of the proposed change. Competition may be so stringent that companies are effectively forced to adopt the 'best' techniques. Alternatively commercial pressure may be so lacking in bite that companies have considerable discretion in the rate at which they adjust to technological change. In practice most industries exhibit a fairly wide gap between the techniques used by the leaders and those used by the majority. This gap is one measure of the delay in utilisation of new techniques.[16] The elasticity of substitution of new for old capital, and capital for labour, will be a major component influencing the rate of change to current technologies. High elasticities of substitution are likely if a particular industry is expanding. Gross investment is likely to be high. New capital equipment is likely to embody recent technological advances and be highly productive. In a period of expansion labour is less likely to be laid off, even if the new plant is very labour saving. Growing demand may cushion the impact on employment levels of a switch to more capital intensive methods of production. In a downward phase, a higher proportion of current investment is likely to be for replacement purposes. The impact on numbers employed of any drop in demand will be aggravated by the adoption of highly productive and labour saving technologies. Labour resistance is likely to be high and management reluctant to institute such an upheaval. Elasticities of substitution are likely to be low and diffusion of new technology slow.

Relative price movements are a further factor in a decision to modernise. Changes in the cost of inputs can have a radical effect on investment decisions. Wage costs may rise relatively faster than other costs. This may heighten the pressure to adopt labour saving innovations. Specific raw material inputs may increase greatly in price. For example, a sharp increase in the cost of iron ore may stimulate interest in lean ore smelting techniques. Alternatively, hitherto neglected production control methods may be brought into service as a management reaction to cost pressure. The expected value of any proposed change is a summary measure of the financial advantages. In a sense this consolidates all the above influences into a single measure. The pressure of competition, elasticities of substitution and relative price movements, will be reflected in the cost and revenue figures used to assess the profitability of adoption. There is a strong presumption that innovations which offer the most favourable prospects are the quickest to be diffused throughout industry. The attraction of high profitability is probably the most powerful of all the commercial stimulants, and probably the most significant single factor explaining the spread of new goods and services.

Before elaborating on the influence of profitability on the rate of diffusion, it is necessary to point out that the discussion has so far concentrated on the spread of industrial products and processes. The decision-making process has been argued from a commercial viewpoint. The company environment has been assumed to be the most relevant. The private individual has been largely neglected. The reason for this emphasis is essentially the result of the bias of empirical studies. Diffusion studies undertaken by economists have largely concentrated on the spread of producer goods. In these circumstances the major customers are business enterprises. Adoption criteria are therefore bound to involve technical and financial considerations. Studies investigating the spread of consumer goods or final products are much less likely to be so concerned with these matters. Private individuals are more likely to be influenced by psychological forces involved in want satisfaction. Newness, emulation, one-upmanship, social status and current and future income, are the type of influences which may be relevant in determining private consumption habits.

In the summary that follows of the economic circumstances relevant to the diffusion process, it is intended to continue this concentration on the spread of industrial products and processes. The primary customers for these innovations are other businesses. The private individual will receive scant attention. The emphasis on the company in the diffusion process arises from essentially practical reasons. Investigators studying consumption patterns of private individuals are faced with considerable data collection problems. There are large numbers involved. There are few agreed units of measurement to determine why consumers behave as they do. Unlike the company decision, an individual's purchasing habits are not heavily influenced by profit and loss consideration. Instead more ordinal and imprecise forces are at work. These require considerable skill in interpretation. Concentration on the company decision is justifiable, however, on two major grounds. First, that a high proportion of innovations are probably in the form of producer goods. They are new goods and processes for which companies are the primary customers. Secondly, even where innovations take the form of entirely new consumption goods, companies are usually involved in the manufacturing process. Thus the adoption of the dish-washer by private individuals is unlikely to be greatly different in character from the decision of a company to adopt numerically controlled machine tools. Both innovations compete for scarce resources and have to lever themselves up the order of priorities by the advantages which they offer. The generality of the S-shaped adoption curve across products and processes is perhaps broad confirmation that there is some parity of behaviour between the types of innovations.

New products and processes vary greatly in the speed at which they are diffused. The time to spread to 60 per cent of relevant producers can take from one to twenty years.[17] The now famous story of the ball-point pen is an extreme example of rapid adoption. For eighteen months the Reynolds International Pen Company enjoyed a virtual monopoly. During this time it was able to recover its original investment a hundredfold. But the wide gap between the manufacturing costs of $0.80 and selling price of $12.50 soon brought a veritable flood of new entrants. The price fell in a matter of months.[18] The attraction of high profitability induced a rapid response and the market soon became competitive. Such a rapid rate of adoption is unusual. The average period of time for the majority of producers in a given industry to become involved with an innovation is probably somewhere near ten years. This figure is based on a study of twelve process innovations in four industries. An average time between first use and use by half of the ultimate users was 7.8 years and ten more years was required before 90 per cent of ultimate acceptance was reached.[19] The industries concerned are bituminous coal, iron and steel, brewing and railroads. The innovations include the shuttle car, the continuous mining machine, the byproduct coke oven, continuous wide strip mill, the pallet loading machine, the high speed bottle filler and the diesel locomotive. The innovations chosen were important. Practically all of them permitted a substantial reduction in costs and in no case did patents impede the rate of adoption. No serious investigator would claim that these twelve innovations are representative of the typical, but nor would he deny the onlooker the luxury of speculation. The typical innovation is probably a relatively minor advance. To this extent the sample is evidently not representative. All twelve of the innovations achieved a considerable advance over the technology then current and all twelve were widely adopted. For the present purpose, however, the importance and wide usage of the innovations is an advantage. In terms of their impact on living standards, it is these which interest the economist. He is not necessarily concerned to assemble a representative sample, but rather to highlight the factors influencing the progress of significant advances.

A company contemplating the adoption of an innovation is likely to assess the change in terms of a number of major considerations. These are likely to include the economic advantage of the innovation; the transition costs and frictions involved in the change; the risks involved in not adopting; doubts about the superiority of the innovation; the rate of reduction of the initial uncertainty; the extent of the commitment required to assess the innovation; the proportion of companies already using it; and the particular industry concerned.[20] The economic advantage offered by an innovation is by no means easy to assess. For companies early in the field, there is a limited pool of experience on which to draw. Few competitors will be using the new knowledge and thus knowhow and hard information will be scarce. Where specification changes are required in the final product, customers may require convincing. The marketing effort required to effect this will be an additional cost to be added to the calculations. The later a company is in adopting, the fewer the problems there are likely to be. Once a new technique becomes widely accepted, a large number of the initial problems will disappear. There will be a considerable number of work people familiar with operation and maintenance problems. Hiring of men who have used the new machines may be a cheap way of acquiring knowhow. They will have been educated at rivals' expense and will thus effectively subsidise the late adopter. Managements will be aware that there is a tradeoff in the timing of adoption. Earlier involvement in a new technique should offer a considerable cost advantage. While the pioneer companies are in a minority there should be little change in the price of the relevant article. Once the innovation becomes a commonplace, this advantage will be eroded by competitive pressure. To be set against the advantage of being early in the field are all the uncertainties associated with pioneering. Doubts about the superiority of the new technique will need resolving, customer reaction is as yet largely unassessed, and labour fears unabated. The tradeoff involves balancing the advantage of leading with those of lagging in the process of diffusion. The way in which this is resolved will be heavily influenced by the calibre of management and the specific economic characteristics of individual companies.

One important method of assessing the economic potential of an innovation is by limited trial. By gradual introduction a company may limit the risk and investment involved. Adoption based on such a phasing procedure, where an experimental start is cautiously built up to full scale commitment, allows time for appraisal and offers management many control opportunities. The fork lift truck provides a good example. Each one involves a relatively modest capital outlay. Consequential investment is limited to palletisation and the provision of suitable warehouses in which the machine may work effectively.

Neither of these requirements is particularly onerous and will probably involve minimum adoption of existing facilities. The purchase of a single machine will only involve a change in the working habits of a few men. If the adoption is successful more machines may be purchased until finally warehousing and in-factory movement of goods is almost entirely handled by this method. The transition should be smooth and should not involve an enormous upheaval. Labour resistance should be minimal. Numbers of machines required can be changed quickly and easily, and the investment expenditure can be closely linked to immediate requirements.

Contrast the fork lift truck with the Wankel engine. This engine is radically different from the normal engine. There are no separate conventional pistons and the familiar reciprocating action is replaced by a circular movement. Adoption of this innovation by a car manufacturer involves radical change. The investment involved is high. Completely new plant is required. The difference between the Wankel and a normal engine is such that it is not practical to produce them in the same factories. A 'green field' start is required where machinery is specificially geared to producing this new engine. On the sales side, customers must be persuaded. They must be satisfied of the superiority of the new propulsion unit. They must be reassured that garages are familiar with maintenance problems. Consumer education and the provision of after sales service is expensive. Any company deciding to adopt the Wankel engine is therefore faced with a considerable upheaval. Production methods have to be altered radically, new plant has to be constructed, considerable sums spent on the education of those concerned with servicing and maintaining the engine, and an advertising campaign launched to persuade the final consumer of the virtues of the new product. Manufacturers' experience with this engine has in fact been mixed. It is now only just begining to emerge as a rival to conventional engines. The development period has been long and expensive. There have been considerable problems with effective sealing of propulsive gases, and a number of companies have suffered heavy losses.

An innovation of the Wankel engine type involves a high degree of interrelatedness.[21] Adoption by a manufacturer induces a chain reaction of consequential alterations. A large lump sum investment of a discreet character is involved. It is one of those 'all or nothing' decisions, where the minimum commitment is large. Opportunities for limited trial of manufacturing experience hardly exist, and the management decision is of a 'go, no go' character. Where production processes are very closely interlinked or related, changes in techniques tend to involve considerable upheaval. An alteration at one stage in a mass production process will induce a large number of consequential changes. The output of one stage is the input of the next. All the stages must remain compatible for a balanced flow of work. Any alteration in the output of one stage may induce a whole reorganisation of inventories, specifications and working schedules both backwards and forwards from the point of disturbance. The Wankel engine is an example of a very large disturbance encompassing virtually the whole of a company's activities. The transition costs and frictions will inevitably reflect the radical character of the investment.

The risks involved in not adopting an innovation relate to the consequences which follow from a deliberate policy of non-adoption. A company decision not to use an innovation may have considerable long-term consequences. Such a decision may of course always be reversed, but the intervening timelag may have important economic effects. The company image for progressiveness may suffer, consumer goodwill may be lost if apparently outdated production methods are retained, and the ability to recruit and maintain a work force may suffer. Where an innovation affects the performance of the final product, tardiness may have a major impact on the revenue earning ability of a company. Adoption requires positive action. Investment and adjustment have to be made. The decision not to adopt may be just as positive in its effects on a company. A company which ignores innovation and opts for the quiet life does not avoid the consequences of technological change. Earning power is likely to suffer and ultimately adjustment may have to be made as an alternative to bankruptcy. Management should therefore make a conscious assessment of the risks associated with non-adoption.

Doubts about the superiority and the rate of reduction of the initial uncertainty associated with an innovation can be an important influence on the diffusion process. Pioneer adopters will inevitably face a higher level of uncertainty than those who follow. For late adopters the major snags will have been eliminated. The quicker an innovation dispels doubt about its technical feasibility and reaches production potential, the more rapid is acceptance likely to be. There are many possible sources of uncertainty with innovation. The long-term effects may be unpredictable. Thus the initial adoption of fibre glass in boat building was cautious. As time has passed, sufficient experience has become available to put the problems in perspective. Developments in pharmaceuticals are always likely to carry a particular degree of uncertainty. In the testing of new drugs there is a crucial phase where experience is transferred from laboratory use on animals to use on humans. There may be side effects which were not present or remained unnoticed at the development stage. The tranquilliser Thalidomide was a particularly unpleasant example. Some women who used this preparation during pregnancy gave birth to deformed children.

The use of chain saws provides another medical example which would have been very difficult to foresee. These saws are an extremely important forestry innovation. Woodcutters' output is greatly increased with them. Unfortunately the vibration associated with their use has in some cases caused serious damage to the bone structure of operatives. As a result there has been a considerable drive by manufacturers to reduce vibration and the UK Forestry Commission has replaced its entire stock of chain saws with improved models to reduce the hazard to its employees.[22] Some techniques have proved persistently disappointing. Promise has been slow to materialise and adoption correspondingly hesitant. One of the best examples of a cussed technology is the generation of electricity by nuclear fission. This has been possible for over twenty years but it has persistently failed to realise its full potential. It is only recently that nuclear generation has become competitive with conventional methods and even now technical problems are by no means all solved. If nuclear generation of electricity in the UK had rested in private hands, development would certainly have been on a much reduced scale. However effort continues to develop and improve the technology as part of a publicly funded long-term strategy to diversify the fuel base of the economy.

Another form of uncertainty to a potential adopter may be a fast rate of technological change. The speed of change may be so rapid as to be a deterrent. The computer industry is an example. The rate of change and consequential obsolescence has been so rapid that potential customers have been deterred from purchase. They believe that delay may allow further development to be incorporated in the model which they finally purchase. This is a major component in the decision by most computer companies to lease and not to sell their products. In this way customer reluctance to current adoption may be sidestepped. Ownership stays with the manufacturing company and usage is purchased on an annual rental basis. Company reaction to the uncertainties associated with new products and processes is likely to vary. Some companies may deliberately wait for innovations to be proved before adopting. They may take the view that the sacrifice in cost advantage or earnings power is well worth the certainty associated with established products and processes. Others may be more adventurous and bias their decision-taking towards early adoption.

The proportion of companies using an innovation and the industry concerned are the remaining influences which may be relevant to the diffusion process. Potential users may feel induced to adopt as the good becomes more and more common. The contagion or band-wagon effect may be real. Companies or consumers may feel comfort in associating themselves with a majority decision. There may however be more than psychological pressure inducing conformity. Manufacturers may find that spares are not available for what has become an outdated technology. Product specifications may change, and the new technology may radically affect the skill and training of the industry's labour force. Conformity may eventually be forced on lagging companies as costs and revenues adjust to the new parameters which have become accepted as normal. Adoption may become obligatory for all companies that wish to remain in the industry. Industries may vary widely in their rate of adoption of innovations. Science based technology-hungry activities may be very quick off the mark. Tradition orientated, old and declining industries may exhibit a conservatism and cautious approach typical of slow adopters. Financial pressures may be so great that funds are not available for what may appear as venture activities. The whole industrial ethos may militate against rapid usage of new products and processes.

These factors in the diffusion process have been summarised in a model based on four hypotheses.[2][3]

1. that the greater the number of firms in an industry adopting an innovation the greater is the probability that a non-user will adopt;
2. that the expected profitability of an innovation is directly related to the probability of adoption;
3. that the probability of adoption is smaller for innovations of equal profitability, where a large investment is involved;
4. that the probability of adoption, holding profitability constant, will vary from industry to industry.

$$\lambda_{ij(t)} = f_i \left(\frac{(M_{ij(t)}}{N_{ij}}, \pi_{ij}, s_{ij} \ldots \ldots \right)$$

$\lambda_{ij(t)}$ = proportion of firms not using the innovation at time t, that introduce it by time $t + 1$.

N_{ij} = the total of firms for the jth innovation in the ith industry. ($j = 1,2,3.$ $i = 1,2,3,4$)

$M_{ij(t)}$= the number of firms having introduced this innovation at time t.

π_{ij} = the profitability of installing this innovation relative to that of other investments.

S_{ij} = the investment required to install this innovation as a percentage of the average total assets of these firms.

The data are drawn from twelve innovations in the bituminous coal, iron and steel, brewing and railroad industries. The model is capable of 'explaining' practically all the variations in the rate of diffusion of the different innovations concerned. Apparently the major influences determining the rate of adoption of an innovation turn on the proportion of firms involved, the probability of the change, and the size of the investment required. The probability of adoption is apparently an increasing function of the proportion of firms already using the innovation and the profitability of doing so, but a decreasing function of the investment required. Where profitability is comparable an innovation requiring a smaller relative investment will be adopted more quickly. There are also significant interindustry differences in the rate of diffusion. These differences are based on only a few observations but are consistent with the view that competitive industries may respond more quickly to an innovation than those where commercial pressures are relatively muted. Supplementary hypotheses receive some passing confirmation. There are weak but not significant indications that the durability of equipment may be relevant to the diffusion process. Longlived equipment may apparently retard the rate of imitation. The rate of expansion of companies may also influence the rate of adoption. Growth in the market may accommodate and further the switch to innovations. Similarly the rate of diffusion may increase over time. The adoption rate may accelerate as experience and information passes between adopters and potential users.

A study of a more recent vintage adds further empirical weight to the conclusions outlined above. This concerns diffusion of numerical control in the tool and dye industry in the United States of America.[24] Numerical control of machine tools involves operating machines by means of instructions recorded on tapes or cards. An electronic system interprets these instructions so that the machine follows the sequence of programmed operations. The numerical control principle is among the most important innovations of this century. Machine tools controlled by numerical means offer considerable advantages over conventional methods. Among these are greater accuracy and uniformity, more complex design possibility and reduced tooling costs and set-up time. Unlike the study of innovations in the bituminous coal, iron and steel, railroad and brewing industries, the diffusion of numerical control is by no means complete. The study was made while the spreading process continued. This offered advantages in terms of freshness of managements' memory, but of course means that the full story will have to wait until the process is complete. Mail survey and interview revealed that numerical control was profitable. Using the payout or payback period as criterion it was found that in about one-third of the cases the payout period was three years or less and the median was five years.[25] In effect the majority of firms found that the earnings could cover the original cost of the investment in five years or less. This may be judged as an attractive proposition when compared with the maximum payback period companies would allow and still invest. A sample from twelve companies revealed that such 'marginal' investment had on average a payback period of 7.7 years. Compared with 4.8 years, investment in numerical control would certainly appear intramarginal.

Using the model outlined above, a comparison is made of the rate of imitation amongst the machine tool firms with those of the four industries mentioned above: brewing, coal, iron and steel and railroad. Values of profitability and investment found in numerical control are used to estimate how the other industries would have reacted if these had applied to them. It is found that with the values relevant to numerical control, the other industries would have reacted less fast. Apparently the rate of diffusion is greater among tool and dye firms for a given profitability and investment, than among the other industries. This suggests that diffusion is likely to be influenced by industrial structure. The tool and dye industry in the USA is composed almost entirely of small firms and concentration is low. Forty per cent of establishments in 1963 employed less than five people and the median shop employed approximately fifteen people. The four largest firms in 1958 accounted for less than 10 per cent of the value of shipments.[26] This highly fragmented structure may be beneficial to the rate of adoption. Low concentration and the associated presumption of a high level of competitive pressure may therefore be a significant factor explaining the apparent speed of diffusion in this industry.

Of the major influences which affect the rate of diffusion profitability is probably the most important. Profitability is an obvious candidate where commercial motivation is involved. All the models explaining adoption by firms include this as a major variable in the estimating equations. To exclude the influences of profits would be to ignore what has been found to be a major influence in the allocation of resources, and to fly in the face of the vast majority of theoretical work on the behaviour of the firm.[27] The most frequent reason given by those who have not adopted numerical control was lack of profitability. Most non-users argued that their work was of a one-off or jobbing character which did not allow runs of sufficient length to make adequate use of the machinery. The basis of their resistance was a belief that the equipment would not be commercially justifiable. Some of this belief was a result of ignorance and probably represents a rationalisation of inertia. Other non-adopters were in firms where the managers were close to retiring age and therefore had little incentive. Nevertheless the hard core of their belief centred on the lack of commercial attraction.[28]

Scepticism of commercial value also appeared important as an influence in a study concerned with the adoption rate of quantitative investment selection techniques such as payout periods, discounted cash flow and composite index for ranking purposes, in nineteen industrial research and development laboratories in chemical, drugs, and the electronics and petroleum industries in the United States.[29] The adoption rate of quantitative selection procedures was found to be relatively slow. The rate of diffusion is only faster in this sample than five of the twelve innovations mentioned above. Despite the small investment required to introduce these selection techniques, their adoption was not fast. Managers were sceptical of their value. The modest investment involved did not apparently compensate for managerial doubts. The major influence would appear to be the value of the change. Where it is considered that this will be low, managerial enthusiasm is muted. In the adoption of Hybrid corn American farmers 'behaved in a fashion consistent with the idea of profit maximisation'.[30] 'The time lag in the first introduction of Hybrid seed into a particular region, the rate at which farmers shifted to the new seed once it became available, and the extent to which the new seeds replaced the old open-pollinated varieties, all turned on questions of profitability.'[31] The predominant and overriding motive in the diffusion of Hybrid corn was profit. In an interim report of a study of ten process innovations in nine industries in Europe broad confirmation is available of the importance of profitability. The emphasis of the study is diffusion between countries, even so this factor is put first in the list of the most probable major influences on the rate of spread of the techniques involved.[32]

The most plausible single explanation of the rate of diffusion of economic products and processes would thus appear to be commercial advantage. Users' response would appear to hinge on two characteristics: first, the larger the stimulus the faster the reaction; and second, in an uncertain environment it takes a shorter time to find out that there is an advantage, if that advantage is large.[33]

Stimulus and reaction are the central threads in most diffusion models. This should not mislead the reader into believing that the industrial characteristics of adopters are unimportant. Reaction to a stimulus is highly dependent on perception and motivation. Powers of perception, economic pressures and incentives vary widely. Some companies react fast, others slowly. Some may be consistently fast adopters, others may exhibit a wide variation in their speed of response to innovations offering similar advantages. The following discussion will therefore be concerned with the economic characteristics of individual companies and their effect on adoption. There are many plausible hypotheses concerning internal influences on diffusion rates. Factors in the arguments include the size of companies, financial health, profit expectations, rates of growth, the dynamism of management, education and achievement incentives, and competitive pressure. For convenience of the discussion, these factors will be collected into three groups: the size of companies, finance, and managerial dynamism.

The size of companies

Large companies should be quicker on average to adopt to a given innovation. The chances of prompt awareness of a new development are good. In a large company the knowledge network represented by the contacts of management and work people is inevitably bigger than that of a small firm. A sizeable company is likely to be involved with consultative bodies and cooperative activities within the industry concerned. Large companies are in a position to buy in expertise relevant to a particular innovation. The acquisition of personnel with the appropriate skills is unlikely to make a large net addition to the wages bill. At any one time, there is likely to be more machinery that needs replacing in a big concern. This will give more opportunities to acquire the most up-to-date productive units. These may be integrated into the production process as part of routine replacement policy. Large investments are likely to be less inhibiting to big companies. Large companies are likely to have diversified outputs. This should provide a better chance of their output being compatible with a given innovation. It should also allow greater scope for experimentation. Commercial success is not dependent on specialised output, and therefore failures in any particular direction should not have catastrophic consequences. There are, of course, potential disadvantages that may be relevant to big companies. Life may be too safe and comfortable to be conducive to change. Conservatism may prevail amongst management. The consequential effects of the adoption of an innovation may cause such an upheaval that large companies are deterred. Their organisations may be more formalised, less flexible and more interrelated than their smaller competitors. The result may be a reluctance to adopt. The weight of evidence from empirical studies suggests that the size of companies is a factor of significance in the diffusion of innovations. There is an inverse relationship between firm size and the average date of first use.[34] The larger the company, the quicker on average will it be to adopt an innovation. There is not necessarily a clash with this finding and the earlier suggestion that diffusion may procced more rapidly in less concentrated industries. It does not follow that because first use tends to be inversely related to firm size that an industry must be highly concentrated to be favourable to diffusion. High concentration comes from a big disparity in the size and market share of companies. An industry composed of large firms is thus not necessarily highly concentrated.

Finance

The financial health of a company is likely to be an important factor in willingness and ability to adopt. A good record of past profits is likely to generate shareholders' confidence and improve access to further capital. Good profits are also likely to permit a high ploughback rate and reduce current liquidity constraints. A sound financial position is a summary verdict of general competence of a company. It is therefore plausible to expect some relationship between the financial performance of a company and its attitude towards current technology. Indicators of financial health, such as liquidity and profit ratios, should be helpful. These ratios should be reasonable proxies for the availability of funds for investment in new products and processes and should be directly linked with a willingness to adopt innovations early. The trend rate of profits, summarising a number of past years' performance, may also yield some insight into the influence of trading results on companies' diffusion habits. By and large, however, these particular financial indicators are disappointing as predictors. Liquidity, profit rates and past profit trends have not yielded statistically significant results. Similarly growth rate figures are just as unsuccessful. They prove to be statistically insignificant.[35] Apparently figures summarising the overall performance of companies are not successful for this purpose.

When interest is switched from the overall financial health of companies to the profit expectations generated by particular innovations the results are more promising. Unlike other financial indicators, profit expectations appear to be a central feature in the speed at which individual companies adopt innovations. The greater the commercial stimulus in the form of improved profits, the more quickly firms are likely to change. When data are collected relating to the expected returns from adopting particular innovations, this pattern is confirmed.[36] The speed of company response is seen to be directly related to the expected financial benefits. The greater the profitability of a particular innovation, the shorter is likely to be the wait before introducing the new product or process. The important point is that a company's response is geared to the specific profit stimulus provided by a particular innovation. It is not related to general financial health and standing. The key stimulant is expectations generated by individual innovations.

Managerial dynamism

The ability of companies to perceive and respond to the challenge offered by innovations is likely to be influenced by the age, education and aspiration levels of management. Measurement of the dynamism of management is bound to be difficult. The age of top management may give a clue to willingness to respond to change. Top executives close to retiring age are unlikely to drive a company along close to its maximum potential. Younger and more vigorous senior management are likely to be imbued more strongly with the need to achieve. They are likely to be more concerned to prove themselves and will be susceptible to the internal competitive pressures generated by those beneath them in the company ladder. Under their leadership a company may well achieve a brilliant commercial performance. Education levels are likely to play an important part. Adaptability to change and appreciation of the benefits of innovation should be a product of improved education. The need for achievement, n-Ach as it is referred to in the jargon of the literature, may not, however, be directly related to observed educational qualifications.[37] The aspiration level of holders of PhDs is not necessarily greater than those with first degrees or more vocationally orientated qualifications. The n-Ach of those with less prestigious awards may in fact be greater. They may feel pressured to compensate for lack of status with achievement. The commercial world offers many opportunities for these drives. It is therefore likely to be a mistake to expect a managerial group with the highest educational rating to be more dynamic and venturesome than one with more modest qualifications. Individuals with the highest qualifications may be imbued with the values and mores of the professional classes. As a whole, professionals exhibit an n-Ach lower than that associated with business men.

A company which has a high proportion of individuals with prestigious qualifications may be lacking in the drive which distinguishes pioneers. In the transfer of technology, the need for achievement is probably a key characteristic. The highest educational qualifications are unlikely to be a reliable indicator of managerial dynamism.[38] Findings on educational qualification and adoption rates should therefore be treated with due caution. In the numerical control machine tool study, the effect of education was significantly related to the average date of first use.[39] Similar caution should be adopted with findings relating to the dynamism of management and the age of a firm's president. There were indications that in the tool and dye industry an ageing president may have influenced the adoption decision. His nearness to retirement may have been a significant factor in the decision not to adopt. In a different study, the age of a firm's president yielded results which were statistically insignificant. In practice this result is likely to reflect the poor quality of a single indicator to show the dynamism of management. The firms concerned were not small like those in the tool and dye industry, and the president's age is therefore unlikely to be representative of the age of the whole management group.[40]

Summary indications of managerial dynamism are clearly difficult to find. Even past behaviour is apparently a poor guide. There would appear to be little consistency in the rate at which companies begin using an innovation.[41] Companies which are fast adopters on one occasion may be slow on another. The classification system used in Fig. 6.3, categorising adopters by their speed of reaction, must therefore be used with caution. The procedure has limited value in describing how companies will react to further innovations. Apparently technical leadership tends not to be concentrated and firms tend not to be consistent in their speed of reaction. Private individuals as final consumers are apparently more predictable in their habits. Within product categories and sometimes between related product categories, there would appear to be some consistency of behaviour.[42] This may be a great help in the early launching of new products. Initial marketing of innovations may be more efficient and general consumer acceptance may be speeded by the example of the early adopters. The reason why companies probably exhibit less consistency in their reaction patterns is likely to include managerial changes, alterations in the competitive environment, and changed expectations. The key factor in adoption decisions is apparently expected profits, but this conclusion does not carry with it the presumption that companies will be consistent in their behaviour. Thus a general statement that the more profitable a particular innovation is the quicker it will be adopted, is likely to mean that an equally profitable innovation will be adopted equally fast. It does not carry with it the corollary that the order of adopters is likely to be the same for both innovations.

Intrafirm diffusion

Discussion so far has concentrated on the rate at which firms begin using an innovation. Diffusion has been treated in terms of a decision relating to the first use of an innovation. This, of course, is only part of the story. The other part is the rate at which the new replaces the old within companies. An innovation will not make a major impact unless it is adopted on a significant scale. The rate at which the new product or process displaces the old, will be a major influence on costs. The faster a cost-saving innovation is adopted and replaces existing technology, the more quickly will average costs of a company approximate to those of the new technique. The faster an industry adopts an innovation, the smaller will be the gap between the best and average practice. Specifically, intrafirm diffusion is the measure of how quickly a firm substitutes the new technique for the old, once it has begun using the technique.[43] If adoption is widening the use of an innovation, intrafirm diffusion is deepening. It is the process beyond adoption, where use is extended more deeply into a company's production function.

A company in the machine tool industry may decide to buy an improved lathe. The first step to begin using the new lathe represents the adoption decision. The second stage where more lathes are bought and the existing machinery is displaced, is the process of intrafirm diffusion. Of course, some machinery has to be introduced on such a scale that the displacement is virtually complete at one stroke. This is the highly interrelated type of investment discussed earlier. In these circumstances measures of intrafirm diffusion become virtually impossible because the investment decision is discontinuous and all-embracing in character. The limits chosen to describe the process of intrafirm diffusion are the time interval when the innovation accounts for 10 per cent of a firm's output and the date when the proportion reaches 90 per cent. The 10 per cent is taken as the time when a company has 'begun' using the technique. The 90 per cent figure represents the time when adoption is complete. These specific figures are arbitrary, but nevertheless should span the period which extends beyond experimentation and up to virtual completion of the change. A study has been undertaken of intrafirm diffusion in the United States railroad industry over the period 1925–61.[44] During this time diesels replaced steam traction as the major locomotive power. The average time taken by thirty randomly chosen firms to go from 10 per cent to 90 per cent was nine years. However, some firms took only three years and others took sixteen. The interesting question is, what factors determine the speed of this transition and why did some companies react so much quicker than others?

The model used to explain the differences in the rates of intrafirm diffusion includes the profitability of replacing the steam locomotive with diesel, the age distribution of firms' steam locos, the apparent risk involved at the time of investment, the size of the firm, and its liquidity at the time when the firm 'began' to dieselise. The age distribution of steam locomotives may require explanation. An age distribution which is old indicates a skewed age weighting where a high proportion of equipment is due for replacement shortly. A young age composition indicates the opposite bias, where the major proportion of capital is relatively new and therefore a small proportion is due for replacement. The practical use of the concept of the age distribution of capital is related to the attitude which management is likely to take towards renewal. If the capital stock is old, a significant proportion of equipment is due for replacement. Management is therefore likely to regard the adoption of innovations as part of its routine replacement. A company with youthful capital will have to take a much more positive decision. Not so much of its capital requires replacing. The existing equipment may therefore have to be displaced rather than replaced to accommodate innovations. The age composition in this instance may consequently be a hindrance to a fast rate of intrafirm diffusion.

Apparent risk is measured in terms of the time interval between the earliest use of diesels by the first firm to 'begin' using them in the United States and the firm concerned. The assumption is that the longer time a company waits the more it will benefit from others' experience. A further strand in assessment of risk, is the nearness to full dieselisation. The nearer a company is to completion of the change to diesels, the less will uncertainty be at the time concerned relative to the beginning of the process. Profitability estimates obtained from firms were based on average payout periods. Liquidity was measured as the average ratio of current assets to current liabilities in the two years prior to the period when diesels reached 10 per cent of total in the firms concerned. Size was indicated by the number of freight ton miles in 1949, and the age composition by the percentage of steam locomotives that were fifteen years and over at the time when diesels reached 10 per cent of the total. The effect of size is not the expected one. The weight of the evidence indicates that the small companies tended to adopt more quickly than the large companies once they had begun to use diesels. The major consideration would appear to be the costliness of operating two kinds of traction systems in a small concern. A large company can probably accommodate the two systems operating side by side. This was apparently less possible with the smaller company. The model performs well in accounting for the variations in the rate of intrafirm diffusion between firms. About 70 per cent of the variations in intrafirm diffusion can be explained by the regression procedure. The most important variable in the model turns out to be the profitability of the change. This is not the overall profitability of the firm, but the particular financial stimulus offered by the change to diesel. When overall profitability is included as an additional variable in the calculations, the regression coefficient has the wrong sign and is statistically not significant. Like the decision to begin using an innovation, the relevant influence in intrafirm diffusion is not the general profitability of companies but their response to the particular stimulus offered by the particular innovation. This would suggest 'that there exists an important economic analogue to the classic psychological law relating reaction time to the intensity of the stimulus. The profitability of an investment apparently acts as a stimulus, the intensity of which seems to govern quite closely a firm's speed of response. In terms of the diffusion process, it governs both how rapidly a firm begins using an innovation and how rapidly it substitutes it for older methods.'[4][5]

Summary

Diffusion is the process by which the use of an innovation spreads and grows. Imitation and emulation are equally good synonyms for the activity which broadens usage from source. In a simplified and highly schematic description of the process of technical advance, diffusion comes after invention and innovation, and is the stage where economic impact really begins to be felt. It is difficult to understate the importance of diffusion. As a gap-closer, a means of upgrading performance, an ally of specialisation, and a servicer of competition, the ability to copy and 'borrow' the technological development of others is of immense relevance to companies and economies. Diffusion involves information exchange. The pattern of adoption over time by users normally exhibits an S or logistic shape. A standard nomenclature has been established which describes users by their time of first adoption. When cast into the non-cumulative form, the distribution of types of users approximates to the normal. Knowledge of the behavioural characteristics of early adopters may help improve the efficiency of the marketing of new products and processes. Behavioural characteristics are, however, only one influence in the rate of adoption by customers. The economic characteristic of the innovation concerned is another. The time taken for innovations to achieve acceptance varies widely. The major determinants of the speed at which adopters first begin to use an innovation are: the expected profitability of adoption, the relative size of the investment involved, the proportion of companies which have adopted, and the industry concerned. Of these influences profitability is probably the most important.

The economic characteristics of individual companies relevant to diffusion include: the size of companies, financial health, managerial dynamism and the need to achieve, profit expectations, rates of growth and competitive pressure. Of these, profit expectation is the most important. When investigation of the diffusion process is switched to the rate at which an innovation displaces existing equipment within companies, a similar conclusion emerges. The rate of intrafirm diffusion is highly dependent on the profitability of the innovations concerned.

7

Diffusion and the multinational enterprise: I. Technology

The previous chapter concentrated on diffusion as a company process, where adoption has been treated as an interfirm and interindustry phenomenon. The approach is now broadened to cover diffusion between countries, but the context still remains at the company level. The role of the multinational enterprise as an agent in the diffusion of technology will be under consideration. In particular it will be argued that the location pattern exhibited by such companies may reflect the character of the goods they sell. The outward pulls to which the multinationals have responded may be a product of an emphasis on innovative activities. This proposition is associated with the work of C. P. Kindleberger and S. Hymer.[1] The model under investigation will test the notion that the technologically orientated company which is large enough to make multinational status a genuine possibility will attempt to enhance and/or defend its own ingenuity by locating abroad. Multinational companies are viewed as an important organisational invention which may help stave off and defer the onset of economic obsolescence of particular products. If this is shown to be a significant influence on location policy, then some indication of the importance of the multinational in the global spread of technology will be indicated.

The diffusion of innovation is essentially an education process. Knowledge of the new product or process must spread from source. Potential users must become aware of the advantages associated with a new good and their resistance to change must be overcome. Knowledge of innovations may be passed by the movement of goods and persons and by the transmittal of documents. The most potent means of diffusion are those which have a strong demonstration effect and which are relatively undemanding on the receiver. This explains the effectiveness of 'person to person' transfers. An individual joining a company, well versed in a new technique, can exercise a strong demonstration effect. He can physically show his colleagues how the innovation works. He can argue and persuade and break down resistance to change by personal contact. In contrast the passage of technical literature is a much less potent persuader. It is dependent on the personal effort of the reader to master the contents. The demonstration effect is minimal and the formal presentation rigid in the sense that once written it makes no allowance for the requirements of particular readers. In general the passage of literature is a less successful means of diffusing knowledge of innovations. This is well understood. Aid programmes to developing countries which merely take the form of cash and technical literature would be most unlikely to succeed. Without the assistance of technical experts the local population would be slow in acquiring the skills necessary for effective technology transfer.

'Person to person' transfers can be effected by a large number of means. Private individuals may switch jobs within industries. They may leave their countries of origin and may form part of what has become known as the brain drain. They may be members of armed forces with widely dispersed bases in different countries. An important means whereby technology may be diffused by 'person to person' contact is the multinational company. International exchange of technical knowledge will take place as a consequence of personnel movement within such companies. It is a direct outcome of the locational structure of the companies. The multinational form of organisation is potentially of great significance to the spread of knowledge. It has all the ingredients making for successful diffusion. A global structure, a unified corporate organisation, a wide source of ideas, a technological endowment independent of host countries, all these are characteristics that should make the international company a potent force in the spread of technology. Before proceeding to the detailed arguments, however, it is necessary to pause and define exactly what is meant by the multinational company.

Definition of the multinational company

A multinational company is defined as 'an enterprise which owns or controls production facilities in more than one country'.[2] This is known as the multinational producing enterprise (MPE). The MPE is distinguished from the multinational trading enterprise (MTE) by the location of producing facilities abroad. A home-based company with world export sales is a multinational trading enterprise (MTE) and is not included within the definition.[3] This is merely a company which sells its products internationally. It has not established production facilities abroad. In practice the distinction between a multinational and a national company is difficult to draw. For example, do companies within a trading block qualify? Are Italian companies located in France multinational? As members of the European Economic Community they are within one trading area. It could therefore be argued that these are transcontinental rather than multinational. In practice these problems are sidestepped by adopting a definition and sticking to it. This requires that actual manufacturing capacity be established abroad and the nationality of the host country should be different from that of the parent. This is an arbitrary definition. It overlooks, for example, intercompany shareholdings across national boundaries. Separate categories such as multinational controlled or multinational owned enterprise (MCE or MOE) are of course possible. Similarly it ignores companies which merely own sales organisations abroad. The arbitrary definition excludes such companies which have only gone part way towards becoming multinational. In practice the arbitrary nature of the definition of the multinational is unlikely to be important, since the typical company under discussion here will be large. It will have many overseas producing subsidiaries and a global outlook. The sort of company under consideration is likely to be amongst those listed by *Fortune Magazine* and be amongst the world's most influential business organisations.

Multinational companies have been growing in importance. This is reflected in the proportion of direct investment overseas in the total private capital outflow. Of the capital outflow from the leading industrial nations, direct investment was approximately 10 per cent of the total in 1914; today this figure is approximately 75 per cent.[4] It has been estimated that the output of foreign subsidiaries of multinationals in 1966 was approximately twice the volume of exports of the major trading nations.[5] In the case of the United Kingdom approximately a quarter of exports of British enterprises are sent direct to their foreign subsidiaries. In 1967 21 per cent of plant and equipment expenditure by United States manufacturing enterprise was undertaken by their overseas subsidiaries.[6]

Locational influences

A major rise in the importance of the multinational has taken place in the last twenty years.[7] This must be a response to strong locational forces. The multinational enterprise is a global organisation. One of its major functions is to reduce the effects of the separation of markets. Countries and trading blocks tend to be distinct in character. Markets tend not to be unified across the world. There are many obstacles to trade. The effects of these is to fragment world demand for products into a series of heterogeneous and specific markets where local characteristics may predominate as sales influences. Such obstacles include tariffs, government regulations, national laws, taxation, the character of competition, capital raising facilities, credit arrangements, and familiarity with the language. By locating within particular markets the multinational producing enterprise (MPE) may secure a number of benefits. Tariffs may be avoided and the knowledge barrier occasioned by language difficulties and lack of familiarity with local practice may be eroded by direct involvement. From the point of view of the parent company it has now reduced some of the effects of market separation. Its subsidiaries should enjoy similar advantages to indigenous producers, yet their allegiance will lie outside the economy of their adoption. This is a form of specialisation where affiliates build up particular knowledge and the parent company acts as the corporate decision centre. There is now a unified organisation interlinking production units across the world. In this sense market separation has been reduced. The benefits accrue in many ways. These will be outlined below.

Companies will opt to produce abroad rather than export, for a large number of reasons. Included in these will be political, tax, tariff and cost considerations. Worldwide location of overseas subsidiaries allows a company considerable tax advantages. By appropriate intercompany pricing, a company may arrange for its profits to accrue where the local tax burden is the least. It can cross tariff barriers by undertaking production within the protected area. It may avoid, for example, the strictures of Anti-Trust legislation by establishing business activities outside the territorial reach of the laws concerned. The attraction of overseas location may, of course, be entirely on the cost side. Cheaper labour may be a strong attraction for companies whose home base is in a high wage economy. Other forces making for multinationals may include enlargement of scale and a desire to take advantage of varying economic conditions between countries. Some economic activities require vast scale. Economic conditions may vary between countries. Some economies may be going through a period of depression, others may not. By having a wide geographical dispersion of production units the multinational may be able to smooth its returns.

Additional locational influences may include a reduction in the costs of using the price mechanism, and the interdependence effects generated by a worldwide organisation.[8] Geographical extension of productive activity may bring with it economies in the use of the price mechanism. The costs of effecting transactions may be reduced. In a sense, a large company may well replace the market for a significant amount of its decisions. It may own most of its raw materials, and resources may be allocated within the organisation by fiat rather than by market forces. The search and enquiry involved in normal purchases may be greatly reduced. A high proportion of needs will be provided within the organisation. Arm's length or market purchases may be relatively infrequent. As a result the costs of using the price mechanism may be considerably reduced. A multinational company may also benefit from interdependence effects. The close link between parent and subsidiaries may represent an example of commercial synergy. The whole organisation may sum to a total which is greater than the addition of the parts. As a consequence, a single subsidiary may be worth more to the parent company than it would be to another company within the host country. This interdependence effect may explain the reluctance of multinationals to have host nationals as equity shareholders. To admit them would merely be to share an advantage which probably arises from the multinational form of organisation.[9]

Economies of scale may be important to the multinational. The home market may be too small to accommodate plant of the minimum efficient scale (MES).[10] This may arise from absolute or relative effects. The number of fellow competitors may reduce the market share to one particular firm. This is the relative effect. The market may not be big enough to support even one plant of MES. This is the absolute effect. Minimum efficient scale is defined as the point where the average cost curve becomes horizontal. The L-shaped cost curve is assumed to be typical. The MES therefore represents an output level which secures minimum average costs. Location of production facilities abroad may secure markets which are large enough to support plant of this size. If overseas markets are not big enough in themselves, a foreign subsidiary may nevertheless help. It may produce goods which have the effect of promoting the sales of parent company output. Aggregate sales, including exports, may now allow the home output to be produced at minimum efficient scale. Strictly these benefits represent a form of marketing economy. Nevertheless they may show themselves in terms of increased output and lower average costs of production.

Other benefits from foreign location showing themselves in terms of improved costs of production, may come from intrafirm specialisation. The division of labour within a firm may be improved. Particular plants may concentrate on highly specific tasks. The new element is the ability to organise this on a worldwide scale. Subsidiaries or plants within individual markets can be highly concentrated in their activities. The commercial risks involved are reduced by the umbrella effect provided by membership of a global corporation. The particular results achieved by individual plants and subsidiaries are not crucial to group wellbeing. The aggregate of activities undertaken by the international corporation can be wide and highly diversified. The potential for cross-subsidisation is therefore considerable. Concentration and specialisation may be taken further than in a normal company. Products or parts of products can be manufactured at the least cost location. These may be sold locally or transported to other companies within the organisation where they may then be sold or processed further. Specialisation can be taken to a very high degree and location of manufacture may be determined solely by cost considerations. The marketing may be handled elsewhere in the corporation and thus these subsidiaries may be left to concentrate solely on achieving low costs of production.

In practice economies of scale may not be an all important locational factor within multinational companies. Such economies may not be a convincing explanation of the geographical dispersion exhibited by such concerns. If economies of scale were particularly powerful this may imply a concentration of plant and not a replication throughout the world. Where affiliates produce what was formerly exported by the parent company, aggregate home output may be reduced and thus the scope for economies of scale may be impaired in the parent company. Economies of scale at first sight would therefore not appear to be a powerful locational influence. This summary conclusion may be unjustified. The assumption lying behind the argument is that foreign subsidiaries are export displacing. This may not be the case, and it will be argued later that the multinational form of company does not necessarily imply that there will be net export displacement. The total value of exports may increase as a result of the establishment of overseas subsidiaries. Economies of scale may also be fostered by intracompany specialisation. Locations may be chosen which heighten concentration on specific sectors of company turnover. The benefits may accrue in terms of economies of scale and lower unit costs. It will also be argued that a major pull inducing overseas location may be market capture. Companies which sell articles which are in the early phases of the production cycle will probably emphasise revenue and not cost considerations. Their concern will be for wider markets. Customers will be attracted by the technological properties of the goods, not necessarily by their low price. This does not imply that economies of scale are unimportant. It may be that considerable cost advantages do accrue from a multinational location pattern. But it is asserted that these are likely to be an additional advantage secured by reducing the separation of markets, not a primary cause of outward investment decisions.

Tariffs may be important to the global corporation. Location within a nation state or inside a trading block may make the subsidiaries equal in legal status to indigenous companies. The impact of tariffs may therefore be avoided or at least reduced. The cost incentive to establish subsidiaries to avoid tariffs may be considerable. Duties with an ad valorem incidence of 20 per cent or more have not been uncommon. Tariff avoidance may thus be a significant locational influence. In practice it is difficult to identify cause and effect in the location decisions of multinational companies.[11] Tariff consideration may well be a primary influence on some goods and a secondary one on others.[12] They are a significant factor in the separation of markets. There is a fairly clear outward pull generated by the cost advantage associated with establishing manufacturing facilities within other countries' tariff barriers. But the importance of this cost advantage is likely to vary considerably with specific circumstances. For present purposes it is accepted that for goods with a high innovational content tariff considerations may be a factor reinforcing an outward tendency based on market capture. For other goods which are in the maturity phase of the product cycle, cost influences may predominate. The price charged is likely to be a crucial influence in sales, and the foreign exporter may be unable to compete with locals if he has to absorb tariffs. In these circumstances it may be plausible to argue that such levies may be a cause of foreign location.

Innovation and location abroad

All the locational forces mentioned above may be part of the explanation for the recent tendency towards multinationalism. However, none of them would appear to go to the heart of the matter. A major clue to an important influence making for multinational location is probably the character of the goods sold by such companies. Technology and multinational firms appear mutually dependent. These companies seem to concentrate in technically advanced activities. Multinationals are predominant in four main sectors. These are vehicles, chemicals, mechanical and electrical engineering.[13] Products typically dominated by multinationals include tyres, oil, tobacco, pharmaceuticals, electronics and motor vehicles. In contrast, cotton textiles, iron and steel, and aircraft are not. Multinationals are hardly in evidence with these products. The absence of the multinational in aircraft production, which is a high technology activity, needs some explaining. The reason probably represents the nationalist character of contract placing by governments. Autarkic considerations may mean that governments favour companies owned by their nationals. The classified or secret nature of a high proportion of this type of activity means that considerations of national security may dictate such prudence. In eight industrially advanced OECD countries eight multinationals accounted for between 30 per cent and more than 50 per cent of all industrial research and development.[14] There are clearly strong forces in action in high technology activities. These may explain the relatively recent drive towards worldwide location of production facilities among the world's leading companies.

A three-stage process has been distinguished in the development of the modern corporation.[15] First the Marshallian firm, with one function within one industry with a single and identifiable entrepreneur. The second stage is associated with large national corporations, with continent wide production and marketing arrangements. The third stage is the multidivisional corporation. Here corporations are decentralised into several divisions, each specialising in a few product lines and organised as an almost autonomous unit. The major cause of this change is probably to meet the conditions of continuous innovation. Multidivisional organisation is highly flexible. It can operate in several industries and adjust quickly to changes in demand and technology. The multinational firm is a geographical extension of the multidivisional form of organisation, and represents an international widening of managerial control. The form of organisation remains the same. There is a central office which is the corporate brain, with a number of subsidiaries with a high degree of autonomy in day to day matters, located around the world. In this representation of the stages of the development of the modern corporation the incentive to go multinational comes from the innovative process. It is the nature of innovation which is probably a major determinant of the multinational form of company. The peculiar properties of knowledge as a 'free' good, lead time, lag time, and the weakness of the International Patent System; these, it will be argued, are major influences. Companies protect their innovations by having a wide geographical production and sales network, and also protect themselves from being overtaken by the innovational activities of rivals by keeping their ears close to the ground all around the world. The multinational is a knowledge network as well as a production and sales organisation. It is asserted that the nature of the innovation process is a primary cause of the multinational type of company. This may be reinforced by tariff and other considerations.

For a company to establish a subsidiary abroad it is reasonable to assume that it must expect to earn a higher return overseas than at home. There are difficulties associated with foreign location. Costs of administration may be higher. The subsidiary is away from the decision-making centre. Communications may be stretched. Lack of familiarity with a new market may raise the risks involved. Influences of this character make it plausible to argue that the parent company should expect a premium return before committing resources. Arguments of a similar character make it equally plausible to assert that the foreign subsidiary should earn a better return on capital than the local firm. If the increased costs involved in running a globally dispersed business are a fact of life, then the competitive advantage of the overseas subsidiary is likely to lie on the revenue side. If the risks associated with foreign involvement are also genuine, then the profit expectations should be greater than those applicable to local rivals.[16]

The way in which superior revenue is generated is related to market imperfections. With perfect knowledge, and perfect markets for technology, and also assuming that there are cost disadvantages for the subsidiary, then local markets would be served by local firms. For a foreign firm to be successful it must therefore have some special advantage. This is likely to take the form of a market imperfection related to the specific advantages secured by companies that innovate and differentiate. Branding, superior sales effort and patent protection for a particular invention all tend to create and protect customer good-will. This creation and maintenance of consumer loyalty is a means of attenuating the encroachment of rivals. By creating something special, the company is generating a specific advantage. This should help it to weaken the blandishment of rivals and lengthen the period of time before the goods concerned enter the maturity phase of the product cycle and sell largely on price considerations.

The character of the goods produced and sold by American companies in Europe suggests that the speciality element is a real consideration inducing overseas location. Drugs, cosmetics, speciality foodstuffs, cars, tyres, chemicals and electrical components are examples. Customers are attracted and retained by branding and by innovation. Newness and distinctiveness are important influences in the marketing of these products. This would appear to support the view that 'in general, horizontal investment abroad can be justified for any unique asset or advantage possessed by an enterprise that differentiates it, or its products, from competitors'.[17] It is thus likely that an important source of competitive advantage among multinationals will be derived from innovative activity. Differentiation which is a weaker form of innovation is also likely to be part of this outward locational pull. Research and development and the successful introduction of new products are likely to provide a major impetus to widen location.

The multinational company is an organisational invention to improve the powers of appropriation of the benefits of innovation. It is a device to improve the ability of an innovating company to capture a large proportion of the benefits of its own ingenuity. It is also a device to strengthen the ability of companies to respond quickly to innovations occuring elsewhere, by having a widespread knowledge network. It is no coincidence that the majority of multinational companies are American. In America the problems of appropriation are relatively acute. The multinational should increase the returns from research. By improving appropriation a company may defend its commercial prospects. The multinational represents a powerful means of improving the yield from research and development and a means of combating product obsolescence. A product which has reached saturation point in America may still be relatively new in Europe and unheard of in India. By having a wide geographical disposition of products among economies with varying economic conditions this should improve the economic life of an innovation.

The alternatives to overseas location of production facilities are licensing arrangements and exporting. Licensing provides an income and avoids the risks associated with establishing new markets in areas which may be unfamiliar. It may also be cheaper in capital, time and energy. The innovating company is saved the effort of establishing overseas production facilities, yet still benefits through the terms of the licence. The example of the British firm Pilkington Bros is relevant here. It developed the revolutionary float technique for the production of plate glass. This was far superior to existing methods. Despite patent protection, major American producers were licensed. Pilkingtons did not establish USA productive capacity to exploit their invention. A number of factors may have been relevant in this decision. At the time, Pilkingtons was a closely controlled family concern which did not have a stock exchange quotation. There may, therefore, have been a capital shortage. In addition the American companies, which would eventually have become competitors, were large and powerful. The spectre of oligopolistic price warfare on expiry of the patents may therefore have been a deterrent. Furthermore, denial of the major American glass producers access to the knowhow may have generated a research effort to improve on and thus sidestep the patent position. In this case Pilkington's market advantage may have evaporated under the stress of innovative competition.[18] In more normal circumstances, licensing may not be an attractive proposition to the company selling goods with a high innovational content. Licensing may not be a viable proposition; it may invite future competition. It may upgrade the licensee's technology by giving him access to knowhow, and also enhance his customer goodwill. Of course, the terms of a licence will benefit the grantor, but these are unlikely to appropriate the full benefit. If they did there would be little or no economic incentive to take out the licence. There certainly appear to be indications that companies are now less willing to license their products.[19]

Exporting may be used as an alternative to licensing or producing abroad. It may also be used by a company as a first stage towards establishing a subsidiary abroad.[20] Once an adequate market has been developed, supporting services like sales and maintenance may follow. Finally, assembly and production facilities may be set up. Exporting as an alternative to overseas location may be unattractive. Tariffs may have to be absorbed. Local producers may be induced to imitate and gain market precedence on patriotic grounds. Overseas location may be a forestalling tactic to reduce market pre-emption by others. By establishing a subsidiary, a foreign company may be able to deter potential entrants by its direct physical presence and may counter patriotic motives by providing employment for nationals. However, the notion that innovation or technological orientation is an important influence making for multinationalism should not lead the reader to believe that overseas producing facilities are necessarily a substitute for exports. It does not necessarily follow that the establishment of productive capacity abroad by a firm will lead to a net reduction in exports to the country concerned. In fact there is considerable evidence to suggest that there is a positive relationship between export performance and the research intensity of the relevant activity. When a comparison is made between USA export performance and the research emphasis of the industrial activity, it is revealed that there is a high concentration of exports in science-intensive product groups.[21] The comparison is made on a 'normalised' base. The data are standardised by relating, for example, United States exports in a particular industry to the export performance of the same industry localised in prospective competitor countries. The calculation is made on a ratio basis to establish the contrast in trade pattern between the countries concerned. The studies reveal that the USA has particular export strength in the research intensive activities. The same is also true but to a reduced degree for the UK and Germany, and to a much less marked extent for France.[22]

The establishment of overseas producing facilities will not necessarily reduce exports, for a number of reasons. Foreign subsidiaries can be export generating, import generating, and export displacing.[23] These terms are used in relation to the parent company. Thus the branches of a multinational company may in fact stimulate exports from the home economy. The subsidiary may be effective in side-stepping tariffs. An increased volume of sales may result. Improved marketing as a result of increased familiarity with local conditions may lead to a higher volume of sales. The parent company may have to provide the bulk of the demand until local capacity has expanded. The parent company may alter the character of its trade. It may now export the basic inputs. These may be processed by the subsidiary and transformed into the final product. The total value of trade may not suffer because of the increased volume of business now being done. The parent company may now have an outlet for a wider range of its goods than before. In the initial situation, where production facilities did not exist and a sales agency had to be relied upon there may not have been sufficient expertise or knowhow to carry the additional products. Once operations encompass production as well as selling, sales economies may result. As a consequence of the increased size of a unit, more lines may now be handled.

Import generation may arise where a subsidiary can produce more cheaply than the parent company. The goods may then be imported back to the home economy and marketed either at an enhanced profit level or at a price that may undercut competitors. This type of trade is most likely to occur when competition is strengthening on the home market and the innovational edge of the products concerned is waning. Products nearing maturity are perhaps likely to induce an overseas pattern of location based on securing a cost advantage for the parent company.

Overseas subsidiaries may, of course, be export displacing. The production of the parent company may immediately reflect the establishment of an overseas subsidiary. There may be a straight substitution of foreign for home production. However, the discussion above indicates that this is by no means an inevitable consequence of multinational organisation. Science-based activities may typically adopt a global location pattern and may also be well represented in export trade. There is no real paradox. Evidence in fact suggests that in value terms production of affiliates, at least of USA companies, is typically greater than exports from parent companies.[24] This does not necessarily indicate export displacement. Nor does it deny that there may be a relationship between R and D intensive activities and exports.

There are, of course, some industries with a natural propensity to locate abroad. Extractive activities are a major example. The main incentive to the multinational firm in this case is likely to be security of supply of their raw materials. Oil, aluminium, lead and zinc are examples where large companies have spread their interests worldwide to secure their commercial future. In these examples the character of the innovative process may not be a plausible explanation. Their major locational influence probably derives from the dispersion of the raw material deposits on which they are dependent. But remember the definition of the MPE. To be multinational, oil companies must refine abroad, and mining interests must smelt or process and not merely import raw materials back to the parent company. Thus even these activities may respond to the market pulls which it has been argued are a major influence affecting the location of high ingenuity activities. When refining and processing takes place abroad to serve foreign markets, then it may be plausible to argue that these pulls are in operation. This will be most persuasive where processing occurs in third countries away from both parent company and raw material sources. In this case the major locational influence is unlikely to involve supply considerations and may well reflect the draw of attractive markets. Consequently extractive industries can come within the scope of the arguments presented here. The establishment of American oil refineries in Europe may perhaps be put forward as an example of customer orientated location decisions. Until the recent discoveries in the North

Sea, there was no significant indigenous Western European source of oil. Despite this, American companies established refining capacity. The process of refining is a complex first stage in an industry which is research intensive in character. Product innovation is important. In these terms, locational pulls independent of supply considerations, are plausible. The natural propensity for such an activity to locate globally does not therefore necessarily deny the market arguments advanced here.

In the particular case of American oil refineries in Western Europe a more convincing explanation may have been tariff policy. Governments were anxious to establish national refining capacity. Tariffs therefore tended to discriminate in favour of crude oil imports and against refined products. Discriminating tariffs may therefore be advanced as a causal locational influence. This does not necessarily destroy the market arguments advanced here. American refineries may have been established in Western Europe without the tariff incentive. Market attraction may have been an underlying factor in the location decisions. The combination of tariff avoidance and good sales prospects may have strengthened the case for overseas location. The cost advantages of establishing subsidiaries may not have entirely supplanted market pulls as a locational influence.

International patenting

There is a further impetus to establish multinational companies. This is the weakness of the international patent system. The International Union for the Protection of Industrial Property was established in the 1890s. The rationale of this Union is to overcome the disadvantages of the 'prior publication' rule applied by patent authorities. In normal circumstances prior publication may disallow the inventor from acquiring a patent. The International Convention, which established the Union, has the effect that an application for a patent in a member country does not amount to prior publication. Because of this agreement an inventor may now make application in all the countries concerned without being excluded on prior publication grounds. The economic reason for this Convention is persuasive. If it did not exist, it would mean that an inventor would have a crucial strategic decision to make. He would only be able to apply for a patent in one country. That application would amount to prior publication as far as all other countries' patent authorities are concerned, therefore he would be excluded from application elsewhere. Consequently the strategic decision to be made would be which country to choose for the single application. Inevitably the inventor would choose the country where a patent would have the most economic power. As a consequence it would be almost inevitable that patent applications would be highly concentrated in the most advanced economies. Effectively, therefore, most patent applications would go to the United States. The effect of the International Convention for the Protection of Industrial Property is to mitigate this geographical concentration effect.[25]

In practice this international patent system has considerable weaknesses. For complete coverage the innovating company has to make application in each and every member country. There are eighty members of the Convention. The physical effort and the costs involved are clearly likely to be considerable. For a private individual, the cost may well be prohibitive. To a company this may also be the case. However, if a company is multinational in status it may not have to go through this process of application. Instead it may merely exploit its economic power knowing that it has widely dispersed production units. The company may therefore be able to avoid the expense and effort of applying for patents. It may use its economic influence to the same effect. Alternatively, the multinational may take advantage of the international patent system. By being so large it may have the resources and energy to make application in all member countries. If so it may establish a powerful patent position to defend itself against potential rivals. With the economic power that comes from size and its ability to defend patents through the courts, the multinational should be in a strong position. The International Convention for the Protection of Industrial Property may, therefore, be another influence adding to the impetus towards multinationalism.

Most countries have as part of their patent law the requirement that a patent be 'worked'. Members of the International Convention for the Protection of Industrial Property require that a patent granted under this Convention should be exploited by local production. The economic rationale of this legal stricture is balance of payments consideration. If there is no home production then the alternative is importation. By requiring that a patent be 'worked', the country is essentially saying that the good concerned should be produced locally. The 'working' provisions may be represented as an important factor, inducing overseas location of production facilities. This, however, would be misleading. The 'working' provisions are rarely applied. Patent authorities would have to be extremely alert to achieve an effective surveillance of applications under the International Convention. This would be an enormous task. In place of the 'working' provisions, compulsory licences or licences of right are more frequently used. The patent-holding company or individual is effectively required to give a local producer the right to use his patent. The inventor is spared the investment effort of setting up plant and machinery, or saved the funds involved in acquiring a local business to carry out the manufacture, and benefits by receiving royalties. The fact that companies tend to set up production facilities abroad to take advantage of their patents, therefore probably reflects not the power of the 'working' provisions but economic forces in action. In order to protect themselves, companies may feel bound to establish production facilities in the major industrial centres. This is probably not a response to the requirements of the patent law, but a defensive attitude based on the fear of rivals' reactions, and a desire to improve appropriation. The effect of the Convention is probably not a primary locational force, but rather an influence reinforcing the tendency towards widespread geographical distribution of production facilities.

Summary

A multinational corporation is defined as an enterprise which owns or controls production facilities in more than one country. This is the multinational producing enterprise (MPE). The ability of such companies to reduce the separation of markets by coordinating geographically disparate subsidiaries brings with it a number of benefits. These may include a reduction of tax and tariff burdens, increased intracompany specialisation and lower costs of production. A major incentive to locate abroad may come from the character of the goods they sell. Global involvement may be the result of an emphasis on innovative activities. Exporting and licensing may not be adequate substitutes for direct involvement in foreign markets.

The next section will examine the proposition that MPEs cluster in technological activities and an attempt will be made to determine the effects on location policy of the character of the goods they sell. The results will be seen to have direct relevance to the diffusion of technology.

8

Diffusion and the multinational enterprise: II. Methodology and statistics

In this chapter an attempt is made to add further evidence to the hypothesis that multinational companies concentrate in technologically orientated industries. The importance of the multinational company to the diffusion of technology, is tested by examining the proposition that such companies predominate in activities with an innovative bias. If it can be demonstrated that international companies typically engage in research intensive activities this will add conviction to the arguments which represent the multinational company as an important agent in the diffusion process. The procedure is to examine the leading manufacturing companies for their ownership pattern and industrial composition. It is assumed, initially, that the world's largest manufacturing companies are multinational in character. This does not imply that only the very largest companies operate subsidiaries abroad, but it does rest on the assertion that the tendency towards global location is likely to be most prevalent amongst the giants. Later this assumption is relaxed.

There are two layers in the procedure to test the technological orientation of multinational companies. The first is to examine the character of the economies from which they come. The second involves examination of the activities in which these companies predominantly engage. Layer one classifies economies by their technological record. Layer two is concerned with the research intensity of the activities of multinational companies. The first layer represents a broad test of the tendency for multinationals to originate from economies with a technological orientation. The second is a more direct test of the character of the activities in which global companies engage. The combination of the two layers should reveal any tendency towards technological orientation of multinational companies. The term technological orientation has been deliberately used. It is a general term summarising the propensity to engage in activities where technology is changing fast. Interpretation is not limited to innovation, but includes adoption and diffusion. Thus, for example, it may be revealed that the majority of multinational companies do not typically originate from economies with the strongest technological record. It may nevertheless be true that they illustrate a high degree of involvement in activities which are considered change orientated. The contrast may be explained in terms of a deliberate policy of fast adoption rather than origination. The double layered procedure is specifically designed to meet this possibility. The role of the multinational as a diffusion agent is under scrutiny. It is not the concern of this study to show that such companies are necessarily the prime originators, but rather that they are important in the spread of technological knowledge. It is hoped to be able to demonstrate that global companies cluster in knowledge generating activities. This does not necessarily assume that they are the major innovators.

Information on the world's largest companies is drawn from *Fortune Magazine.* To be listed by this publication companies must derive more than 50 per cent of sales from manufacturing or mining activity, and be among the top 500 American companies or top 300 non-USA companies. The primary indicator used to rank companies is total sales in dollars in 1971. The two separate *Fortune* lists have been merged to compile a list of the world's largest manufacturing companies. All the 300 non-USA companies are included and those American companies that are greater in size than the 300th non-USA company. The total number involved is 664 firms. There are a host of statistical problems involved in the compilation of the *Fortune* list. Included among these are the adequacy of official exchange rates as indicators of the dollar value of overseas sales and the problems associated with changing exchange parities and floating exchange rates. A particular problem associated with the requirements of this study is the identification of the major activity of the companies concerned. This information is needed to establish their degree of involvement in areas of innovative or research intensive activity. Notice that the word 'activity' has been deliberately used instead of 'industry'. With companies of such size it is probably inappropriate to expect them to confine operations to one industry. Giant companies are big enough to enjoy the advantages associated with large-scale operation in particular activities, and yet spread their involvement over a large number of commercial interests. The classification procedure is thus inevitably arbitrary. Definition of the nationality of companies is also arbitrary, and follows *Fortune Magazine* in determining it by the country of registration. The shareholding structure is ignored in apportioning the nationality of companies. Broad justification for this blunt approach is sought on the grounds that it is probable that the head office and corporate decision centre of companies will be located within the boundaries of the country of registration. The flavour, emphasis and technological endowment of companies is likely to be that of the parent country.

Layer one in the testing procedure involves establishing the technological orientation of the economies which own the world's leading
companies. Several different indicators are used. These include expenditure on research and development, success in innovations, receipts for
technology, and foreign patenting activities. Table 8.1 summarises this
information. It represents an attempt to classify economies by their
technological orientation. There is a mixture of input and output
measures. Thus R and D indicators summarise an expectation of future
benefit. Receipts for technology and patents are indicators of success
already achieved. The overall level of agreement between the indicators
is reasonable. The coefficient of concordance between the nine rankings
is 0.63. There is apparently quite a degree of communality between the
indicators. The table inevitably emphasises the origination aspect of
technological orientation. There are few satisfactory direct indicators of
countries' willingness to be involved in innovations developed elsewhere. Payment for licences and patents may be one example.
Unfortunately it is not at all clear how such figures should be used. A
low figure for payments to acquire knowledge may indicate either a
high degree of technological self-sufficiency or a relative lack of interest
in applying ideas developed elsewhere. The figures are thus open to
interpretation and the ranking procedure is consequently uncertain and
subjective. In 1963 payments for technology by the USA were $87.3
million.[1] This figure was below that for most of the advanced nations.
Interpretation in the special case of the United States is relatively easy.
The top ranking achieved on all of the indicators in the table make it
convincing to argue that the relatively low payments figure by the
United States indicates a high degree of technological self-sufficiency.
But it may be equally plausible to argue that the low payments figure
reflects the tendency of American companies to be multinational.
Payments may be registered in the accounts of other nations acting as
hosts to American subsidiaries. In this case expenditure to acquire
foreign technology may in fact be very much higher than indicated. In
1963 Japan paid $130.2 million for technological knowledge. This high
figure should not necessarily indicate a low ranking for technological
orientation. Payments on this scale for proprietary knowledge do
indicate a keenness for early involvement. Patents have a limited life.
Once they have expired no payment is necessary. A high figure for the
acquisition of knowledge may therefore be interpreted as an input
measure indicating an early adoption policy. Within the meaning of the
term technological orientation, a fast follower should qualify for a high
ranking. There is a further complication. The high figures for the
acquisition of technological knowledge in Japan may be a byproduct of
the deliberately tough government policy towards direct foreign
investment. The establishment of foreign subsidiaries within the
Japanese economy has been severely limited, although since 1967 a

Table 8.1 Technological orientation

Country	R and D as a % of net industrial output By rank (a) 1963	1967	GERD/GNP at market prices By rank (b, c) 1963/64	1967/70	Countries of origin of 1012 major inventions, discoveries and innovations since 1750 By rank (d)	Location of first commercial exploitation of 110 innovations since 1945 By rank (e)	Patents originated locally as % of all countries patents on local invention By rank (f)	% total foreign patents issued by country By rank (f)	Receipts for technology By rank (a)	Overall rank
Belgium	9	10	9	10	8	9	7	11	9	10
Canada	10	9	10	8	11	10.5	10	10	6	11
France	7	4	4.5	3	3	8	3	5	5	3
Germany	8	7	7.5	6	4	3	4	2	4	5
Italy	11	11	11	10	5	7	6	7	8	9
Japan	3	5.5	7.5	7	9.5	5	2	9	11	7
Netherlands	5.5	3	4.5	2	9.5	10.5	11	6	7	6
Sweden	5.5	8	6	9	6.5	5	9	8	10	8
Switzerland	4*	5.5	3*	5	6.5	5	8	4	2	4
UK	2	2	2	4	2	2	5	3	3	2
USA	1	1	1	1	1	1	1	1	1	1

*Estimated

Sources. Based on: (a) OECD *International Statistical Year*; (b) OECD *Gaps in Technology Analytical Report*, 1970, Table 1, p. 120; (c) United Nations *Statistical Yearbook 1971*; the years concerned relate to any single year in the period 1967-70; (d) C. K. Streit, *Freedom Against Itself*, Harper, 1954; (e) OECD *Gaps in Technology Analytical Report*, 1970, Table 8, p. 198; (f) J. Shipman, 'International patent planning', *Harvard Business Review*, March-April 1967.

more liberal attitude has been taken. Thus the expenditure figures by Japan to acquire knowledge may reflect the constraint applied by government policy. Other nations which have adopted a more open attitude towards foreign investment may have found that they did not need to be so heavily involved in the purchase of knowhow. A considerable technological endowment may have been provided by foreign subsidiaries, and thus expenditure avoided. Because of the problems involved in interpreting the payments figures for technological knowledge, and also the uncertainty as to the ranking which should be given individual countries, this data has not been used in the table.

Table 8.2 indicates the number of companies by country of origin, and their technology ranking. An alternative ranking is available from an OECD publication.[2] It is important to draw attention to the differences in the technology ranking procedures adopted in columns C and D. Column D, which is drawn from the OECD study, uses 'normalised' data in calculating technology ranking. An attempt is made to allow for size-related influences. Location of significant innovations and monetary receipts indicators, are adjusted by dividing the absolute figures by the working population in manufacturing in each country, and transforming the resultant figure into an index based on USA = 100. The absolute figures of patents taken out in foreign countries are adjusted or normalised by dividing by the respective country's percentage share of total exports, and again expressing the

Table 8.2 The world's largest manufacturing companies

Country	A Numbers* (a)	B Rank	C Technology ranking	D Alternative technology ranking (b)
USA	365	1	1	1
Japan	75	2	7	11
Britain	67	3	2	3.5
Germany	45	4	5	3.5
France	32	5	3	7
Canada	17	6	11	10
Sweden	14	7	8	6
Netherlands	9	8	6	5
Italy	8	9.5	9	8
Switzerland	8	9.5	4	2
Belgium	6	11	10	9
Others	23	—	—	—

*There are five jointly owned companies. Each has been given two entries:
Rank correlation coefficient between B and C = 0.60 NS at 5 per cent
Rank correlation coefficient between B and D = 0.21 NS at 5 per cent
Sources. Derived from (a) *Fortune Magazine*, May and August, 1972 (ref. 6); (b) OECD, *The conditions for Success in Technological Innovation*, (ref. 2), p. 146.

resultant as an index based on USA = 100.[3] The rankings in column D are also based on a much wider range of measures. Extra indicators included qualified scientists and engineers (QSE), income *per capita* data, size of firm and size of market indicators, and proxies for the quality of research done in the sciences like the number of scientific abstracts or the number of Nobel prize winners in designated subjects. All these additional measures are normalised using an appropriate population denominator.

The purpose of presenting two versions of technology ranking in Table 8.2 is to draw attention to the shortcomings of such an exercise. The concept of 'technological orientation' of economies is extraordinarily broad and open to wide interpretation. The number of plausible indicators that could be used is large. The way in which they should be presented is also open to debate. There is a case for normalising data. There is also a case for using absolute figures. For present purposes the absolute values are preferred. They are more in accordance with the requirements of this study. The multinational company is under investigation. Normalising for the size of the home market or strength of national R and D effort may have little relevance. These companies operate on a worldwide scale and may have a techological endowment independent of their home country.

The rank correlation coefficients between the number of companies per country in the *Fortune* lists and the two versions of technological orientation are disappointing. They are low and neither is significant at the 5 per cent level. The most obvious explanation for the low level of association is the apparent nonconformity of Switzerland and Japan. In their cases technology rankings and number of companies exhibit wide disparities. The explanation for Switzerland may lie with the smallness of the country. Thus, on the normalised figures, population adjustment may tend to overstate technology ranking. Alternatively, the size of the home market may militate against a large number of giant companies. For Japan the explanation may be the lack of sensitivity of the technology rankings. The figures used in Table 8.1 are weighted towards the early 1960s. But since 1962 the number of Japanese companies in the top 200 non-USA *Fortune* list has increased from 31 to 43 in 1967, to 48 in 1972.[4] No other country has experienced a similar rate of increase. Research and development expenditure has increased by approximately seven times over the period 1958 to 1968, and has risen to 1.7 per cent of national income.[5] The figures available to indicate technological orientation may be too dated to reflect these recent changes. However, no attempt will be made to adjust the figures in the hope that improved correlations will result. Rating countries by their technological orientation is bound to be a somewhat insensitive procedure, and adjustment in this case may be represented as special pleading to achieve the desired result. Rather than resort to any such manipulation, further information is sought in the second layer of the testing procedure.

The second layer in the testing procedure involves a more direct test of the association between multinational companies and research orientated activities. Companies in the sample are examined in detail. The assumption that they are multinational in character is relaxed, and each company is scrutinised to establish involvement in overseas production and research intensive products. The macro approach of layer one is abandoned. The broad presumption that the technological orientation of whole economies will be reflected in their constituent companies, is left behind. Recourse is made to detailed information on each company, in an attempt to discover the predominant locational influences.

Information on companies is drawn initially from the *Fortune* magazine.[6] Additional detail has been obtained from a wide variety of sources. These include *Moodies Investment Books of America, Britain and Europe;*[7] *Stock Exchange Year Books* of the countries concerned; *Jane's Major Companies of Europe;*[8] *Extel Statistical Cards;*[9] *Extel-Nomura Statistical Cards of Japanese Companies;*[10] *Diamond Japan Business Directory 1971;*[11] *The Times 1000;*[12] *Who Owns Whom,* continental edition;[13] individual company accounts, and discussions with stockbrokers,[14] and direct contact with individual companies.

Procedure has been as follows. American companies have been scrutinised using the Moodies *'Handbooks'*. These are abridged versions of the full publication or the 'big Moodies'. Where the handbooks give insufficient information use is then made of the full version of Moodies and also the widespread sources of information available in the City Business Library, Moorgate. This two stage procedure has been adopted with the American companies because the full sized Moodies was not available in Exeter. British and European companies are scrutinised using the *Moodies Investment Book of Britain and Europe.* Confirmation and additional information is obtained from *Jane's Major Companies of Europe,* and the *Stock Exchange Year Books* of the countries concerned. Information on the Japanese companies would have been a problem but for the co-operation of Extel Statistical Services, and Nomura Securities, London. These two organisations were extremely helpful and between them provided all the information required. *Extel-Nomura Statistical Cards,* which are English language profiles of the major quoted Japanese companies, were provided free of charge. The *Diamond Japan Business Directory* of 853 companies was also made available. This is a very detailed source book which is used in the compilation of the *Extel-Nomura Statistical Cards.* Where companies were not included in the *Diamond Japan Business Directory* or the statistical cards, direct enquiries via teleprinter were made to the Tokyo office of Nomura Securities. If the answers were not known, then contact was made with the companies concerned and the replies made available within days. Information on other non-European companies was gathered from a miscellany of sources. Canadian companies were scrutinised using *Extel Statistical Cards*. The *Year Book of the Johannesburg Stock Exchange* was used for South African companies. Australian companies were classified using information provided by the City Business Library. The few remaining companies were mostly South American. Fortunately tracing these was not necessary as nearly all of them were state owned and thus excluded.

At the beginning of this study it was hoped to obtain the accounts of every company in the *Fortune* lists. Early on however it became clear that the time taken, expense incurred, and the frustrations involved with postal contact would make this approach impractical, and that secondary sources would have to be used. Fortunately these secondary sources which have been described above are almost equivalent in quality to the originals. The detail given by such publications as the *Moodies Investment Books, Stock Exchange Year Books, Jane's Major European Companies*, and the *Diamond Japan Business Directory*, is copious. This opinion is not just an impression based on hunch, but is backed by a limited sample procedure. The accounts of approximately thirty companies in the *Fortune* lists, which were available in the Economics Department, University of Exeter, were compared with the secondary sources. This showed that for the purposes of this study they were equivalents. In terms of identification of companies' product mix, and ownership of foreign subsidiaries, there was no sacrifice of information. The favourable outcome of this 'spot check' suggests that accuracy and detail have not been lost by the procedure adopted and adds confidence to the belief that the resultant classifications are in no way inferior.

Classification: research intensity

The second layer in the testing procedure involves classifying the world's largest companies by activity. To establish that there is a bias towards research intensive products, a definition is required. There is no single, uniform and entirely satisfactory definition. The classification procedure is bound to be arbitrary. Thus, for example, it is clear that at the extremes electronics, aircraft and pharmaceuticals are the most research orientated and paper, food and drink are the least. In the middle range and at the margins, the distinction is bound to be blurred and will reflect the criteria adopted. Table 8.3 sets out those industries which have been defined as research intensive by three studies.

A major difference between the three definitions of research intensive industries in the table relates to the classification of vehicles. In col. 2 vehicles are not included. The scheme used in the OECD 1970 publication to classify industries is as follows: Science based, Mechanical and Other. Vehicles, with the exception of special motor vehicles (SITC subgroup 732.4), are classified within the mechanical and not the science-based group. Schemes 1 and 3 however do include vehicles. Scheme 3 has the advantage that the classification criterion is made explicit. To qualify, an activity must have research and development expenditure which is 2 per cent or more of sales, or scientists and engineers employed in research and development activities amounting to 1 per cent or more of total employment. The definition relates to 1962 and only to United States companies. This is an important and ingenious qualification. Research intensity within the United States is used as the criterion for research intensity elsewhere. It is assumed that activities in other countries will have research or employment figures which are similar at least in terms of ranking, compared with other activities. Alternatively, it is assumed that even if there is no parity of research expenditure and employment between countries the character of the activity is essentially similar. Similarity in this instance means dependence on technological inputs. The internationality of science-based activities is thus explicitly acknowledged. The advantages of this definition are considerable. It sidesteps the problems associated with establishing the 'research exchange rate' between countries, and standardises procedure.[15]

The research exchange rate involves establishing a satisfactory valuation procedure for intercountry comparisons of research effort.

Table 8.3 Activities defined as research-intensive or science based

1 (a)	2 (b)	3 (c)
Aircraft	Aircraft	Aircraft
Electronics	Electronics	Electronics
Other electrical	Electrical machinery	Electrical engineering
Chemicals and	Chemicals, drugs and	Chemicals, pharmaceuticals
allied products	petroleum	oils and petroleum
Machinery	Instruments	Mechanical engineering
Vehicles		Motor vehicles
Instruments		Rubber products

Sources. Definitions used in (*a*) OECD, *Science, Economic Growth and Government Policy*, 1963; (b) OECD, *Gaps in Technology, Analytical Report*, 1972; (*c*) Dunning and Pearce, 'The world's largest enterprises' (ref. 15).

Differing salary levels for scientists and research personnel, and varying input costs between countries are unlikely to be satisfactorily allowed for by the official rate of exchange. As a result a valuation procedure would normally have to be adopted which uses exchange rates more appropriate to the purpose in hand. Thus in a study comparing research and development in British and American industry a rate of exchange of $4.93 per pound was used instead of the official rate of exchange of $2.8 per pound.[1 6] The difference between the exchange rates reflected higher salary level and other research costs in the USA compared with Britain. Valuation problems of this character can be avoided in the present study if American activities are used as the standard. Research intensity in other countries is thus defined, not by their adjusted figures but by involvement in the activities concerned. In this sense, the classification procedure is standardised by taking research intensity in American activities as the world model.

The definition of research intensive activities used in this study follows the general procedure adopted in col. 3 of Table 8.3. Emphasis is placed on the international similarity of science-based industries. An activity rather than valuation approach is adopted. But the particular activities selected as research intensive are broadly those outlined in col. 2. The attraction of col. 2 arises from the exclusion of vehicles from the research intensive class. Vehicle manufacturers are well represented among the world's largest companies. They are also highly multinational in character. Table 8.3 indicates, however, that their claim to research intensity is somewhat marginal. By resisting the temptation to include them any results which then indicate an association between multinational status and research orientated activities will be strengthened.

Details of the classification procedure are given in Appendix 1. Appendix 2 lists the results of the classification procedure for individual companies. In broad terms, aircraft, electrical engineering, scientific instruments, chemicals, petroleum, and pharmaceuticals, are classed as research intensive activities. All other activities are classed as not research intensive. Major exclusions are domestic electrical appliances, developed cinematographic film, and essential oils, perfume and flavour materials. Although these are part of the research intensive groups, they are not included. They are activities with low R and D spending. Use of the Standard International Trade Classification to subgroups of five digits, should not mislead the reader into a belief that the classification procedure is precise. This is not the case. Companies almost inevitably have a wide and mixed product base. The proportion that particular activities represent in the total is not always revealed. Judgment is involved. The basic criterion is that the majority (more than 50 per cent) of a company's sales should be derived from research intensive activities. The details given in the Appendices 1 and 2 represent the decisions which have been arrived at in the process of classifying companies.

Classification of multinationality

Companies have been classified by their degree of multinationality. Companies are assigned to one of three categories. These are: MPE 2, MPE 1, and not MPE. MPE 2 companies are those which are the most international in character. MPE 1 concerns are less globally orientated, and those in the not MPE class are essentially not involved in overseas production. The abbreviation MPE (multinational producing enterprise) has been used to stress that the emphasis of the classification procedure is on overseas production. Companies with worldwide exports, but no foreign manufacture, will be classed as not MPE. Qualification for the status of multinational, turns on owning or controlling foreign subsidiaries which actively engage in manufacture. Sales agencies are thus excluded. Control is defined as 51 per cent of the voting equity.

Specific criteria used are as follows:

MPE 2 are those which are clearly international in character. They are defined as having more than five producing subsidiaries in different countries, or more than 15 per cent of total group sales accounted for by overseas manufacturing activity.

MPE 1 are companies which are less globally orientated. They have more than two, and up to five subsidiaries, each in different countries. Where sales figures are available, then between 5 and 15 per cent qualifies.

Not MPE are companies which concentrate production almost exclusively within their national boundaries. They have two or less subsidiaries abroad and a sales figure of less than 5 per cent.

A few cautionary remarks are appropriate. The criteria used may give an impression of precision. This should be immediately dispelled. The criteria are a rationalisation of an essentially subjective process. The sources of information are searched to determine the flavour of company operation. Unfortunately, borderline decisions have to be clarified and arbitrary cut-off points decided. The numbers given represent the criteria which have been evolved during the search process. The procedure is essentially ordinal in the sense that companies in each category are required to have different foreign involvement, but no effort is made to indicate precisely the degree of difference. The procedure is dependent on a number of arbitrary rules. These will be made clear below.

The definition of manufacturing activities abroad is fraught with difficulties. Overseas involvement may progress from sales agencies merely handling exports, to wholly owned self-contained manufacturing concerns. At the extremes, the distinction between a sales organisation and a producing unit is clear. But during the transition from one to the other, the distinction is bound to be blurred. The difficulties are similar to those experienced by the tax authorities in administering tariffs which are levied on finished goods, but not on raw materials. Fortunately, nearly all companies make the distinction between sales agencies and foreign producing units. Whether definitions are consistent between different companies is, of course, not known. Despite this, in classifying companies the following procedure is adopted. The description given as background information to the accounts are accepted at face value. However, joint ventures and minority interests are ignored. These categories of overseas involvement are theoretically capable of raising the effective status of a company to that of MPE 2. With enough joint ventures or minority interests, a plausible case could be made to class a particular company as highly multinational. For present purposes, however, companies have to own or control producing subsidiaries to be classed other than not MPE.

Numbers of subsidiaries relate to foreign producing units which are located in different countries. A Netherlands company which has a controlling interest in ten firms in France would only be classed as having one foreign subsidiary. The selection procedure attempts to distinguish between companies with a worldwide location pattern, and those which are essentially national in character. Where subsidiaries are concentrated in a few countries it is plausible to class the parent company as less multinational than a concern which has exactly the same number of affiliates but which spreads them more widely across the globe. This argument is accepted. Subsidiaries are required to be in different countries to be counted in the classification procedure.

Mixed criteria are used to classify companies. Numbers of subsidiaries, or the percentage of group sales accounted for by foreign producing units, are used. It should be stressed, however, that the numbers and percentage indicators are not equivalents, nor are they true alternatives. The senior indicator is numbers of subsidiaries. The sales percentage figure is very much the junior. It is only used where the background information in companies' accounts is sparse. Thus, where it is stated that there are a number of overseas subsidiaries, but no detail is given, use is made of the percentage figure if it is available. This figure is never used on its own. There must be indications in the description of companies' activities that there are a number of foreign producing units. Only in these circumstances is the figure used. The sales figure is also junior in the sense that it is not used to reappraise the impression given by the numbers of subsidiaries. To take an example, where a company has only three foreign subsidiaries, but over 80 per cent of total sales accounted for by these affiliates, then it will still be classed in the MPE 1 group. The large percentage figure will not upgrade the status of the company to MPE 2. The example is not unrealistic. There are a number of companies where this occurs.[17] Reasons for the apparent disparity in the indicators will include the contrast in market size between that available for the parent company and subsidiaries, and a change in the major market which is not accompanied by a change in the nationality of the company. Thus Canadian companies may find themselves with a very high proportion of their trade and manufacturing activities in America. For all practical purposes, such concerns could be treated as American. However, while registration remains in Canada, they are classed as Canadian. Similarly Netherlands companies may find themselves subjected to strong outward locational pulls because of the limited size of their national market. In these circumstances a single foreign subsidiary in a large market could easily represent a very high proportion of group activity.

Jointly owned companies like Shell and Unilever have been treated as follows. The value of sales has been divided equally between the countries concerned, and in terms of numbers, each country has been given one entry. Thus the grand total of companies in the sample will exceed the actual number by an amount equal to the extra entries occasioned by jointly owned concerns. State owned or controlled companies are excluded from the sample. It is assumed that such concerns are not so free to respond to locational forces as their private enterprise counterparts. Inclusion of them might obscure or bias the results. They have therefore been deleted. There are some companies in the *Fortune* USA and non-USA lists which are owned or controlled by other companies in the population.[18] Where this occurs they are deleted from the sample. In this way, double counting is avoided and also the conceptual problem of assessing the degree of multinationality of a subsidiary independently from that of the parent company. Where there is only a minority holding companies are classified as independent concerns. This procedure is plausible where say 10 per cent of the voting equity is held by another company. It becomes less plausible as the percentage rises towards 50 per cent. In such circumstances a minority holding may amount to effective control and independent assessment may be somewhat misleading.

The rules of thumb enumerated above in classifying companies by multinationality, are clearly open to question. In practice these arbitrary classification procedures are forced on the investigator. Detailed information on the locational pattern of companies is limited. Legal obligations to divulge such information varies from country to country. Interpretation of figures like overseas production, or profits earned by foreign subsidiaries, is rarely simple. For the purpose in hand, the procedures are required to identify, in a broad fashion, companies which are international in character. These, it is hoped, will be distinguished from those which are essentially national in orientation, and those which are in the intermediate category. However, it should be pointed out that the MPE 1 category has been deliberately used as a safety device. If it transpires that the discrimination between types of companies is poor, then it may be possible to improve this by eliminating the middle group MPE 1. This category is in a sense on standby as a potential means to heighten the contrast between the extreme types of company in the sample.

Tables 8.4 and 8.5 give a general flavour of the data. By total value of sales from all companies, research intensive activities account for 46.7 per cent. The equivalent figure on numbers of companies is 37.8 per cent. When companies are cross-classified by categories more detail is revealed. Tables 8.6 and 8.7 summarise the information. A classification of research intensity and multinational status shows that MPE 2 concerns are approximately evenly distributed between RI and not RI activities. This holds on both a numbers and value basis. In the lower categories of multinational status (MPE 1 and not MPE) entries in the not research intensive class, on numbers and value, are approximately three times as large as those in the research intensive class. When the companies are classified by multinational status and research intensity, then of all the companies within the RI class, approximately 75 per cent by numbers and 83 per cent by value are MPE 2 by character. Figures 8.1 and 8.2 are a graphic representation of the

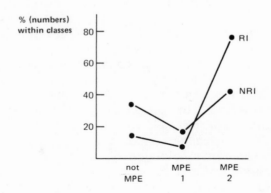

% within classes of RI and not RI. Thus MPE 2
+ MPE 1 + not MPE within RI sum to 100%

Fig. 8.1 Graphical presentation of Table 8.6

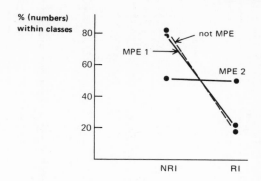

% (numbers)
within classes

% within classes of multinational status which
are RI or not RI. Thus RI + not RI within MPE 2
sum to 100%.

Fig. 8.2 Graphical presentation of Table 8.7

information in Tables 8.6 and 8.7, respectively. There is such a close correspondence in the pattern between numbers and value that the figures are presented on numbers of companies only.

Tables 8.8 and 8.9 present the information from Tables 8.6 and 8.7 in a different form. The figures in each cell of the contingency tables are now expressed as a percentage of the grand totals. Instead of calculating them as a percentage of the column marginal frequency, they are now related to the aggregate of companies or value of sales. Thus the 173 companies which are MPE 2 RI in character now represent 28.2 per cent of the total rather than 74.6 per cent. This form of expression makes direct comparison between cell values easier and has the added advantage that the columns total to the percentage figures shown in Tables 8.4 and 8.5. Figures 8.3 and 8.4 summarise the information in Tables 8.8 and 8.9 respectively in graphic form. Again there is such close correspondence between numbers and value, that the figures have been presented on numbers of companies only.

The following would appear to summarise the general position reasonably well. The most globally orientated companies (MPE 2) appear to spread themselves evenly between research and not research intensive activities. But there are approximately three times by numbers and five times by value as many companies in the RI class which are MPE 2 in status, as those which are MPE 1 plus not MPE. To reinforce the point, there are a quarter of the number or one-seventh of the value of sales from research intensive companies in the not MPE class, as compared with the MPE 2 category. Apparently MPE 2 status is not the prerogative of the technologically orientated company. Global status has been achieved by just as many companies selling items which are not research orientated. But while this seems to be true, it is also

Table 8.4 Numbers of companies classified by multinational status and research intensity

	Numbers of companies	Numbers in MPE 2 class	Numbers in MPE 1 class	Numbers in Not MPE class	Numbers in research intensive class	Numbers in not research intensive class
USA	352	210	41	101	136	216
Japan	68	10	15	43	29	39
Britain	65	47	12	6	21	44
Germany	41	25	8	8	20	21
France	26	16	2	8	9	17
Canada	16	4	7	5	–	16
Sweden	13	12	1	–	3	10
Netherlands	7	6	–	1	4	3
Italy	5	5	–	–	3	2
Switzerland	8	7	1	–	3	4
Belgium	5	5	–	–	3	2
Others*	7	2	1	4	–	7
% of total	613	349	88	175	232	381
		56.9	14.4	28.7	37.80	62.20

*Spain, Luxembourg, Australia, South Africa.

Table 8.5 Companies classified by multinational status and research intensity — value $000

	Total	MPE (2)	MPE (1)	Not MPE	Research intensive	Not research intensive
USA	461,135,776	342,149,585	29,593,502	89,392,689	221,216,345	239,919,431
Japan	58,952,648	15,828,415	9,366,388	33,757,845	25,327,617	33,625,031
Britain	63,722,158	53,929,720	6,726,217	3,066,221	27,242,669	36,479,489
Germany	51,926,240	40,236,580	5,370,537	6,319,123	24,806,290	27,119,950
France	26,305,413	20,012,402	922,076	5,370,935	11,781,607	14,523,806
Canada	9,812,051	3,594,123	4,325,340	1,892,588	—	9,812,051
Sweden	7,622,524	7,026,306	596,218	—	1,936,708	5,685,816
Netherlands	19,290,881	18,675,408	—	615,473	14,558,711	4,732,170
Italy	8,790,389	8,790,389	—	—	4,665,052	4,125,337
Switzerland	10,585,523	10,268,863	316,660	—	5,576,380	5,009,143
Belgium	3,852,430	3,852,430	—	—	2,585,403	1,267,027
Others*	5,755,207	3,704,471	621,816	1,428,920	—	5,755,207
	727,751,240	528,068,692	57,838,754	141,843,794	339,696,782	388,054,458
% of total		72.60	7.90	19.50	46.70	53.30

*Spain, Luxembourg, Australia, South Africa.

155

Table 8.6 All companies by research intensity and multinationality

	MPE 2 Nos	%	MPE 1 Nos	%	Not MPE Nos	%	MPE 2 Value $000	%	MPE 1 Value $000	%	Not MPE Value $000	%
Research intensive	173	49.6	20	22.7	39	22.2	283,630,570	53.7	15,135,388	26.2	40,930,824	28.9
Not research intensive	176	50.4	68	77.3	137	77.8	244,438,122	46.3	42,703,366	73.8	100,912,970	71.1
	349	100.0	88	100.0	176	100.0	528,068,692	100.0	57,838,754	100.0	141,843,794	100.0

Table 8.7 All companies by multinationality and research intensity

	Research intensive Numbers	%	Not research intensive Numbers	%	Research intensive Value $000	%	Not research intensive Value $000	%
MPE 2	173	74.6	176	46.2	283,630,570	83.5	244,438,122	63.0
MPE 1	20	8.6	68	17.8	15,135,388	4.5	42,703,366	11.0
Not MPE	39	16.8	137	36.0	40,930,824	12.0	100,912,970	26.0
	232	100.0	381	100.0	339,696,782	100.0	388,054,458	100.0

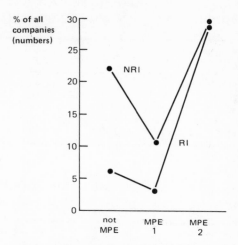

RI and not RI companies within classes of multinational status as % of all companies in the sample.
Thus figures within RI by multinational status, plus
similar figures with not RI aggregate to 100%.

Fig. 8.3 Graphical presentation of Table 8.8

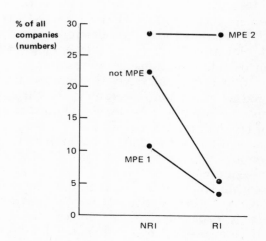

As 8.3 but by classes of multinational companies.

Fig. 8.4 Graphical presentation of Table 8.9

Table 8.8 Percentage of companies of a given research intensity that are classed amongst the various grades of multinational status*

| | On numbers % | | | On value % | | |
	RI	NRI		RI	NRI	
MPE 2	28.20	28.74		38.99	33.58	
MPE 1	3.25	11.07		2.10	5.86	
Not MPE	6.35	22.39		5.61	13.86	
	37.80	62.20	= 100.0	46.70	53.30	= 100.0

* Based on all companies in the sample.

Table 8.9 Percentage of companies of a given multinational status that are classed as research intensive or not research intensive

| | On numbers % | | | On value % | | | |
	MPE 2	MPE 1	Not MPE	MPE 2	MPE 1	Not MPE	
RI	28.22	3.27	6.37	38.99	2.07	5.64	
NRI	28.68	11.13	22.33	33.61	5.83	13.86	
	56.90	14.40	28.70 = 100.0	72.60	7.90	19.50	= 100.0

apparently true that companies which are RI are much more likely to be international (MPE 2) than national (not MPE) in character. Such companies are rarely in the not MPE class. Furthermore companies which are not MPE in status, apparently cluster in the not RI class. The phenomenon where there are few RI and many NRI companies in the not MPE class is referred to as the relative scarcity effect. It would appear that the locational influence of technological activities is not revealed by an overall predominance of research orientated activities amongst international companies. Verification occurs in a more subtle way and is a product of the contrasts revealed by the cross-classification procedure. This conclusion is provisional and must await more detailed examination of the data and tests of significance.

Detailed examination of the data is undertaken by subdividing the information for all companies into groups. Tables are presented by country and area grouping. Whenever possible these are arranged so that there are a reasonable number of observations. The contingency tables are presented in 2 x 3 form. Verification of the provisional conclusions advanced above is dependent on the consistency exhibited by the subgroupings. If countries and area groupings exhibit erratic patterns of behaviour, then the generality of the information summarised in the tables for the whole population would be suspect. In fact there is a remarkable degree of consistency in the country data. This is why the information is presented without comment on individual tables.

Table 8.10 USA companies by research intensity and multinationality

	MPE 2 Nos	%	MPE 1 Nos	%	Not MPE Nos	%	MPE 2 Value $000	%	MPE 1 Value $000	%	Not MPE Value $000	%
Research intensive	108	51.4	11	26.8	17	16.8	186,808,773	54.6	9,239,955	31.2	25,167,617	28.2
Not research intensive	102	48.6	30	73.2	84	83.2	155,340,812	45.4	20,353,547	68.8	64,225,072	71.8
	210	100.0	41	100.0	101	100.0	342,149,585	100.0	29,593,502	100.0	89,392,689	100.0

Table 8.11 Japanese companies by research intensity and multinationality

	MPE 2 Nos	%	MPE 1 Nos	%	Not MPE Nos	%	MPE 2 Value $000	%	MPE 1 Value $000	%	Not MPE Value $000	%
Research intensive	5	50.0	6	40.0	18	41.9	7,099,570	44.9	3,993,700	42.6	14,234,347	42.2
Not research intensive	5	50.0	9	60.0	25	58.1	8,728,845	55.1	5,372,688	57.4	19,523,498	57.8
	10	100.0	15	100.0	43	100.0	15,828,415	100.0	9,366,388	100.0	33,757,845	100.0

Table 8.12 European companies, by research intensity and multinationality

	MPE 2 Nos	%	MPE 1 Nos	%	Not MPE Nos	%	MPE 2 Value $000	%	MPE 1 Value $000	%	Not MPE Value $000	%
Research intensive	60	48.4	3	12.5	4	16.0	89,722,227	54.6	1,901,733	13.7	1,528,860	9.5
Not research intensive	64	51.6	21	87.5	21	84.0	74,674,342	45.4	12,029,975	86.3	14,572,773	90.5
	124	100.0	24	100.0	25	100.0	164,396,569	100.0	13,931,708	100.0	16,101,633	100.0

Table 8.13 Britain, France and Germany by research intensity and multinationality

	MPE 2		MPE 1		Not MPE		MPE 2		MPE 1		Not MPE	
	Nos	%	Nos	%	Nos	%	Value $000	%	Value $000	%	Value $000	%
Research intensive	43	48.9	3	13.6	4	18.2	60,399,973	52.9	1,901,733	14.6	1,528,860	10.4
Not research intensive	45	51.1	19	86.4	18	81.8	53,778,729	47.1	11,117,097	85.4	13,227,419	89.6
	88	100.0	22	100.0	22	100.0	114,178,702	100.0	13,018,830	100.0	14,756,279	100.0

Table 8.14 All companies less Japan, by research intensity and multinationality

	MPE 2		MPE 1		Not MPE		MPE 2		MPE 1		Not MPE	
	Nos	%	Nos	%	Nos	%	Value $000	%	Value $000	%	Value $000	%
Research intensive	168	49.6	14	19.2	21	15.8	276,531,000	54.0	11,141,688	23.0	26,696,477	24.7
Not research intensive	171	50.4	59	80.8	112	84.2	235,709,277	46.0	37,330,678	77.0	81,389,472	75.3
	339	100.0	73	100.0	133	100.0	512,240,277	100.0	48,472,366	100.0	108,085,949	100.0

Consistency

The pattern which occurs most often and most consistently is illustrated in Fig. 8.5.

	MPE 2	MPE 1	not MPE
RI			
	≃	∧	∧
NRI			

(≃ approximately equal, > greater than, < less than.)

Fig. 8.5

The only near exception to the pattern in Fig. 8.5 is Japan. The inequalities relating to MPE 1 and not MPE, hold but they are weak. In the 3 x 2 form a less uniform pattern is revealed. Figure 8.6 is a reasonable summary.

	RI	not RI
MPE 2		
	∨*	∨*
MPE 1		
	∧	∧
not MPE		

Fig. 8.6

The inequalities with asterisks in Fig. 8.6 are well exhibited. The others are less uniform. If the classes MPE 1 and not MPE are aggregated, then in the not RI class, MPE 2 is not always greater than the new combined class. But in practically all circumstances in the RI class, MPE 2 outweighs MPE 1 plus not MPE. A major exception to the representation in Fig. 8.6 is Japan. The inequalities are sometimes reversed and when a comparison is made with the MPE 2 and the combined MPE 1 and not MPE class, then the direction of both inequalities is always firmly reversed. Thus, in the RI class, the new combined class is 4.8 times MPE 2 by numbers, and 2.6 times by value. In the not RI class the corresponding figures are 6.8 times and 2.8 times respectively.

	MPE 2	MPE 1 + not MPE
RI		
	>	
NRI		

Fig. 8.7

Figure 8.7 illustrates cross relationships. These involve a comparison of the diagonal cell frequencies. Thus, for example, in the 2 x 3 form A_{11} (RI, MPE 2) is compared with A_{23} (NRI, not MPE) and A_{21} (NRI, MPE 2) with A_{13} (RI, not MPE). For convenience of exposition the MPE 1 and not MPE classes have been amalgamated in the diagram. The most consistently exhibited cross relationship is that illustrated. The other diagonal comparison between RI MPE 2 and NRI and the amalgamated MPE 1 and not MPE, does not show great consistency. The direction of any inequality tends to be influenced by the basis of comparison. Numbers and value comparisons tend to give conflicting results. Japan is the only exception to the pattern shown in Fig. 8.7. Here the relationship is firmly reversed on both a numbers and value basis. Thus in general the overall impression given by a comparison of the diagonal cell frequencies suggests that there is a marked scarcity of research intensive companies which are only national in orientation, relative to not research intensive companies which are international in status. The overall impression from Figs. 8.5, 8.6 and 8.7 is that the relative scarcity effect is consistently exhibited by the data.

Significance

The contingency tables are tested for statistical significance using the χ^2 test. The hypothesis under investigation is that there is a dependency relationship between companies' research intensity and location policy. It is therefore necessary to reject the null hypothesis that companies' tendency to locate abroad is not related to the character of goods they sell. A comparison is made between observed and expected frequencies using the formula:

$$\chi^2 = \Sigma \frac{(f - fc)^2}{fc} \qquad \begin{array}{l} f = \text{observed frequency} \\ fc = \text{expected frequency.} \end{array}$$

Where there are less than 50 companies in a contingency table χ^2 is not calculated. Table 8.15 indicates the groups of countries for which the calculations have been done. Where cell frequencies are less than 5 particular care is required in interpreting the χ^2 values. This is only relevant to the Britain France and Germany group, and the European group. To overcome the problem of low cell frequencies in the case of these groups χ^2 has also been calculated with the values for MPE 1 amalgamated with those for not MPE. The pattern revealed in Fig. 8.1 suggests that the hybrid companies (MPE 1) are more like 'not MPE' concerns, than global corporations (MPE 2). This opinion based on the visual impression given by the diagram is substantiated by an auxiliary test. When χ^2 is calculated on just MPE 1 and not MPE, by classes of research intensity for the whole population in this study, then χ^2 on numbers is 0.011 and on value of sales is 0.150. Apparently there is no significant difference in the distributions exhibited by MPE 1 and not MPE. On these grounds it would seem reasonable to amalgamate the two classes. As already stated however this has only been done where cell frequencies are low.

Table 8.15 χ^2 values

Contingency tables of	By numbers	By value	Excluding MPE 1	
			By numbers	By value
USA	37.16	23.43	33.95	19.79
Britain, France and Germany*	13.63 (13.54)	14.91 (14.86)	6.77	9.51
Europe*	17.28 (17.21)	19.14 (19.02)	8.91	12.01
Japan	0.27†	0.04†	0.22†	0.03†
All countries less Japan	58.37	42.23	45.37	31.05
All countries	47.36	38.43	36.51	27.68

*The figures in brackets represent χ^2 where MPE 1 has been amalgamated with not MPE.
† Not significant.

The results in Table 8.15 are satisfactory in that the majority are highly significant. With the exception of those marked, all are significant at the 1 per cent level and a considerable number are significant at 0.1 per cent. The null hypothesis is rejected at a high level of significance in nearly all the cases. The odds on these results occurring by chance are low. Even when the calculations are done without MPE 1, the general picture remains the same. The fear that the results are heavily influenced by this particular classification is apparently groundless. Of course the satisfactory values for the χ^2s does not necessarily indicate that the results are meaningful, nor do they relieve the investigator of the burden of analysis. Cause and effect have still to be argued, even though the tests indicate that chance can be rejected as a plausible explanation. To pass the test of statistical significance, expected and actual frequencies merely have to differ by large amounts. This may occur in a way which exhibits no consistency between countries and areas. The results may therefore be statistically significant but of no economic consequence. Thus the evidence provided by the χ^2 tests is accepted as powerful refutation of chance as an explanation. But conclusions are based on the consistency of the behaviour pattern within the total sample, and the quality of the causal logic.

Japan

A major exception to the results achieved in Table 8.15 would appear
to be Japan. The values for χ^2 are not significant and the odds on these
results occurring by chance are high. Apparently the Japanese companies are distinctive. At a descriptive level there is considerable
evidence to support this opinion. There are few MPE 2 companies;
approximately 15 per cent by numbers and 27 per cent by value of all
Japanese companies are in this class. There are relatively more
companies in the MPE 1 class; 22 per cent by numbers and 16 per cent
by value, compared with 14 per cent by numbers and 8 per cent by
value for the whole population. Companies in the not MPE class
predominate; by numbers and values these are more important than
MPE 2 plus MPE 1 companies. Finally, in the research intensive not
MPE class, there are thirty-nine observations for the whole world; of
these eighteen are Japanese companies. Apparently Japanese companies
are independent of the locational influences which induce other
concerns in the population to locate abroad. Classification by multinational status and research intensity, reveals a pattern which is
seemingly unlike that in the rest of the world.

In order to substantiate the belief that Japanese companies are
distinctive, an auxiliary test is conducted. The procedure is to compare
these companies with all the companies in the sample less the Japanese
concerns. The expected frequencies are now derived from the rest of
the world, and these are contrasted with the observed frequencies from
the Japanese companies. A 2 x 3 table is sliced horizontally, and
separate tests are undertaken on the research intensive companies, and
the not research intensive companies. Specifically, the proportions of
RI companies which are MPE 2, MPE 1, and not MPE for the whole
world less Japan, are compared with the proportions pertinent to
Japanese companies. A similar and separate test is then conducted on
the proportion of not research intensive companies in the cells relevant
to MPE 2, MPE 1, and not MPE, comparing the proportions relevant to
the Japanese companies with those of the remainder of the world. The
proportions relevant to the remainder of the world have been chosen to
enable a comparison to be made, where the standard used is not
influenced by the Japanese companies.

The 2 x 3 table has been sliced horizontally, and thus transformed
into two 1 x 3 tables. The reason for conversion is related to the nature
of the χ^2 test. Where the usual contingency form is used, the expected
values (fc) are derived from within the distribution under investigation.
Thus the column marginal expected and actual frequencies will be
equal. The same will be true of the row marginal frequencies. When an
outside standard is used to establish the expected frequencies and these

are not derived from within the distribution, then a problem arises. If the 2 x 3 table is retained the expected and actual row marginal frequencies will not be equal. The same will apply to the column marginal frequencies. The contingency form is therefore violated. The grand totals of expected and actual frequencies will be equal, but the respective marginal totals by column and row, will not. To sidestep this problem the 1 x 3 form is used. For each 2 x 3 table, there are now two tables each composed of one row with three observations. The contingency form has been re-established by eliminating a row. The χ^2 test is now:

$$\chi^2 = \Sigma \left(\frac{p - \pi}{\sqrt{\dfrac{\pi(1 - \pi)}{N}}} \right)^2$$

where p = the proportions relevant to Japanese companies
 π = the proportions relevant to the remainder of the companies
 N = numbers of companies in the remainder of the world.

This form is the square of the Z statistic, where n is large (>100) and where κ (the degrees of freedom) = 2. Z is the value assumed by a random variable having approximately the standard normal distribution. The square of the Z statistic where $\kappa = 2, = \chi^2$.

The hypothesis under consideration is that the Japanese distribution is the same as that exhibited by the remainder of the world. If this is rejected, then this is further evidence that the Japanese companies are a distinctive population.

The values of χ^2 found by the procedure outlined above, indicate that the 'similarity' hypothesis is firmly rejected. Apparently the Japanese companies in the sample are distinct in both the research intensive and not research intensive classes. The difference is most marked in the research intensive class, but even in the other class, the 'similarity' hypothesis is rejected at the 0.1 per cent level of significance. The Japanese companies do not exhibit the location pattern found in the remainder of the world. For reasons which will be speculated below, Japanese companies are apparently not subject to the same locational pulls as the majority of companies in the rest of the world.

Plausible explanations for the distinctive behaviour of the Japanese companies may include four reasons. First, shortcomings in the classification procedure and inadequacies in the data; second, the particular character of Japan's trading strength; third, the state of development of the economy; and fourth, government regulation of outward investment. These reasons will be dealt with in turn. The classification procedures used in this study may be inappropriate. In particular, the identification of research intensity by activities rather than actual research expenditure, may misclassify Japanese companies in the sense that they may not be subject to the postulated locational pulls. For example it may be wholly inappropriate to classify a company which is involved in research intensive activities as research intensive, if its actual R and D is low. With little research expenditure and presumably modest powers of innovation, the appropriation arguments advanced here may not be relevant. It may therefore be proper to class such companies among the not RI class even though their particular activities may suggest otherwise. If it is true that Japanese companies typically have low R and D, then their distinctive properties may be a product of the classification procedure and have no particular economic meaning. This is an objection of considerable weight and is accepted as such.

A major weakness of the data used here is the absence of a time variable. Information relates only to 1971. Cross-section data are used, where time series data may have been more appropriate. The location pattern of multinational producing enterprises will inevitably evolve over time. A one-year snapshot may therefore misrepresent what is essentially an historical process. Current location patterns are likely to represent an amalgam of past influences. Today's most powerful forces may only be partly reflected. Change is likely to be relatively slow and the general pattern exhibited by the data may reflect an adjustment to forces which are no longer in operation. In other words, the marginal or current forces may not have been in operation long enough to influence general behaviour. The data may thus reflect past forces where it is today's influences that are really of interest. This may be particularly relevant to Japan. Major companies may already be responding to the forces postulated here, but there may have been insufficient time for this to show in the data.

The second explanation for the singular behaviour of the Japanese companies, may relate to the particular character of their trading strength. If it is assumed for the moment that they are 'fast-followers' of innovations occurring elsewhere in the world, and also that they have a relative cost advantage in their home economy, then they may not be subject to the outward locational pulls postulated here. As imitators rather than initiators, the pressure to appropriate markets by overseas location may be weak. The fast-follower may have a twin benefit. Such companies are selling goods which they have not had to develop and these items are in the early part of the product cycle. They are new and can command a price premium reflecting their novelty and/or technological superiority. Anxiety to appropriate is therefore reduced. Fast followers are likely to have a cost advantage which the innovator is unlikely to possess. He has to recoup fixed expenses incurred in creating the innovation. This cost advantage relating to development expenses may be reinforced if there is also a labour cost advantage within the home economy. The net result may be a location pattern where Japanese companies engage in research orientated activities, but do not feel an outward pull. Overseas markets tend to be served by exports and the impetus to locate abroad may be weak. These arguments have been deliberately overstated to make the general point that cost influences may predominate as a location force, even when relatively new products and technologies are being sold. In the past Japanese companies have been notable as imitators. This is less true now. As has already been explained, R and D has been rising fast in recent years, and Japan's contribution to world technology is growing. In these new circumstances it is plausible to argue that as Japanese companies become more involved in research expenditure, and the problems associated with defending successful innovations, they too will begin to respond to outward locational pulls and spread production facilities around the world.

A third explanation may relate to the state of development of Japan. This economy may not yet have reached the degree of maturity exhibited by the rest of the countries represented in the sample. The majority of companies among the world's largest manufacturing concerns come from America or Europe. In other words, they come from countries with a long history of industrial involvement. A major general influence inducing outward location may come from the maturity of the home economy. Resource constraints may arise as a result of the advanced state of industrialisation. A major escape from the cost of such constraints may be innovation.[19] It may therefore be reasonable to argue that economies which have a long history of industrial involvement will tend to emphasise activities where the knowhow input is high and locate globally to capture the benefits of their ingenuity. Japan has become a major industrial nation in a relatively short period of time, so the resource constraint arguments may not apply with great force. Japanese companies may not feel obliged to locate around the world. For convenience of presentation, detailed exposition of the mature economy arguments will be deferred until later. For the moment the general point is being advanced that the distinctive character of the pattern exhibited by Japanese companies may to some extent be explained by the state of development of their home economy.

The fourth possible explanation is the most prosaic. The Japanese government has kept a fairly tight rein on the investment policy of their companies. Direct foreign investment has been controlled until recently. In July 1971 official control on outgoing investment was lifted.[20] It should not, however, be assumed that this regulation has been restrictive. The existence of the Overseas Economic Co-operation Fund, which encourages the establishment of affiliates, suggests that there is a desire for involvement in foreign ventures.[21] Nevertheless, government intervention may provide part of the explanation for the absence of Japanese companies among the world's multinationals.

The four reasons advanced to explain the apparently atypical behaviour of Japanese companies are not intended to be exhaustive, but are merely intended to give a flavour of the considerations that may be relevant. A full treatment of the topic would require a detailed investigation of the Japanese economy, and this is beyond the scope of the present study. The χ^2 tests indicate that within the limitations of the data being used, Japanese companies in this sample would appear distinctive. This conclusion is accepted. The rejection of the 'similarity' hypothesis is so firm in statistical terms that it would require a great deal of reclassification to make the pattern of behaviour correspond to that exhibited by the rest of the world. In these terms there seems to be little doubt that by comparison with other companies Japanese concerns are different in character.

Size bias

The distinctive nature of the Japanese companies may help to make an important point. All of the contingency tables and other calculations have been conducted on both a numbers and a value basis. This has been done as a precaution to meet the possibility that the results may merely reflect a size effect. It may be that the largest companies in the sample have a pattern of behaviour, which will bias all the results if they were based on the value of sales alone. Use of numbers may counterbalance this possibility, but nevertheless it remains a spectre lurking in the background. However, the unusual character of the Japanese companies may perhaps help in exorcising this worry. There are only five out of a total of sixty-eight concerns which are classed as international in status (MPE 2). It is apparently not a necessary condition to qualify for inclusion in the *Fortune* list that companies should be global in character. Large size can apparently be achieved without resort to heavy involvement in overseas location. It may be that this is a result of the peculiar circumstances relevant to the Japanese economy. Nevertheless it does add a degree of conviction to the argument that the results are not prey to overwhelming size bias effects.

The fear of size bias is not a whim. The size distribution of companies is very positively skewed. The mean size lies to the right of both the mode and the median. The mode occurs in the size class $300 to $400 million. The median company size is $664.4 million and the mean is $1187 million. In order to add a degree of conviction to the belief that the results are not prey to size bias a further precaution has been taken. Besides presenting the results on a numbers and value basis, the sample population has been halved. Table 8.16 shows the results of slicing the sample into two sections. The general pattern illustrated in Figs. 8.5 and 8.6 still persists through both halves. Nearly all the values for χ^2 are significant at 1 per cent. The exception is marked NS and is not significant at 5 per cent but would qualify at 7.5 per cent. This exception indicates that concern at possible size bias effects is proper. It also indicates the wisdom of not relying on value figures alone. Particular caution is suggested when interpreting results based on sales. A wholesale reappraisal of the provisional conclusions is not, however, called for. An explanation for this low value of χ^2 may be the importance of the larger Japanese companies in the bottom half of the sample. By numbers Japanese companies represent 8.8 per cent of the top half and 13.4 per cent of the bottom half. By value of sales the corresponding figures are 6.9 per cent and 13.4 per cent respectively. If χ^2s are calculated on the subdivided population with the Japanese companies excluded, then the values are as follows: Top half $\chi^2 = 22.12$ on numbers, 24.00 on sales values. Bottom half $\chi^2 = 33.16$ on numbers and 9.63 on values. All of the χ^2 are now significant at the 1 per cent level. The change in the last figure from 5.63 to 9.63 is perhaps indicative that the explanation advanced above is plausible. It has already been argued that the Japanese companies are distinctive. Subdividing the whole population to search for possible size bias effects, may in fact merely increase the influence of this group of companies on the results in any particular section. This is what appears to have happened.

Shortcomings

Discussion of the Japanese companies has drawn attention to the shortcomings of the classification procedures used here. This needs emphasising. The arbitrary nature of the procedures, the activity definition of research intensity, and the absence of a time variable are a real source of concern. There are others. These include specific explanations for particular industries' location pattern, and identification problems. It may be that the preference for a multinational structure exhibited by research intensive companies does not reflect the market pulls argued here. The explanations may be much more prosaic. Government influence within most countries may pre-empt normal

Table 8.16 Upper 306 companies by research intensity and multinationality

	Numbers						Value $000					
	MPE 1	%	Not MPE	%	MPE 2	%	MPE 1	%	Not MPE	%	MPE 2	%
Research intensive	8	23.5	15	24.2	106	50.5	9,451,445	29.3	28,975,813	31.1	258,483,949	55.0
Not research intensive	26	76.5	47	75.8	104	49.5	22,859,258	70.7	64,157,772	68.9	211,420,939	45.0
	34	100.0	62	100.0	210	100.0	32,310,703	100.0	93,133,585	100.0	469,904,888	100.0
	$\chi^2 = 19.0$**						$\chi^2 = 23.6$**					

Lower 307 companies by research intensity and multinationality

	Numbers						Value $000					
	MPE 1	%	Not MPE	%	MPE 2	%	MPE 1	%	Not MPE	%	MPE 2	%
Research intensive	12	22.2	24	21.1	67	48.2	5,683,943	22.3	11,955,011	24.6	25,146,621	43.2
Not research intensive	42	77.8	90	78.9	72	51.8	19,844,108	77.7	36,755,198	75.4	33,017,183	56.8
	54	100.0	114	100.0	139	100.0	25,528,051	100.0	48,710,209	100.0	58,163,804	100.0
	$\chi^2 = 24.5$**						$\chi^2 = 5.6$ N.S.					

** Significant at 1 per cent
NS = Not significant at 5 per cent

market forces. The example of Aerospace has already been mentioned. Government concern for secrecy and security virtually eradicate free market forces.

Government regulation may be a significant influence in the location pattern of the computer industry. An anxiety to preserve an indigenous computer industry may lead to severe restrictions on the penetration of the market by foreign concerns. Japan has exercised very strict control of direct investment by foreign companies in this industry. France and Britain have exercised less influence but have nevertheless taken positive steps to secure the desired results. Pharmaceuticals may be equally open to government influence. It may be that the market pulls operate, but they may be outweighed by other more specific considerations. Direct involvement in foreign markets may be virtually forced on companies if they are to make any sales impact. Official regulations governing the sale of medicinal products may be so complex that local involvement may be the only effective way of acquiring the desired expertise. In addition, where there are national health services, government purchasing policy may favour locally produced items. Overseas location may therefore be a defensive measure to enable competition on equal terms with local producers.

These specific explanations of location policy are not necessarily confined to research intensive activities. Thus multinational status may be rare in steel making, not because opportunities are lacking but because individual governments will not tolerate significant foreign involvement in an industry which is considered so basic to economic wellbeing. Autarky may predominate and may virtually prevent steel companies becoming global in character.

These examples of specific explanations for particular location patterns are all plausible. The importance of government regulation and influence on market forces is emphasised. The activities of governments are among the factors which separate markets. A major function of the multinational company is to reduce this separation. It would seem that the character of goods sold by companies may have an influence on their location policy. But it must be remembered that the market pull arguments advanced here, are merely one of a number of plausible explanations. The separation of markets caused by institutional, language, fiscal and legal barriers may provide the rationale for overseas location. But the predominant reasons inducing particular decisions may vary widely with specific circumstances.

Identification problems may be considerable. The classification procedures adopted here may be suspect. The distinction between research intensive and not research intensive activities may not have identified technologically orientated companies. Instead it may have identified firms which face high tariffs in overseas markets and separated these from concerns where tariffs are more modest. In this case the RI and NRI classification may be acting as a proxy for tariff cost incentives to locate abroad. Market pull interpretation may therefore be inappropriate. It is not immediately obvious that high technology goods carry the highest tariffs, nevertheless this argument has to be accepted as a possible counter-explanation for the results found here. There are considerable identification problems and these make interpretation cautious. The distinction between the grades of multinational status, MPE 2, MPE 1 and not MPE, may not in fact have separated companies which are national in character from those which are globally orientated. The procedure may have actually graded companies by their age, so that those in the international category may be the oldest, and those in the national class the youngest. Alternatively, the classification procedure may merely have separated firms by their size, so that the largest are MPE 2, and the smallest not MPE. These possibilities are real, and are recognised as such. Some attempt has been made to meet the size bias arguments, but the others remain as disquieting shadows lurking in the background. Generalising in such a complex field as company location policy is fraught with difficulties. Any conclusions that emerge must recognise this.

Technological orientation again

Before summarising the conclusions, it may be instructive to return to Table 8.2. In this table an attempt was made to measure the association between the broad indicators of technological orientation of economies and the numbers of companies in the *Fortune* list. With the greater information which is now available, further tests may be conducted. Table 8.17 summarises a few of these.

Rank correlation coefficients have been calculated between the two technology rankings, and rank information of numbers of MPE 2 companies by country and the rank numbers of companies in the RI MPE 2 classification by country. The correlations seem to indicate a closer degree of association than when the exercise was undertaken within Table 8.2. However before there is any indulgence in self-congratulation, it is necessary to look more closely at the results relating to column D. When the rank proportions of a country's companies which are MPE 2 in character is related to the indicator of technology ranking the resultant correlations are low and negative. Apparently the plausible notion that a high proportion of a country's manufacturing concerns in this sample will be MPE 2 in status when technological orientation is high, is rejected. There are a number of explanations for this curt rebuttal. However, it is not worth rehearsing

Table 8.17 The world's largest manufacturing companies

Country	A Technology ranking	B Alternative Technology ranking[a]	C Numbers in MPE 2 by rank	D % of country's companies in MPE 2 by rank	E Numbers in MPE 2 and RI class. By rank.
USA	1	1	1	8	1
Japan	6.5	11	6	10	5
Britain	2	3.5	2	7	2
Germany	5	3.5	3	5	3
France	4	7	4	6	4
Canada	10	10	11	11	11
Sweden	8	6	5	9	8
Netherlands	6.5	5	8	3	6.5
Italy	9	8	9.5	1.5	8
Switzerland	3	2	7	4	6.5
Belgium	11	9	9.5	1.5	8

Rank Correlation Coefficients: between A & C = 0.841**
between B & C = 0.659*
between A & D = −0.145 NS
between B & D = 0.173 NS
between A & E = 0.866**
between B & E = 0.655*

** Significant at 1 per cent
* Significant at 5 per cent
NS Not significant

Source [a]. OECD, *Conditions for Success in Technological Innovation,* 1971.

these because column D has served its purpose. It is a strong reminder that this exercise is very susceptible to the particular measures used and that unscrupulous selection may yield a set of apparently convincing results. The correlation coefficients relating to column D put things in perspective. The exercise summarised in Tables 8.2 and 8.17 is interesting in its own right, but capable of yielding only limited results. It can do no more than hint at explanations. It does not search deeply, and can only provide a broad overview of the factors that may be relevant in the location pattern of multinationals. A more detailed approach is necessary. The later portion of this chapter has been an attempt to provide this.

Conclusions

Within the limitations of the data and the arbitrary nature of the classification procedures, there would appear to be support for the arguments that postulate a link between research orientated activities and global location. The evidence does not show that technological activities predominate among international companies. Support comes in a more indirect way. This has been called the relative scarcity effect. The cross-classification procedure reveals fairly striking contrasts in the cell frequencies. Thus companies which are MPE 2 in status are evenly distributed between RI and not RI activities. But in the not MPE class there are approximately 2.5 to 3.5 times as many observations in the not RI class as in the RI class. Furthermore there are between 3 and 5 times as many RI observations in the MPE 2 class, as in MPE 1 plus not MPE. By contrast NRI companies do not cluster in this way. These companies appear to exhibit no particular preference over MPE 2 or MPE 1 plus not MPE. Examination of subdivisions of the sample population suggest that these patterns of behaviour are reasonably consistent. There is enough evidence of consensus to be fairly confident that the contingency tables relating to all companies, provide a reasonable summary of the typical position. Tests of statistical significance reject the null hypothesis that companies' tendency to locate abroad is not related to the character of the goods they sell. Chance is a most unlikely explanation for the observed data. One major exception is the subpopulation relating to Japan. Japanese companies are apparently free of the location forces which influence others. Confirmation of this opinion is provided by an auxiliary test. There is firm rejection of the hypothesis that Japanese companies exhibit a pattern of behaviour which is the same as that for the remainder of the world. Thus with this exception, the conclusions outlined above are accepted. There is apparently a fairly general relationship between research orientated activities and multinational status. Interpretation of this finding and speculations about cause and effect follow.

9

Diffusion and the multinational enterprise: III. Interpretation

In this chapter an attempt will be made to interpret the conclusions that have emerged from chapter 8. In the process causal mechanisms will be postulated. These will be linked with further discussion of the mature economy thesis.

Mature economies

The evidence in chapter 8 at least does not deny, and may even support, the argument that multinational location is linked with the type of goods being sold. This evidence may also permit the speculation that the multinational enterprise tends to be the product of mature economies. This line of thought will now be pursued. The purpose is to indicate the type of considerations that may affect the product mix and location policy of the MPE.

Mature economies are those characterised by a high standard of living but a slow rate of growth. They are highly industrialised nations which suffer from severe resource constraints.[1] There are few spare resources in the sense that a high proportion of the factors of production are in current employment. In the process of industrialisation of economies there is a tendency for labour to be drawn away from agricultural employment. In a mature economy this process is largely complete. These spare resources are no longer available to service industrial expansion. There is a tendency for unit labour costs to be high and for industrial effort to turn towards innovative activity. Technological change becomes recognised as of prime importance. It is no accident that it is amongst the developed economies, that pressure to innovate is at its highest. Economic forces conspire to make innovational effort an increasingly important prerequisite for economic growth. Mature economies generally rely on resource substitution for improved economic performance. A high proportion of available factors of production is already engaged in economic activity, therefore increased production tends to be secured by using improved methods and new products. In this way innovations offer an escape from resource constraints which would otherwise tend to make developed economies less competitive. New goods and processes are thus major ways round the erosion of competitive advantage. Sales of technological goods are not particularly price elastic. Competition takes a non-price form where the performance characteristics of the goods on offer predominate as a sales influence. A mature economy, therefore, tends to be characterised by a relatively high R and D effort. It also tends to have well-developed tertiary industries. These are activities which market services and expertise. Standards of living in such economies tend to be high because industrialisation has been going on so long.

Two economies which it is agreed have reached maturity are the USA and Britain.[2] Another possible candidate is Belgium.[3] Unfortunately precise definition of the broad concept of maturity is not easy. Most highly industrialised countries could advance a legitimate claim to this status. On these grounds the majority of European countries could be included. For the present purposes this does not matter. The general flavour of the arguments is being rehearsed to indicate possible locational influences. The archetype may be assumed to be the typical, and definitional problems set on one side. The USA and the UK are therefore taken as the model. It should, however, be pointed out that the importance of maturity is not unchallenged. For example, it has been argued that during the 1960s Britain could have secured a higher growth rate than other major European nations if a higher rate of innovation had been achieved. In these circumstances inefficient management and not economic maturity is seen as the predominant cause of the disappointing performance.[4] There may be an element of truth in the argument, but it does little to explain the equally disappointing performance of the USA over the same period. The United States is without doubt the most technologically orientated and innovation conscious economy in the world. In addition, it is renowned for the quality of its management. Economic maturity is therefore taken by the present author to be an explanation of some importance, but the reservations of those who resist this point of view are kept in mind.

Escape and capture

An association between multinational companies and mature economies is not implausible. It may well reflect what will be called the escape and capture mechanisms. The escape mechanism describes a tendency for companies to invest overseas to avoid the slow rate of growth in the home economy. The capture mechanism reflects an anxiety to appropriate the benefits of companies' own innovations and those originated by others, on a worldwide scale. The model predicted here postulates a centrafuging effect in mature economies, and an outward pull generated by involvement in research intensive activities. The level of industrial development of advanced economies probably puts an emphasis on technological effort to secure an international competitive advantage. The slow rate of growth of mature economies may also induce a search for improved commercial prospects elsewhere. Firms may set up foreign subsidiaries abroad rather than export or license competitors, in order to capture the benefits of their innovational effort. The incentive to take this action is considerable. Invention and innovation are activities which have large external economies. They generate knowledge. This is expensive to create but cheap to copy. Devices to protect proprietary knowledge do exist, but they can be weak. In an attempt to appropriate the benefits of their ingenuity, companies are likely to establish overseas production facilities. The other aspect of the capture mechanism is the necessity to keep up with rivals' technology. Thus the escape mechanism would predict that it is inevitable that a mature economy will have a high rate of direct overseas investment. In contrast, the capture mechanism would predict a high rate of inflow of foreign capital into such an economy. Other mature economies are anxious for sales outlets and an ideas base. They will choose economies likely to buy their sophisticated goods and those which have a compatible technological environment. In these terms a research and development and innovationally orientated economy is an obvious choice. A locational mix is predicted where there is a two-way flow of capital, both into and out of mature economies representing the escape and capture mechanism in operation. In the jargon of the literature this two-way investment is known as intra-penetration or cross-penetration.

It is possible to classify countries in three ways to illustrate the effects of foreign investment.[5]

1. Net colonisers. Here foreign operations of domestic companies exceed by a substantial margin those of foreign enterprises located within the country. Switzerland and the United States provide examples.
2. Colonisers and the colonised. Here there is a high two-way flow of investment. Britain, Holland, Sweden and Germany are examples.
3. The colonised. Here foreign owned companies are extremely important in the economies. There is a subclassification to be made here, between high income low population countries, like Canada and Australia, and the less developed economies with low income and low usage of technology. These are typically economies which

use what is known as intermediate technology. This is technology which has become part of history for the advanced economy, but which is useful in the environment of a less developed country.

In Britain there is a considerable two-way investment. Thirty per cent of the profits of British owned enterprises are derived from overseas operation, and at the same time foreign multinational firms in the United Kingdom account for approximately 25 per cent of manufacturing exports, and may account for 25 per cent of manufacturing output by 1980.[6] The reason for this two-way investment may be explained by the escape and capture mechanisms. The dynamic large company may feel constrained by the growth rate within the United Kingdom. Its response may be to invest elsewhere. Pressures to do this are considerable, especially when these companies are research intensive. Imitation rates may be fast and lead times short. A defence against this erosion of economic advantage is a production and sales network across the world. The same mechanism also causes inward investment into the United Kingdom. Foreign companies are anxious to appropriate the benefits of their innovations and to share in the technological advances that tend to be generated in such a mature economy. Research and development efforts are at a high level, and where the development gap is large opportunities for the ambitious foreign company are considerable. By locating within the United Kingdom it may in fact pick up ideas which are neglected by national companies. It may also enhance its potential output of innovations by employing local R and D personnel.

The position of the United States economy is somewhat anomalous. This is probably the most mature and also the most technologically advanced of all economies. In terms of the mechanisms, there ought to be a high two-way flow into and out of this economy, yet the United States is a net coloniser. There is a large net outflow of capital from this economy. The explanation probably lies in the enormous scale difference in the figures between the countries concerned. The gross national product of the United States is so much greater than that of other countries that it is hardly surprising that the capital exports are very much larger than capital imports. A further reason may be the daunting character of the United States market. There may be a crucial size before companies go multinational. In addition non-American companies may have to be even larger before effective location in the United States is possible. There may be a progression in the life of a non-American company, whereby it takes the first step towards multinationalism by locating in foreign markets, but outside the USA. Concentration on softer markets may allow a gradual extension of the geographical scope of activity without too much commercial peril. Once size and confidence have risen the next step may be location in

America. Here size and financial strength may be crucial and such a step may represent the hallmark of a company that has arrived in the world of international business.[7] Cross-penetration of the American market may therefore be limited by a size and confidence barrier which only the largest non-American company can overcome.

Evidence for the escape mechanism in operation has to be inferred from the behaviour of multinational companies. In a study of international big business 1957–67, the author found a considerable 'country effect' in explaining the growth rates of the world's leading companies.[8] Theoretically, the growth rate of a company can be independent of the rate of expansion of its home market. But in practice there may well be a parity between company and economy performance. A large company is likely to be responsible for a significant proportion of industrial activity and may well be directly affected by the prevalent growth rate of the whole economy. There is evidence that this may be the case.[9] Results from regression analysis indicate that the nationality of these major companies has been a significant variable explaining growth. Apparently there has been a fairly strong 'country effect', even though the companies concerned were often multinational in character.

The behaviour pattern of the Japanese companies in this study may also provide broad support for the escape mechanism. One explanation for the lack of Japanese multinationals may be the fast rate of growth of their home economy. This has been so rapid that location overseas to promote expansion may not have been an influence of any force. The scarcity of international companies originating from Japan may, therefore, be represented as a form of support for the escape mechanism, and a direct outcome of a strong 'country effect'.

Evidence for the capture mechanism in operation is more difficult. The location of US companies in the United Kingdom in considerable numbers, even though the UK rate of growth has been slower than that of America, is perhaps indicative. Equally, capital investment of British companies in the USA is suggestive. These companies are deliberately going into markets which the United States multinationals locate overseas to escape. Evidence for the capture mechanism should be most clearly exhibited among research intensive activities. On the definitions used in this study it has not been revealed that such activities are predominant among international companies. But the contrasts revealed by the cross-classification procedure do suggest that the outward pull exerted on companies in technological activities may be considerable. If a wider definition is adopted, however, then this pattern is exhibited. Thus if mechanical engineering, motor vehicles and rubber products are added to the list of research intensive activites the dominance of the multinational in technological areas is revealed. In 1967 United States firms in the high technology activities were more international in scope than American firms in other industries. Nearly two-fifths of assets in research intensive activities were owned by firms with 25 per cent or more of their operations overseas, and 87 per cent of all sales of such companies were in the research intensive industries. Furthermore, the success of internationalism in technologically orientated activities was testified by faster growth and higher profitability.[10] 'This pattern would generally support modern theories of internationl investment, which emphasise that overseas activities can only be successfully exploited by the investing company if it possesses specific technological and marketing advantages, coupled with the ability to maintain their lead by R and D.'[11] In terms of the capture mechanism, the tendency for internationalism to be most prevalent in research orientated activities is broad confirmation of locational forces of the general character outlined here. It is among innovationally orientated activities that the pressures to locate on a global basis would apparently less in other activities.

Figure 9.1 illustrates the experience of the largest American manufacturing companies during 1957–67. Stylised facts for this time period may be represented as follows:

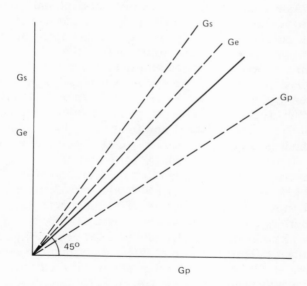

Sources. Based on Fig. 9.1 Rowthorne, *International Big Business*, 1957–67 (ref. 8); Hymer and Rowthorne, 'The multi-national corporation: the non-American challenge' (ref. 7).

Fig. 9.1 The performance of U.S. Multinationals

Gs > Ge ⩾ Gp, where Gp = growth rate of the United States parent firms including subsidiaries, Gs = the growth rate of overseas subsidiaries, and Ge = the growth rate of non-US firms. In essence the American multinational has been able to secure a faster rate of growth for its subsidiaries overseas than achieved by the parent company.

US companies have come into the fastest growing sectors in the UK and EEC. They have also exhibited a strong bias towards high technology activities.[1 2] Fig. 9.1 illustrates the combined effects of successful escape and capture. By locating abroad the US multinationals have enhanced their overall growth rates, have presumably increased profit earning, and have probably achieved a rate of expansion in excess of that typically enjoyed by their more domestically orientated counterparts. These benefits were presumably a direct result of successful escape and capture.

Diffusion and the multinational

By reducing the separation of markets the multinational company is likely to be important to the diffusion of innovation. These companies have a worldwide spread of subsidiaries. They are coordinated through head office. Assets may now be allocated on a global basis. Multinationals with headquarters in the technologically advanced nations have an enormous potential to unify and speed the rates at which new products and processes spread from source. The rate of adoption normally varies between advanced and developing countries. Thus, for example, in plastics, where the pace of change is fast, two to three years may be taken by the United States and Germany, and more than twenty years in others, for diffusion from the originating company.[1 3] However, foreign subsidiaries of multinationals have a technological capability which is largely independent of the economy in which they are located. Their skill and knowledge are based on the endowments of the economy from which they have come. Consequently their rate of adoption is likely to reflect not the attitudes prevalent in their current location, but those of the head office. The impetus to adopt will come from headquarters and not from some 'natural' process of diffusion. Percolation will be hustled by fiat, and will not necessarily reflect local market conditions. Thus the rate at which they take up new products and processes is likely to be independent of their host economy. Diffusion rates may therefore approximate to those typical in the home economy and will presumably be faster.

The costs of acquiring technological knowledge may also be reduced. The multinational may be effective in acquiring knowhow cheaply. The bargaining power of a large global company may reduce payments necessary to become a licensee of a particular technology. Information exchanges, patent diplomacy, economies of scale in handling proprietary knowledge, are the type of considerations that may reduce the cost. If proprietary knowledge can be acquired cheaply this may encourage early involvement in new products and processes. The ability of the global corporation to reduce costs in this way may therefore be another factor contributing to faster diffusion.

Analysis of data on the flow of technology suggests that the spread of innovation is increasingly due to direct investment across national boundaries, mainly from the USA to Canada and Europe.[14] If, as seems likely, there is an association between research intensive activities and multinational companies, it is probable that they will speed the diffusion of innovation around the world.[15] One author is of the opinion that the most impressive characteristic of the global corporation is the speed with which it channels advanced technologies into the far corners of the world.[16] If this is accepted, then the more important multinationals become, the faster and more uniform is the rate of adoption likely to be. The international perspective of such companies and the enormous investment resources available to them is likely to make a major impact on the spread of technology.

A plausible case can be argued that innovative competition may be fostered by competitive oligopoly.[17] The reasoning hinges on a modification of the rigour of the competitive process to permit adequate appropriation and the avoidance of the lethargy likely to be associated with monopoly. The virtues of size are recognised and a 'big firm, few firm' type of competition advocated. On an international scale, the multinational company may be an energetic vehicle of technological change. It may be effective in generating its own ideas, be vigorous in copying those of others, and may spread usage quickly throughout the world. One commentator believes that this is likely to be the case.

> The record of the United States shows that one certainly cannot fault oligopoly on the grounds that it does not provide a very rapid rate of technological change and product innovation. Indeed it is easier to argue that the rate of change is too high. One can expect international oligopoly via multinational corporations to provide the same kind of dynamic environment for the world economy as a whole.[18]

In effect it is being argued that the innovative dynamism associated with oligopoly will be made global by the activities of the multinational.

Summary and conclusions

It is tentatively suggested that the multinational enterprise may be the product of mature economies. By 'escape and capture' such companies may reduce the influence of the home economy on their own performance. They may also defer the onset of economic obsolescence of their own innovations and put themselves in a powerful position to respond quickly to the developments of others.

At a less speculative level, the results in Chapter 8 point to the central role played by the multinational in the worldwide circulation of technological knowledge. There is evidence that involvement in research intensive activities is associated with multinational status. Interpretation of this conclusion must, however, be cautious. The shortcomings of the procedures must be remembered. With these in mind, it would seem that the character of goods sold by companies may have an influence on their location policy. Companies in prosaic activities are by no means excluded from global status, but those with a technological orientation are much more often international than national in character. It would therefore seem not unreasonable to conclude that the multinational producing enterprise is an important agent in the diffusion of technology. The international character of high technology may have its counterpart in the global corporation.[19]

10

Diffusion and the multinational enterprise: IV. The direct investment package

Introduction

The preceding chapter has put forward the suggestion that outward direct investment may be a response by companies originating from economies that have achieved economic maturity. This chapter leaves that particular speculation behind, and concentrates on the nature of the direct investment package and its relation to the transmission of technology. A somewhat wider definition of the term diffusion will be used. The discussion in Chapter 6 was deliberately limited to the spread of specific innovations. Diffusion in that context meant the widening adoption of a particular article or technique. It is now appropriate to use a somewhat broader meaning. The discussion will incorporate some of the effects induced by technology transfer. In particular, emphasis will be given to the role of the multinational enterprise in diffusion and the impact on the host economy. The penetration of a foreign market by subsidiaries is likely to have a considerable influence on the recipient economy. This will be especially marked where the strangers come from an advanced nation and bring products and techniques which are virtually unknown in the new environment. The most important effects will be outlined in this chapter, but no attempt will be made to compile a balance sheet of the costs and benefits of direct foreign investment to the host economy. Instead effort will be concentrated on revealing the unique nature of the package and its connection with the diffusion of technology.

The word package is used as a form of short-hand to refer to the endowment of capital, technology and management which a foreign subsidiary brings to its chosen location. Included in the package is an 'extra-territorial' dimension. This refers to the transplant of an alien organisation into a host economy, where allegiance and control lie outside the country of adoption. The extra-territorial dimension raises a number of problems. Included amongst these are the possible loss of a nation's economic and political sovereignty, the effect on the allocation of national resources, and the general fears of host governments. As already indicated a micro approach has been adopted in this study. The company is under investigation as an agent in the creation and spread of technology. The wider problems are not discussed. A similar casualty of the micro approach is a treatment of the balance of payments consequences of direct investment in the originating country. The country-wide approach adopted for example in the Reddaway Report[1] or the Hufbauer-Adler report[2] is not appropriate to this study. The exclusion of these topics is not intended as a comment on their importance. It is merely a product of the approach adopted.

A further exclusion has been made. The role of the multinational enterprise in spreading technology to developing or less developed countries (LDC), is not covered in the treatment. Justification for this procedure is sought on four grounds. First, is to limit the discussion to manageable proportions. Second, this study is essentially concerned with the spread of new or relatively new technology. The major industrial activities of the LDC are in mature products; at least this is what their export trade suggests.[3] Such countries are unlikely to be early adopters of innovations. They perhaps concentrate on goods which have capital intensive standardised production processes in which change has virtually ceased.[4] They are likely to be on the fringe of technological activity, and new technologies may be largely irrelevant to their needs.[5] The factor mix appropriate to production processes and the type of good produced may not be compatible with the requirements of developing nations. The quality of local labour and scientists may militate against early involvement. There may be none of the external economies available to companies in advanced nations, where there is a pool of industrial and scientific know-how available in a significant proportion of the work force.[6] Third, in technological transfer between advanced nations there are few of the additional complications which make diffusion to the LDCs hesitant. Political upheavals, expropriations, lack of supporting technology and trained personnel are unlikely to be constraining influences on the developed nations. It is admitted that the transmission of technology to the world's poorer countries is of great importance, but in studying the international diffusion of products processes and know-how, it is reasonable to assert that a concentration on the advanced nations will reveal the essence of the process. The differences, special difficulties and complications of transplants to the LDCs may in this sense cloud the issue. The transfer of technology to developing countries has virtually become a separate subject and a specialist literature has grown up around it.[7]

Fourth, it is the author's impression gathered during the process of classifying companies by their degree of multinationality, that the location of producing subsidiaries in developing nations by the world's largest manufacturing firms, is comparatively rare. It must be stressed that this is only an impression. It has not been tested by a strict geographical count. An analysis has not been made of the particular location of subsidiaries. Nevertheless during the process of classifying companies for this study, the conviction arose that developing nations were comparatively rare choices for the affiliates of multinational enterprises. Location in the advanced nations appeared much more frequent. This would suggest that as the world's largest companies are almost entirely owned or controlled by the leading nations, there is a general preference for direct investment in economies with broadly compatible cultural and economic backgrounds.[8] Technological interchange induced by the multinational enterprise, is probably concentrated amongst the advanced nations. The LDCs are on the fringe of the process, and the location of subsidiaries would appear to reflect this.

The package

When a foreign company establishes a subsidiary within a host economy, a transplant is involved. There is a transplant in the sense that an organisation is established which draws its initiative and impetus from alien and not indigenous sources. Allegiance and control lie outside the country of adoption. At first sight the affiliate of a multinational enterprise may appear similar to its national counterparts. Local resources of capital labour and management may be used in operations. Productive activities and methods of organisation may be like those used by national companies. But when the extra-territorial dimension is remembered, the likeness is revealed to be deceptive. In these terms, a subsidiary of a global company is only superficially comparable to indigenous rival producers. It is a transplant which has been grafted into a new environment, but which nevertheless remains distinctive because of its ownership characteristics.

There is an additional meaning to the word transplant. Not only has the company come from elsewhere, but it has in a sense arrived complete. It is an entity which in effect already exists. Physical construction of buildings, lay-out of plant, and recruitment of personnel have, of course, to be carried out, but the major features are predetermined. As an offshoot of a global corporation, a high proportion of management, capital, expertise and product design will be supplied from within the parent company. They arrive as part of the package. They already exist and are merely transposed into their new environment. This availability is not dependent on local supply and their form and characteristics may be independent of that which is typical in the host economy.

The ramifications of direct foreign investment can be very wide indeed. Local producers may be shaken out of their competitive lethargy, new technologies may be introduced, managerial methods may be revolutionised, industrial relations and methods of working may be radically changed; all of these are examples of the type of influence that may follow an injection of alien capital and know-how. However, before outlining likely effects, it is necessary to pause for some background definitions. The first relates to the contrast between portfolio and direct investment, and the second to initial as opposed to continuing effects of direct foreign investment. Portfolio investment is essentially a transfer of money capital for use in a foreign economy. There is a transfer of purchasing power from the lender to the borrower. The borrower puts the capital to work to earn the interest and profit required to make the transaction viable.[9] Direct foreign investment is different in character. Instead of there being a transfer of money capital to locals, there is now a mobilisation of all the factors required for the economic activity with control remaining in the hands of the initiators. In the typical situation, the foreign investor establishes a subsidiary in the host economy and retains ownership of the assets concerned. The initial as opposed to the continuing effects contrasts the immediate impact of establishing a subsidiary in a host economy, with the long term and continuing effects of that investment.[10] The distinction relates to time periods and draws attention either to the immediate influence of the arrival of a foreign affiliate, or the longer term effects of the subsidiary, once the initial period is over.

In order to appreciate the likely effects of the arrival and operation of a foreign subsidiary in a host economy on the diffusion of technology, it will be helpful to set out the major characteristics of these companies. The list that follows indicates the major features of subsidiaries, and also the features of multinational enterprises. The first portion sets out the special properties of affiliates. The second portion deals with multinational companies. The list is confined to the special qualities that have a bearing on the diffusion of technology. Furthermore it is not meant to imply that all such companies have all of these characteristics, nevertheless it is reasonable to suppose that a fairly high proportion will apply. The list is based on academic studies, but the reader should not assume that the features are 'proven'. Some have only limited evidence in their support, others are highly plausible but lack empirical support. Even those which have received considerable investigation may no longer apply even though they were correct at the time concerned. In effect all the normal and proper academic cautions must be remembered when interpreting the list of findings.

CHARACTERISTICS OF AFFILIATES

1. Approximately 50 per cent of the world's direct foreign investment in manufacturing activity is probably carried out by the leading 50 multinational companies; the next 50 largest probably account for another 25 per cent.[11]

2. Numerically and by size, American companies are predominant amongst the world's largest manufacturing companies, and also amongst those companies that come within the MPE 2 category. In fact, Table 8.4 (p. 154) reveals that 'other nationalities' have only 139 companies in the highly multinational class compared with 210 from America. By numbers of MPE 2 companies, nations other than the USA come in the order: Britain, Germany, France, Japan and Sweden.

3. The technological orientation of economies indicates with little doubt that America is ranked first.[12]

4. Multinational companies favour 100 per cent ownership of their affiliates. Intermediate holding and control arrangements are not preferred.[13]

5. Involvement of foreign capital in host economies varies widely from industry to industry.[14]

6. UK experience suggests that foreign subsidiaries tend to come into fast growing and profitable areas of activity.[15]

7. US owned affiliates tend to be more profitable than their indigenous UK counterparts.[16] The same would appear to be true of the affiliates of other nationalities in the UK.[17]

8. Participation by US affiliates in particular UK industries is a higher percentage of gross output of the activity concerned the greater the distinctive advantage of the subsidiaries relative to indigenous firms.[18]

9. The superior profitability of the US affiliates referred to in item 7 is not merely a composition effect, but may reflect superior efficiency within given activities.[19]

10. An additional influence in profitability may well be a heightened form of specialisation referred to as intra-company specialisation[20] or truncation.[21]

11. The true profitability of subsidiaries may, however, be masked by parent company backing.[22]

12. Because affiliates are not autonomous and independent companies, but part of a larger organisation, they may be able to act independently of their immediate commercial environment. This will be explained in detail later.

13. American subsidiaries in the UK would appear to modify their capital output ratios and working times towards those of the host

economy.[23] Nevertheless they would appear to be more capital intensive than that typical in the activity concerned.[24]

14. Affiliates are likely to produce differentiated goods. This is reflected in a tendency for them to spend an above average amount on advertising and also to be members of companies which are international oligopolies.[25]

15. Affiliates of multinational enterprises relative to local producers are probably more diversified in their output.[26]

16. US subsidiaries in UK are generally to be found in export intensive industries and may well be more export orientated than their local rivals.[27]

17. Subsidiaries of foreign affiliates may possibly have a restricted import and export franchise; at least this is what experience in Australia may suggest.[28]

18. Foreign affiliates would appear more responsive to government regional location policies, than their indigenous counterparts.[29]

19. The skill and endowment of host countries has a vital bearing on direct foreign investment. This may explain why involvement of multinational companies tends towards nations with similar economic and technological backgrounds.[30]

20. Subsidiaries of foreign companies tend to be in technologically advanced industries.[31]

21. In terms of R and D spending, US affiliates in Britain appear research intensive.[32] However, UK subsidiaries in the USA would appear modest spenders on research. The cost of establishing and running a research department in America is apparently an inhibiting influence.[33]

22. Experience in the petrochemical industry suggests that the size of foreign markets is an important influence in the decision to establish manufacturing facilities abroad.[34]

23. The form and timing of investment by multinational companies may be influenced by the stage in the product cycle of the article concerned.[35]

24. There are indications that the lag in establishing US overseas production in Europe is decreasing.[36]

CHARACTERISTICS OF MULTINATIONAL ENTERPRISES

Turning now to the features of multinational corporations as a whole rather than the characteristics of their subsidiaries, there are indications that global corporations are distinctive relative to their counterparts from within the home economy.

1. US global companies relative to their national counterparts might well be more profitable and grow faster.[37]

2. American multinational enterprises appear to spend relatively more on research and advertising than other US companies which are not so globally orientated.[38]

3. The American multinationals referred to in item 2 would also appear to be bigger, more diversified in their product structure, export more and pay higher wages in the US.

4. With the possible exception of Japanese companies, there would appear to be a tendency for firms of all nationalities from amongst the world's largest manufacturing concerns which are research intensive in character, not to be national in status. This has been referred to as the relative scarcity effect in this study.[39] In this special sense the 'outward urge' would appear to be demonstrated by companies which are involved in technological activities.

5. It is reasonable to assert from item 4 that direct foreign investment may be important in narrowing technology gaps.[40]

6. Case studies in a number of industries suggest that the multinational enterprise is an important agent in the diffusion of technology. Included amongst these are scientific instruments, electronic components, electronic computers, plastics, pharmaceuticals, non-ferrous metals and synthetic materials.[41] Motor car manufacture, chemicals, oil, office machinery, tyres, and tobacco are also areas of activity in which the multinational enterprise is heavily involved.[42] Appendix 1 indicating those areas which have been classified as research intensive, also provides candidates where direct investment is likely to be important.

7. The global corporation may well be the fastest and most effective means of achieving inter-country diffusion of technological knowledge.[43]

8. Direct investment by the global corporation may be an important factor inducing a parity of industrial structures amongst leading industrial nations.[44]

Caveats

Before elaborating on some of the features of the multinational enterprise and their affiliates a few cautionary points are necessary. First, the evidence from which the lists have been compiled is heavily biased towards the characteristics of American companies. This emphasis reflects the importance of US firms in world economic activity and also the number of studies which have investigated them. There is little evidence on European multinationals. Almost all of the empirical work has been concerned with American companies. In terms of discovering the representative this bias may not matter, but it may nevertheless highlight distinguishing characteristics which may not apply to the companies of other nations. European firms, for example, may have different properties, or the same properties but to a different degree. This study has suggested that Japanese companies may be distinctive; at least in terms of the scarcity of the multinational form of organisation amongst their leading concerns. The emphasis towards the American multinational must therefore be kept in mind when interpreting the results, and generalisation must be circumspect.

Second it is important to appreciate the basis of comparison being used to indicate the special features of multinationals and their affiliates. The first part of the list draws attention to the properties of subsidiaries. The basis of comparison is not companies of the same nationality which adopt different structures of trading, but companies of different nationality where the contrast is between foreign affiliates located in a host economy, and other firms in the same economy. In other words the comparison is particular to the country under investigation and emphasises differences between foreign subsidiaries and that which is typical in the host economy. Because the comparison is particular in this sense, generalisation has to be cautious. The majority of the empirical evidence cited above relates to American subsidiaries in the UK. To widen the findings to apply to the performance of US subsidiaries in other economies, or to the foreign affiliates of companies of all nationalities, is clearly hazardous. If and when such a generalisation is made, this must be remembered.

Problems of this type are not so severe in the second portion of the list. The general characteristics of multinationals are being cited. A comparison is being made between companies of the same nationality which adopt different types of organisation. Thus, for example, American multinational companies are contrasted with American national concerns, to identify distinguishing features in their inputs, economic ratios and performance. The consolidated results of the two types of companies are being compared. Thus the performances of all subsidiaries are included, and not merely those in a particular country. This gives a firmer basis on which to build conclusions. The results are not so specific to the country of location of affiliates, and in the case of the multinational enterprise represent an aggregation of all home and overseas activities. Confidence in the generality of the results is also increased by their geographical scope. The findings in 1, 2 and 3 are applicable to companies from America, Israel, Holland and Denmark.[4][5]

Third, the findings especially those relating to the economic superiority of affiliates in host countries, may only be temporary. At the time when the studies were undertaken, it may well have been true that the subsidiaries of foreign companies were markedly better in their economic performance than other companies in the host economy. It does not follow, however, that this disparity will remain. As already pointed out earlier in this chapter, the arrival of foreign producers may shake locals out of their lethargy, managerial methods may be revolutionised, and product mix and techniques of production may be radically changed. The effect of the challenge and response may be a narrowing or elimination of any performance disparities. In effect the operation of the competitive process suggests that the findings of such studies should be treated as a static insight into a dynamic situation. They may reveal a situation pertinent to a given time period. They do not carry with them the implication that things will remain unchanged. Interpretation of the apparent superiority of particular types of companies should keep this in mind.

An elaboration

In the discussion that follows the features presented in the lists above are given some elaboration. The method of treatment will not take each point in turn but will cover them as a whole. The purpose is to indicate the likely effects of foreign subsidiaries on host economies, in terms of the diffusion of technology. The claim that the multinational enterprise is an important agent in the spread of technological knowledge is under investigation. The special characteristics of these companies will help to indicate why this claim may well be substantiated.

The nature of the investment decision taking process of multinational companies is as yet poorly understood. A great deal more empirical work has yet to be done before a clear picture emerges. Nevertheless it is possible to speculate on its character guided by the evidence that is available, and currently accepted theories.[4,6] The major influences which induce overseas location are likely to include, the stage in the product cycle of the article concerned, the size of the market in the contemplated location, and the compatibility of the business environment. The discussion in Chapter 2 suggested that overseas production may be influenced by the stage in the product cycle. Chapter 7 took the argument somewhat further and argued that where a company has proprietary knowledge, the preferred method of exploitation of overseas markets may well be direct investment over exporting or licensing. The discussion centred on patentable innovations. 'When' and 'where' affiliates would be located was not covered. This deficiency must now be rectified to the extent of indicating the predictions which arise from the product-cycle thesis, on the timing and location of overseas investment. These will help clarify the characteristics of the multinational enterprise and their affiliates.

The product-cycle theory argues that manufacture will be initially located in the country of discovery. Production facilities will be established for the innovation in the home economy and the goods sold there. Market success will raise the possibility of overseas sales and in Phase I these are likely to be served by exports. As the product becomes more standardised in its production and sales characteristics, overseas manufacture is likely to be undertaken and depending on entry barriers this may be done by home or foreign rival companies or by affiliates of the originating firm. Assuming that there is a well-protected patent position, then the discovering company will be able to deter others, and so confine overseas manufacture to its own subsidiaries. From these offshoots yet other markets may be served by exports. In essence Phase II of the product cycle would predict, that given an imperfect market, production facilities will be established in suitable markets abroad, and that these will belong to the originating company. By Phase III, the mature good stage, the proprietary knowledge embodied in the product will have been eroded. Patents will have expired or have become less daunting. Competition will be much less imperfect and producers are likely to be price takers and quantity makers. Cost considerations are likely to be a major determinant in location decisions taken in this Phase. Production will have stabilised and is likely to involve large scale methods. Because techniques are unlikely to evolve further, and because normal running requires only supervisory management skills, products in the mature stage are suitable for transplant into Developing Economies. The skills and techniques required for their successful operation are not too demanding on local resources, and relatively cheap labour may confer an international competitive advantage in products from such locations. At this stage of the product cycle, the theory would therefore predict the establishment of production facilities in the emergent nations, and importation back into the originating country. It would also suggest that the company that developed the good would, by this time, have diversified its product base, so that it would not be totally reliant on a single product which is now sold in a highly competitive world market, from economies that may well have a labour cost advantage.

Assuming that the initial innovation was developed within a technologically orientated, high income, high consumption economy like the United States of America, then the 'when' and 'where' predictions would appear as follows. Production is at first home based. Gradually, however, it is likely to be established in other nations. In the early stages of the life cycle of the product, the economic and technological environment of the potential host economy must not be too far removed from that prevalent in the originating nation. Production methods have by no means stabilised, and innovative competition may be prevalent. There must therefore be highly skilled management to incorporate these changes. If this is available locally overseas, this will reduce the drain on the parent organisation. In addition, there must be a sufficient level of demand for this relatively sophisticated good. Both of these factors suggest that direct investment, at least in the early stages of the life of a product, will take place in rich advanced nations. Only later is there likely to be involvement in the less developed countries.

This exposition of the direct investment process is, of course, highly simplified. The process of transference of production to overseas locations is inevitably complex. Nevertheless it should help reveal the essence of the process. Clearly the timing of location decisions will be affected by the character of the innovating company. If this is already a multinational enterprise, then a significant proportion of the required organisation will already exist to effect transfer to overseas manufacture. Presumably foreign production of a new article will be established relatively quickly. If the innovator happens to be merely national in status, then it is likely that the process will be more leisurely. A company which is not already organised on an international basis will have all the delays associated with establishing overseas facilities, and the inevitable managerial reluctance associated with a change in corporate organisation. The product cycle draws attention to the pattern of trade and investment that may evolve as a given article passes from novelty to maturity. Obvious locational forces like security of supply of raw materials, the type of company involved and strategic considerations are not denied. They are merely set on one side to highlight the core of the argument. The more subtle effects associated with the economic characteristics of a good over its lifetime are under scrutiny. It is these which yield considerable insight into the forces which induce foreign direct investment and help to create multinational companies.

The general prediction from the product-cycle thesis on the location of production, is a penetration amongst advanced wealthy nations in the early stages. Later direct investment will spread to others. The actual timing of location decisions is specific to the product concerned. In broad terms, however, the time scale is likely to be measured in years rather than months, and in the case of the LDCs may well be decades.[47] Where the initial discovery is located in a high income, large market, technologically well-endowed economy, this pattern and timing of the spread is plausible. The product-cycle approach may, however, be less convincing in explaining the pattern of trade when an innovation originates in a low income, small market, relatively backward economy.[48] The initiating company may feel a conflict of interest between investing in other similar economies and those with larger and more wealthy markets. The company may feel daunted by the prospect of investment in the advanced nations, and may in fact settle for production in economies which are less inhibiting in their economic and technological background. In spite of this difficulty the product cycle thesis serves to draw attention to two important factors in international investment. These are: imperfect markets; and the multinational enterprise. Imperfect markets are created by proprietary rights in innovation, company specific knowledge, differentiation and barriers to entry. The multinational enterprise is one vehicle for the international exploitation of a trading advantage. A major attraction of overseas location is probably based on market penetration and prolongation, and may be part cause and part effect of the apparent superiority of foreign affiliates over their local rivals. The lists above suggest that this superiority is realised in practice. Its relevance to the package and the diffusion of technology must now be explained.

The lists indicate that in numerical terms, the typical affiliate of a multinational enterprise, is likely to be US owned. It is likely to be in a technologically advanced industry and even if it is not, it is still likely to possess a considerable degree of company specific knowledge. It has originated from the most industrially advanced country in the world and is, relative to its counterparts in the host economy, likely to have a wider and deeper fund of general know-how. Such know-how may be reflected in superior management, better production methods, and more effective sales selection and marketing. This fund of knowledge may be a major explanation of the apparently superior performance of US foreign affiliates. Their industry selection favours the faster growing and more profitable sections, and even within a given activity the superiority of performance remains. When special care is taken to standardise for the industrial composition of US and local rivals, on a wide range of economic ratios, the American companies still exhibit superior performance. A major element in this must be managerial ability.[49] An additional element in the explanation of economic performance is also likely to be the multinational form of organisation. The special advantages referred to in Chapter 7 amount to a formidable array of favourable influences. The parent company may reach forward to markets (forward vertical investment), it may secure raw materials (backward vertical investment), and it may heighten specialisation by horizontal integration.[50] All of this investment may take place unhindered by national boundaries, and may show itself in an advanced degree of truncation in particular subsidiaries. Furthermore it may be co-ordinated on a highly interdependent basis.

Truncation or intra-firm specialisation will normally be associated with a high interdependent form of company organisation. Without the co-ordination provided by the parent company, such a heightened degree of specialisation would not be possible. In effect truncation is a geographical or spatial concept. From the viewpoint of the host economy, such subsidiaries may appear very narrow in their range of activities. To the multinational, however, these affiliates are merely a co-ordinated part of a large organisation where geographical separation of individual units does not carry with it the implication that they should encompass the normal range of activities.

Truncation and interdependence make for considerable difficulty in interpreting performance data. When investigators compare the performance of foreign subsidiaries with other companies in a host economy, they face considerable problems. In effect they are not comparing like with like.[51] Parts of companies, namely foreign affiliates, are being contrasted with other concerns which are more likely to be autonomous. To validate the comparison, attempts should therefore be made to allow for truncation, for inter-company pricing decisions which may be organised so that the accounts of subsidiaries reflect tax avoidance strategy rather than local results, and for the subsidy element that may arise from parent company backing. Without such adjustments, the results of studies which show an apparent superiority of foreign subsidiaries, should be treated with caution. Certainly the figures should not be taken at their face value and they should not necessarily be interpreted as prima facie evidence of superior economic efficiency. In effect it is being argued that subsidiaries of foreign companies are likely to appear superior to their local rivals. If, however, it were possible to make allowance for their special features, then this superiority may evaporate.

Fortunately the interpretation problem created by the lack of comparability between subsidiaries and autonomous companies, can to a certain extent be resolved. Evidence presented in the second portion of the list, would appear to confirm that multinationals achieve superior results, to their counterparts which are merely national in character. Apparently companies which are global in status do achieve better results. Presumably their foreign affiliates are responsible for a significant proportion of this performance. Disaggregating in this way, it is perhaps possible to infer something about affiliates in their foreign locations. In effect, the two sets of studies would appear to support each other in the sense that multinationals seem superior to nationals and foreign subsidiaries to locals.

The purpose of stressing the economic performance of subsidiaries and multinational companies, in the list above, is to indicate something of the commercial environment in which they operate. Despite the problems involved in interpreting results it is probably true that, in general, the subsidiaries of global companies do achieve considerable success in their host economies. It is also probably true that multinationals outperform their national counterparts. In effect it is being inferred from the studies that the commercial environment is favourable for such companies. This leads on to the assertion that the diffusion of technology has and will benefit from such a favourable economic climate. The argument is inevitably somewhat circular. The propitious environment is likely to be part cause and part effect. Multinationals may have created their success by innovative and other excellence. Equally they may have taken advantage of the particular benefits which their form of organisation may bring. In practice both types of influences are likely to be in operation. Despite this element of circularity, an important point emerges namely that innovations developed or adopted in such companies are likely to inherit two advantages. Firstly, they will be created or handled within companies which are likely to be wealthy. They are therefore likely to be brought to the market quickly. Secondly, they will be part of the product structure of a firm which already has a world-wide network of affiliates. A high proportion of the organisation required for overseas market penetration already exists. Furthermore, the knowledge barrier normally associated with transfer to a foreign location is likely to be reduced by the communication network and organisational unity achieved within global corporations. The speed of diffusion between countries is therefore likely to be faster than usual. The combination of a propitious economic climate and the organisational properties of the multinational enterprise suggests that the world-wide spread of new products and processes should be favourably affected. The arguments outlining the effects of the reduction in knowledge barriers will be developed later in this chapter.

The commercial independence effect

Part of the favourable influence on the diffusion of technology may arise from what may be termed independence effects. These are subdivided into commercial and technological factors. The commercial independence effect refers to the influence of parent company backing on the performance of subsidiaries. The technological independence effect draws attention to the contrast in the source of know-how of foreign affiliates compared with their rivals in local markets. Commercial independence will be dealt with first.

The commercial independence effect describes the ability of subsidiaries to act in a way which would appear unrelated to their immediate commercial environment. The assertion that affiliates are distinctive in their economic behaviour arises out of a study, the full details of which have never been published. The study was based on

411 UK-based foreign subsidiaries which were obliged to make returns of their accounts to the Registrar of Companies. The period covered was 1959–66. Only thirty of the companies had a quotation on a British Stock Exchange. The initial results of this study, relating to the problems in assessing the economic performance of subsidiaries using published accounting data, have already been cited.[52] The later results which come from additional processing of the data have not, however, appeared. Point 12 in the first portion of the lists above summarises the findings. The reason for the delay in publication was a period of study leave in the USA of one of the co-authors, and subsequent diversion of interest into other fields. In spite of the age of the data, however, it is appropriate that the results should now appear. They have considerable bearing on the arguments being presented, and yield further insight into the special character of the affiliates of foreign enterprises.

In the original study, data from 411 UK-based foreign-owned subsidiaries were processed to discover the effects of using definitions of profitability more appropriate to the type of company under consideration. Attention was drawn to the folly of using a Net Assets definition of profitability, where the ratio is expressed in terms of gross profits over total capital minus current liabilities. The effect of this definition is to exaggerate the apparent success of subsidiaries. On average, current liabilities represented approximately 40 per cent of foreign subsidiaries total assets, as against 23 per cent for industry in general. The logic of deducting current liabilities from the capital figure may have some force where independent companies are under consideration and where the investigator is attempting to discover the return on shareholders' assets. In the context of affiliates this justification has small value. Use of the definition is convenient because the Net Assets figure is provided in the standardised company accounts, which have been processed by Companies House. To find the total capital figure involves extracting data from the work sheets of companies, and is a time-consuming and tedious job. The effort is, however, justified because a definition of profitability emerges which avoids the risk of deducting parent company loans from the assets figure. It also goes part way towards meeting the argument that profitability of subsidiaries will be overstated because of the inevitable subsidies arising from parent company backing. It does this by making the capital denominator in the profitability calculations larger than in the Net Assets version.

Additional processing of the data after the original article was published revealed evidence of the effects of parent company backing. When the mean growth of the subsidiaries is calculated on a Total Assets (TA) and Fixed Assets (FA) basis, their growth rate appears to be higher than their host industries in practically every case. The only major exception is in Miscellaneous Services. Table 10.1 shows the results. The expression 'all quoted independent' refers to the growth performance of quoted indigenous companies. The capital figures used in calculating these percentages have been adjusted to exclude the quoted foreign subsidiaries which came within the study sample. It should be pointed out that the basis of comparison of the mean growth figures for subsidiaries, and their host industries is different. The figures

Table 10.1   Subsidiaries mean growth (per cent p.a.) by industry 1959–65

Industry	US	Others	All quoted independent	Industry	US	Others	All quoted independent
Food				*Textiles*			
FA	20.4	9.4	14.1	FA	11.5	9.1	6.8
TA	12.4	14.9	12.2	TA	12.2	10.0	5.6
N (in 1965)	16	3		N (in 1965)	5	4	
Chemicals				*Bricks, paper, glass, cement*			
FA	19.4	13.7	9.6	FA	17.2	–	15.3
TA	19.5	13.7	8.0	TA	15.8	–	12.1
N (in 1965)	52	17		N (in 1965)	5	–	
Metal manufacturers				*Paper, printing, publishing*			
FA	17.3	16.1	6.6	FA	3.5	20.2	12.8
TA	16.0	13.3	5.9	TA	2.9	9.4	10.9
N (in 1965)	9	4		N (in 1965)	8	7	
Non-electrical engineering				*Other manufacturing*			
FA	14.7	15.1	7.8	FA	10.8	10.5	6.7
TA	12.0	15.6	7.2	TA	10.2	10.6	6.6
N (in 1965)	80	20		N (in 1965)	19	6	
Electrical engineering				*Wholesale distribution*			
FA	21.0	16.1	10.5	FA	17.3	17.8	7.8
TA	14.6	12.0	8.3	TA	13.5	12.3	6.2
N (in 1965)	26	3		N (in 1965)	17	23	
Vehicles				*Misc. Services*			
FA	20.9	15.7	7.0	FA	9.0	11.6	18.5
TA	13.7	16.7	4.0	TA	10.0	14.4	12.4
N (in 1965)	7	2		N (in 1965)	18	3	
Metal goods n.e.s.							
FA	16.9	8.8	10.3				
TA	13.0	13.0	9.5				
N (in 1965)	15	5					

Drink, Retail Distribution. Tobacco, Transport and Construction have not been shown separately because there are so few observations in each group. In all cases, subsidiaries' mean growth rate is faster than their industry's rate of expansion.

FA   = Fixed Assets (Total tangible fixed assets gross of depreciation.)
TA   = Total Assets (Fixed assets plus current assets.)
N   = Number of Companies

used for all quoted independent companies are calculated from what was then the Board of Trade's 'Income and Finance of Public Quoted Companies'. The growth figures are derived by taking a mean of the year to year percentage change in the aggregate capital values, for each industry group. The growth rate of subsidiaries on the other hand, is an average of the mean growth rate of each individual company in each industry. Justification for this procedure is largely practical. First, to derive an 'all industry' mean based on the performance of individual companies rather than aggregated capital values, would have involved separate calculations for every member firm in each industry. The total number of companies involved would have been in the thousands. Second, the quoted industry mean is effectively an average weighted towards the performance of the largest companies. This is appropriate in the sense that the performance of the most important members of a given industry will tend to be revealed. The growth figures for subsidiaries is not weighted in this way. Each company has equal weight in the calculations. Again this is appropriate. Size measured by capital involvement of a subsidiary, is unlikely to be a useful indicator of its importance within an industry. Parent company backing may belie the impression given by normal size criterion.

Within the limitations of the comparisons and remembering that without strictly comparable data any conclusion is bound to be tentative, it would appear that foreign subsidiaries of all nationalities within the UK, appear to grow at a faster rate than their industrial environment. Explanations for this will presumably centre on the special circumstances created by parent company backing. Proven products, tried management, access to group capital, know-how and research techniques, all of these may well be part of the reason for a commercial performance which is superior to their indigenous counterparts.

A more sophisticated way of establishing the distinctiveness of subsidiaries, is to examine the relationship between achieved mean profit and growth rates. Table 10.2 summarises the results of this exercise. When growth and profitability are correlated a very low level of association is indicated. In statistical terms, the explanatory power of the independent variable is approximately zero. Apparently there is no link between achieved profit rates and achieved growth rates. Even when the calculations are done on the more appropriate Total Assets basis, the conclusion remains the same. It would therefore appear that subsidiaries achieve a performance which is to all intents and purposes independent of their immediate commercial environment. Confidence in this interpretation arises from a comparison with more normal companies. When autonomous concerns rather than subsidiaries are investigated, correlation coefficients of between 0.5 and 0.7 are usually

Table 10.2   Coefficients of correlation of growth and profitability of foreign-owned UK subsidiaries

	All foreign subsidiaries		USA subsidiaries		Other foreign subsidiaries		Quoted subsidiaries	
	N = 245		N = 179		N = 66		N = 33	
	P/TA	P/NA	P/TA	P/NA	P/TA	P/NA	P/TA	P/NA
G on FA	0.014	0.041	0.017	0.048	0.019	0.078	0.010	0.011
G on TA	0.097	0.062	0.038	0.076	0.012	0.000	0.000	0.000

Notes: 1. P/TA = Profitability on Total Assets 1959—66 mean values.
P/NA = Profitability on Net Assets 1959—66 mean values.
2. G on FA = Mean Growth of Fixed Assets 1959—66
G on TA = Mean Growth of Total Assets 1959—66
3. Only companies with three or more years profitability figures are included.

found. A large number of studies using data from different countries, indicate that a relationship of this strength amounts to what may be termed a 'rule' of growth.[53] The low correlations found in the present sample may therefore be taken as evidence that the companies under investigation are unusual. Their peculiarity would appear to arise from their subsidiary status. The normal constraints which apply to ordinary companies do not seem to operate. They are apparently able to secure above average growth rates, without obeying the normal rules of the game. Figures for the regression coefficients have not been presented in Table 10.2. With such low and non-significant correlation coefficients, there can be no confidence in the lines of best fit. If normal correlations of between 0.5 and 0.6 had been achieved for these subsidiaries, the values of the regression coefficients could have been investigated for signs of distinctive performance. For example, the evidence could have been tested for indications that a given average profit rate yields, on average, a higher than normal growth rate. As it is, such an exercise would be fruitless because all the normal commercial relationships would appear to have broken down.

One objection of considerable weight to the evidence from such correlation procedures relates to the dual interpretation put upon the results. The investigators would appear to want their cake and eat it. They appear to be arguing on the one side, that accounting data from subsidiaries are likely to be highly misleading, and then on the other, that the results of correlations can be interpreted at their face value, even when the same suspect data are used in the calculations. This is indeed an objection of considerable weight. Answers to this charge take two forms. First, considerable trouble has been taken in handling the data to avoid obvious pitfalls. The investigators have done their best to ensure that the results are not the product of extreme observations. Artificial constraints have been placed upon the growth rate that individual companies may record in any given year. A limit of 100 per cent has been placed upon the annual expansion rate of individual companies. This to a certain extent meets the problems associated with the effects of take-overs, when only a relatively short run of data is available. Furthermore the correlations have been re-calculated to exclude all the rogue values. This has been done by plotting the values for growth and profitability, and then excluding the observations which are obviously 'wild'. A box procedure has also been adopted, where all the values outside given limits are excluded. In spite of these precautions the correlation coefficients remain consistently and obstinately low.

Second, appeal is made to the frequency and consistency with which correlation coefficients of between 0.5 and 0.7 are normally found. Even with Italian companies, which have valuation problems of a fearsome order, the expected and normal values are found.[54] It therefore seems not unreasonable to conclude that the low r^2 found in this study, represent a real not a shadow effect. This, it is asserted, is a product of subsidiary status. The expectation that parts of companies should behave like their autonomous counterparts, is not verified. Apparently subsidiaries are distinctive and do achieve results which suggest a degree of independence from their immediate economic environment. A convenient name for this phenomenon is the commercial independence effect.

It should be made clear that the effect described above is not necessarily confined to the affiliates of multinational enterprises. In all probability the independence exhibited from the normal association between growth and profitability would also be found in the home subsidiaries of indigenous companies. The scrutiny of affiliates in isolation from their parent organisation is bound to heighten the problems associated with disaggregation. The distinction with the affiliates of foreign companies probably lies in their apparent autonomy. They are physically and legally removed from their parent organisation in the sense that they are located in different nation states, and by the conventions of local procedures, they are required to publish separate accounts. They therefore give the appearance of autonomy, when in fact this may be far removed from the truth. This is a trap for the unwary and many have been snared.[55]

The commercial independence of foreign subsidiaries may have a considerable influence on the diffusion of technology. It is part of the 'package' which foreign direct investment is likely to bring to a host economy. In broad terms, the economic performance of affiliates may not be constrained to that which is typical in the activity concerned. The establishment of a foreign subsidiary is not analogous to the birth of a normal company. Parent company capital, products, management and expertise is available. Success is not immediately dependent on results in the local environment. In effect the launch phase can be expedited. Evidence that this happens should show up as deviant behaviour. In the study of 411 foreign subsidiaries in the UK described above, one form of deviant behaviour has been identified, namely the lack of association between growth and profitability. Amongst the firms in the sample there were four newly-established chemical companies. These recorded very high loss rates, but also achieved very high growth rates. In effect their expansion was undeterred by their apparent failure. Few independent companies could have sustained such a performance; at least this is the inference to be drawn from other studies. Direct inspection of scatter diagrams for normal companies, reveals only one comparable observation in the quadrant where losses combined with growth are recorded.[56] Market penetration and the accumulation of physical capital by these four companies apparently proceeded in complete contravention to normal patterns. Without parent company backing it is almost certain that this could not have happened. The effect of subsidiary status for these four companies was presumably to enable a take-off to viable size to be achieved at a rate that few autonomous companies could have achieved.

In terms of the continuing effects, the inference to be drawn from the low values for r^2 between growth and profitability is that the deviant behaviour is not necessarily confined to the early years. This inference must, however, be cautious. The sample has not been sub-divided by the age of establishment of companies. If this had been done and the correlations recalculated for new comers, and those which are well established, it may have been revealed that the low values could be attributed to the newly located concerns. Certainly there is some support for this contention. The foreign subsidiaries that most closely approximate to indigenous companies would appear to be those which have a quotation on a UK stock exchange. They have a profitability and asset holding pattern which is similar to that of industry in general.[57] Nevertheless it is unlikely that such a neat subdivision would be exhibited by such a procedure. The correlation coefficients are very low and are therefore unlikely to contain many observations for companies which are normal in their behaviour. In addition the age of establishment is unlikely to be a reliable proxy for autonomy. It does not follow that a subsidiary will become independent of the parent company over time. It has been stressed that a major feature of the multinational company is a close organisational interdependence between parents and affiliates. One way in which this may be revealed is in persistent atypical behaviour.

An additional element in commercial independence is the type and character of the market environment relevant to affiliates of a multinational corporation. Local market conditions will not necessarily be a major determinant of the form of competition adopted by subsidiaries. Because they are members of a world-wide group it may be that the flavour of their commercial strategy is determined by the international perspective of their organisation. A plausible case has been argued in Chapter 4 that innovative competition may be fostered by competitive oligopoly. The reasoning hinged on a modification of the vigour of the competitive process to permit adequate appropriation and the avoidance of the lethargy likely to be associated with monopoly. The possible virtues of size are recognized and a 'big firm, few firm' type of competition advocated. Extending the argument, the affiliates of a multinational enterprise may be members of a company which is an international oligopoly and where the prevalent form of rivalry is innovative competition. Under these circumstances, subsidiaries may adopt a form of commercial behaviour which reflects their twin personalities. They may be members of a highly competitive local market, and yet be part of a larger organisation where international oligopoly is prevalent. The result may be that the competitive response by affiliates is less predictable and also that they may be initiators of new forms of commercial rivalry. As part of an international oligopoly they may favour innovative competition. With parent company backing this may be fostered against all the normal auguries. The OECD study in electronic components provides an interesting example of the influence foreign direct investment may have on the character of competition. During the early 1960s, in a relatively short time, the old patterns of moderate competition were completely disrupted. American companies located in Europe radically altered the type and character of the competitive environment. As a result of their entry, innovative competition became prevalent. Technological change became a major factor determining sales, and local companies had to adjust rapidly to changed conditions.[58]

It is plausible to assert that the commercial independence effect has a beneficial influence on the diffusion of technology between nations. The risk reducing influence implied by parent company backing is likely to favour a more aggressive initial marketing effort, and a tolerant attitude to losses. Once the decision has been made to establish a foreign subsidiary in a new country, it would seem reasonable that the time taken to affect this is likely to be short. Market penetration during the early years is likely to be deep and concern for immediate profits not over-riding. If it is assumed that a discovery has been made within a company which is already of multinational status, then the existence of a global network of affiliates is likely to provide a propitious environment for inter-country diffusion.

The technological independence effect

The multinational is capable of reducing the separation of markets. It is thus likely to be important in the diffusion of technology. These companies have a global spread of subsidiaries which are co-ordinated through head-office. Where headquarters are in the technologically advanced nations, this suggests a potential to unify and accelerate the rate of spread of innovations. Adoption rates normally vary between nations. The example of plastics illustrates the wide range of times taken to spread between different countries.[59] However, the foreign subsidiary has a technological capability which is effectively independent of its local environment. Its skill and knowledge base is derived from the parent company, not from the host economy. This is the technological independence effect. Consequently the rate of adoption of innovations is likely to reflect not the attitudes prevalent in overseas locations, but those in head office. Impetus and timing may be dictated by headquarters, and is unlikely to reflect some 'natural' process of diffusion. Knowledge of innovations is unlikely to be much affected by geographical separation from the home environment. Intra-company movement of personnel should reduce knowledge barriers. Percolation of ideas and products will be hustled by fiat, and will not necessarily reflect local market conditions. The rate at which innovations are taken up will probably reflect parent company attitudes, and is likely to be very different from that typical in the host economy. Diffusion rates may therefore approximate to those typical at home. Where this is an advanced industrial nation like the USA, the rate of spread will presumably be faster.

The importance of technological independence to the host economy is considerable. It means in effect that an economy can become an early beneficiary even when it has had no part in the development of the innovation concerned, or even when there is complete ignorance of the relevant technology. This is the power of the transplant. An affiliate which draws its knowledge base from outside its locational boundaries, is not dependent upon local indigenous sources for inspiration. The transferring, producing and applying of an innovation is facilitated because it is being affected within one and the same company. The geographical separation of subsidiaries may have little effect on the rate of spread, and the particular state of local technology may not be an inhibiting influence. The multinational is in a position to transfer innovations quickly. The form and method of transfer may, however, have a considerable bearing on the impact in the host economy. Space must now be taken to describe in further detail the likely effects arising from technological independence in subsidiaries of multinational companies.

A major determinant of the effect of the establishment of subsidiaries in foreign countries is the form of the industrial involvement. It has been assumed throughout this discussion that manufacturing activity is likely to create the greatest impact. This presumption arises from the contrast with other means of transfer. A foreign company can export, it can licence producers, it can locate assembly facilities and it can set up complete production and manufacturing units. The presumption in favour of 'full blown' manufacture arises from the level of involvement of local personnel. Production involves not only familiarity with the article concerned, but also a depth of understanding which extends to the details of manufacture. Technical knowledge is required which is not necessary if the product has merely to be assembled from pre-fabricated parts, or if it has been imported complete and ready for sale through an agent. Operatives have to be trained, and local personnel are likely to become involved in management. Furthermore the effect is not merely confined to the subsidiary itself. Indigenous suppliers may well have to upgrade their technology and standards to meet the requirements of their new customer. Provided the technology gap is not too wide between the giver and receiver, there is likely to be a transfer.[60] This may be embodied in machinery, or disembodied in techniques of production and working. The influence outside the firm concerned and in the host economy in general, can be considerable.

A foreign subsidiary brings with it a technological endowment different from that of its local counterparts. Because its technical heritage is independent of that typical in the host environment, there is likely to be a contrast. Where innovations in the most research intensive areas of technology are transplanted, the knowledge transfer is likely to be forward from the parent company to the subsidiary and into the host economy. However, once the initial effects have worked their way through, it is likely that a two-way flow will be established. For example, a subsidiary may well evolve useful modifications in the products concerned, and or, may establish its own R and D department. Equally it may 'capture' the ideas of local rivals, and repatriate these back to the parent company. One report suggests that this may be a major part of the rational of American companies research effort in Europe.[61] In such cases there is likely to be a backward transfer of knowledge to the home company. In effect it is being argued that manufacturing activity by foreign affiliates is likely to have the greatest impact in the host economy because understanding of techniques of production has to be fundamental, and because local personnel may become involved at all levels in the company hierarchy. In addition it is assumed that local suppliers may well respond to the technological challenge. Full-blown productive activity by a foreign subsidiary also raises the possibility of knowledge generation. Involvement may progress beyond technology usage to technology production. This is most likely when affiliates graduate to a position where research and development becomes part of their activities.

An important feature of technological independence is the cost of knowledge acquisition and transfer. The global company may be effective in both creating and spreading knowledge cheaply. Large size may confer benefits in terms of economies of scale in research. The bargaining power of such companies may reduce payments necessary to become a licensee in particular technologies. Information exchange between firms, patent diplomacy, expertise in handling and marketing proprietary knowledge; these are the types of considerations that may be relevant to the costs of acquiring knowledge. The arguments presented earlier in this book indicate that large size beyond some threshold does not emerge as a crucial prerequisite for success in innovation. Later arguments, however, suggest that if a company is an innovator, then there may be very special benefits associated with multinational status. In particular, prolongation and attenuation has been stressed in preserving the earning power of novel goods. An additional benefit may be an ability to transfer knowledge of new products and processes cheaply between locations. Low cost transfer may help speed the diffusion process.

Cheapness of transfer may arise through low education costs. Knowledge of innovations within the company can be passed by the movement of personnel. 'Person to person' contact is probably the most potent form of knowledge transmission. There is a strong demonstration effect and resistance to change is likely to be overcome most readily by this means. Before innovations can be incorporated into production, a considerable familiarization programme has to be implemented. Personnel in management, production, and sales must be educated. When this is an intra-company activity, it may well be achieved relatively cheaply and quickly. Low costs may arise from the effectiveness of person to person contact as a medium of knowledge transmission, and the possible economies of scale associated with information exchange within a large organisation. Repeat performances of an educational programme amongst subsidiaries may become progressively cheaper, as the individuals concerned become more expert in their role. Speed may be achieved because the transfer is being affected within a single organisation, even though this may be geographically fragmented. Without such organisational unity, the rate of spread is likely to be more leisurely. Outsiders would have to become aware of the relevant innovation. They are unlikely to be helped by the originating company unless there is a licensing arrangement. In other words there may be considerable communication and proprietary barriers to be overcome. These may be aggravated where companies wishing to become adopters are located in different countries. Under these circumstances, geographical separation may have a considerable effect on the rate of diffusion. Differences in technological endowment and physical separation from the source of the innovation, may be elements which help to explain why the spread of technologies between countries has been slow in the past. This would suggest that as the multinational enterprise becomes more prevalent throughout the world, inter-country diffusion will quicken. This seems to be happening.[62]

Analysis of data on the flow of technology suggests that the spread of innovation is increasingly due to direct investment across national boundaries and mainly from the USA to Canada and Europe.[63] If, as seems likely, there is an association between research intensive activities and multinational companies it is then probable that they will speed the diffusion of innovations around the world. This may well be the most impressive characteristic of the global corporation.[64] The more important multinationals become, the quicker and more uniform adoption is likely to be. The enormous investment resources and the international perspective of such companies, is likely to make a considerable impact on the diffusion of innovations. An element in the process, which is part of technological independence, may be the low cost of effecting such transfers.

SOME EXAMPLES

Some examples of the role played by multinational enterprises in the production and spread of innovations may help. The development of what may be termed the oil-refining industry has had enormous ramifications throughout the world. The technology of catalytic cracking was commercialised almost entirely in America.[65] The international diffusion of these techniques has been largely via direct investment. There are, of course, obvious forces inducing a global outlook in this industry. Sources of oil are geographically widespread. Nevertheless foreign refining capacity has tended to be located in the final market, not at the oil fields. Political, security, foreign exchange considerations, as well as market pull influences have played their part in shaping this pattern. The UK government took deliberate steps, begun in 1948, to establish refining capacity in Britain.[66] Other European governments have taken similar action. The effect of oil refining in host economies is enormous. It is difficult to understate its importance. Oil refining provides the raw material base for the petro-chemical industry. Plastics, synthetic rubber, chemical solvents, and man-made fibres are examples of intermediate products which are dependent upon the outputs resulting from oil refining technology. The motor vehicle industry, and shipping and shipbuilding are equally reliant on the products and requirements of this industry. One author has shown that in various important petro-chemicals, direct foreign investment was the major form of technology transfer while the products were in the early stages of their economic life. Later when they became mature, licensing became dominant.[67]

The computer is another area of technology which has been largely developed in America. With the exception of Japan, a major vehicle of diffusion has been direct investment.[68] Computers lie at the very heart of automation. Without the feedback and control mechanisms made possible by electronic data processing, production methods would probably not progress much beyond mechanisation. Automation which implies the control of machines by machines, would be severely limited in its scope and application. In modern industry the computer is all pervasive, and has had an incalculable effect on all advanced economies. The 360 line of computers by IBM is an interesting case study of the role of the multinational enterprise in technology production. This range of computers was developed within what must be one of the most international companies in the world. The research programme was not conducted solely in America, but the European laboratories were integrated into the effort. Particular missions were allocated and thus, for example, the medium-sized machine was designed in England, and the smaller one came from Germany.[69]

Pharmaceuticals are an example of a research intensive activity where the prevalent form of company organisation is the multinational enterprise. The technology is less American dominated than in the industries cited above. The European contribution has been marked.[70] In the sample of companies used in this study, only one that has its major area of activity in pharmaceuticals, is not in the very multinational class (MPE 2). The UK pharmaceutical industry reflects this tendency for organisation on a world-wide basis. A high proportion of the companies are subsidiaries of overseas firms.[71] It does not do violence to the facts to represent this as an international industry. Current R and D is likely to be conducted in firms with a world wide spread of production facilities. Rapid diffusion of findings is therefore almost inevitable. Identifying the raison d'être and separating this from current locational forces is, of course, difficult. However, it is probably true that in this industry, innovation provided the original impetus for world-wide involvement, and that this is being continually reinforced by the type of competition. Fast diffusion of technological knowledge, under these circumstances, can be both an explanation and a by-product of the multinational form of organisation.

A specific case from a different industry will help clarify the arguments. Pilkington Bros. has become a multinational company on the strength of the float glass process. It is reasonable to assert that international involvement is a product of that particular innovation. The company was not really a multinational before the float process was developed. The incentive to go abroad came from the prospects associated with the advanced technology, and its proprietary knowledge. Without the innovation, direct investment overseas is unlikely to have been as large or in so many different locations. Under these circumstances, the raison d'être of global involvement is clear. In essence this company went international on the strength of the float process. The innovation was not made in a company that was already an MPE. Once established, this form of structure can, of course, facilitate the inter-country spread of 'follow-on' and subsequent developments. As innovative competition is not prevalent in this industry it is plausible, however, to assume that subsequent developments would not, on their own, have provided sufficient incentive to go multinational. Their rapid diffusion might therefore be viewed as a by-product and not the raison d'être.

Evidence on the importance of the multinational enterprise in the production of innovations is scarce. Some broad indicators are, however, available based on an analysis of the character of the companies responsible for a sample of innovations in the USA in petroleum, steel, bituminous coal, pharmaceuticals and chemicals. Lists have been compiled giving the identity of firms that first introduced each innovation commercially.[72] Information from Moodies Industrials has been used to determine if the firms concerned had subsidiaries or other productive facilities outside the United States, at the time when the innovations occurred. In other words the geographical scope of operations at the time of the innovations, is under investigation. The results are summarised in Table 10.3.

The author of the table is careful to point out that this attempt to quantify the importance of the innovative role of the multinational is very broad in character. The time span of the table does not go back beyond 1950, and the definition of foreign involvement is not particularly demanding. Thus a single foreign plant would classify a company as having productive facilities outside the United States.[73] In the investigation described in Chapter 8, involvement in more than five different countries is required before a company is classed as MPE 2. In these terms, the entry under bituminous coal preparation would be zero. Other adjustments in the percentage figures would probably also be required to comply with this more strict definition. However, in spite of the comparability problems the table is interesting. It suggests

Table 10.3   Percentage of innovations introduced in the United States by firms with productive facilities outside the United States

Industry	Time Interval	Percentage
Iron and steel	1950–58	51
Bituminous coal preparation	1950–58	33*
Petroleum	1950–58	85
Pharmaceutical	1950–62	94
Chemicals	1960–69	100

In the case of the pharmaceutical innovations, only the 20 most important innovations during 1950–62 were included. See Mansfield, Rapoport, Schnee, Wagner, and Hamburger, *op. cit.*

* This percentage is non-zero due entirely to the fact that a single firm, which carried out 33 percent of the innovations, was owned by another firm with a very small proportion of its productive facilities in Canada.

Source. E. Mansfield. 'The Multinational Firm and Technological Change', in J. H. Dunning (Editor) *Economic Analysis and the Multinational Enterprise*. Allen & Unwin 1973.

that where innovation is an inherent part of an industrial activity, the companies concerned are likely to have overseas involvement. The industrial groupings petroleum, pharmaceuticals and chemicals, all come within the research intensive definition described in Chapter 8. The percentage of firms with productive facilities outside the United States would appear to be markedly higher in these areas, than in the more prosaic activities of bituminous coal preparation and iron and steel. Caution is appropriate, nevertheless the findings are perhaps indicative. At least they do not deny the general tenor of the arguments advanced here.

Structural alignment

The direct investment package may be an important unifying influence amongst economies. One manifestation of the power of the multinational enterprise as an agent in the diffusion process, may be a degree of alignment of the industrial structures of advanced nations. There is certainly a suggestion that this may have occurred.

The multinational company may be an influence inducing a parity of industrial structures between leading nations. Direct investment between countries and cross penetration indicates that there may be a convergence of industrial structures and trading patterns. The predominance of US multinationals amongst the world's largest companies would suggest that there is likely to be an alignment towards the American pattern. There appears to have been such a convergence, at least in terms of the structure of European net exports over the ten

year period 1955 to 1965.[74] Net exports are defined as exports of
Europe minus imports from the USA. There has been an increase in the
net exports of high research intensive products amongst nearly all
European countries, and a fall in the share of low research intensive
products.[75] The convergence of net exports towards the American
pattern carries with it the implication of a corresponding movement
towards parity of the underlying industrial structures. This will
presumably reflect the influence of direct investment by US
multinationals in Europe, and the challenge and response of local
companies in closing 'technology gaps'.

A complicating factor in the pattern of trade may be a restricted
import and export franchise imposed on foreign affiliates. In effect the
pattern of trade may be dictated from outside the host economy.
Export markets may be designated to protect other subsidiaries and/or
parent company interests. Similarly imports may be dictated by
considerations relevant to the multinational concerned, and not the
recipient economy. Evidence of these types of restrictions is limited.
There are suggestions, however, that they may be relevant to
Australia.[76] Canada is another possible candidate.[77] Figures of
American exports are pertinent. Thus for example 25 per cent of all US
exports are shipped within or to the subsidiaries of American-owned
international corporations.[78] Multinationals are in a position to dictate
the type and destination of trade to and from their affiliates. Europe is
clearly not beyond the reach of such arrangements.

The mechanism of convergence between countries is likely to be
complex. Means by which technology is transferred across national
boundaries will include licensing, joint ventures, movement of
personnel with the required know-how, emulation and direct
transplants via subsidiaries of foreign companies. The signals inducing
the closure of 'technology gaps' will include the profitability of the new
areas of activity, and the decline in earning capacity in competing but
outmoded rival products. It has been established in Chapter 6 that
within a nation, a major influence in the diffusion of new products and
processes is profitability. Between nations profitability is almost
inevitably of equal importance. A new factor, however, when
technology spreads between countries, is the multinational producing
enterprise. Conventional diffusion models do not find that the
particular type of company is a major influence on the rate of
adoption. When the approach is broadened to cover technology transfer
between nations, this is no longer the case. The type of company
becomes important. Attention is drawn to the role of the MPE in the
spread of technology.

The finding indicated in 24 (page 190) above that there would
appear to be a decrease in the lag in establishing US subsidiaries in

Europe, is not based on a study of the time elapsed before overseas manufacture is undertaken. It is an interpretation of the evidence that suggests technology gaps are closing.[79] The alignment of net exports towards the American pattern, indicates European involvement in areas of activity which were previously a US preserve. Part of this convergence has been induced by direct investment in Europe and part by the reaction induced amongst locals. It is believed, however, that perhaps the major part of the movement towards parity has been due to the American investment.[80] The reaction of indigenous producers is thought, with the possible exception of the UK,[81] to have played a relatively minor role.

A bonus which foreign direct investment may bring to the host economy, is a 'footloose' attitude towards location. Affiliates of overseas companies are likely to be less inhibited by location away from the main industrial centres in their new environment. Governments are likely to find that they are relatively easy to attract to special areas designated as in need of industry. The centre of gravity for a subsidiary is unlikely to be the same as that for a home company. They are often so far removed from their parent organisation, that location 'in the sticks' may well make very little difference. Where high value added goods are produced, long distance transport to the industrial centres, is unlikely to upset the profit arithmetic. The importance of US electronics firms in Scotland is a case in point. Local activity has benefited considerably.[82]

This study has indicated the relative scarcity of research intensive companies which are merely national in status, and the tendency for companies in prosaic activities not to be global. Apparently firms which are involved in knowledge generating activities tend to locate around the world. Their locational pattern is bound to have an influence on the industrial structure of recipient countries, and is also likely to affect the speed of access of a host economy to innovations which are channelled through their foreign affiliates. The presumption is that the MPE is a unifying influence causing and inducing an alignment of industrial structures, and a reduction in differences in the speed at which technologies are diffused between nations.

Conclusion

The presumption in favour of the direct foreign investment package as a most powerful agent of diffusion arises by contrast with other mechanisms of transmission. One author has listed ten channels for the international transfer of technology.[83] These are: trade in producer and consumer goods; purchase of specialised services; personal contacts; technical assistance and joint production agreements; the presence of foreign military troops in a country; involuntary leakage of technological information; observation and imitation; licensing agreements; joint ventures; and the multinational firm. With the exception of a military presence, the major advantage possessed by the multinational is that it can incorporate most of these mechanisms of transfer within its ambit. The establishment of manufacturing activity by a foreign company will inevitably involve practically all of these transfer agents. The MPE can function as a producer, an innovator and a vehicle of diffusion. The unique properties of the package summarised by commercial and technological independence, structural alignment, and the multiplier effects on rival and other organisations, suggest that the global corporation is a most effective agent of transmission. Ally these arguments to those which indicate that the multinational enterprise is likely to be involved in innovative activities, and the case becomes stronger. They are not merely good transmitters, but they are apparently also involved in activities where the production of new knowledge is occurring at a fast rate. It is the combination of the ability to transfer and involvement in activities where knowledge generation is rapid, that strengthens the case so much. It transforms the arguments from those which suggest that the MPE is a most important agent in the diffusion of technology, to those which assert that this structural form of company organisation, is the most important of all the mechanisms, when transfer between nations is under scrutiny.

In terms of the direct investment package, a major benefit to the host economy is likely to be an earlier involvement in advanced technologies, than may otherwise have occurred. This does not imply that particular nations will suffer if they exclude foreign direct investment as part of their economic strategy. For example, it is difficult to argue that Japan has slowed its rate of advance by the virtual exclusion of foreign subsidiaries.[84] Nevertheless this conclusion draws attention to the possible risks involved in not admitting foreign companies. It may, and probably does, imply a larger indigenous effort to acquire and generate know-how. It also implies a presumption that local personnel are capable of closing any technological gaps. Furthermore it has not been the purpose of this discussion to emphasise the possible disadvantages associated with foreign direct investment. The balance sheet summarising the costs and benefits of a liberal attitude towards foreign companies may not be particularly favourable. However, if attention is focused on the multinational as an agent in the diffusion of technology, then the signs are that this is an instrument of exceptional power. Economies that deliberately exclude the direct investment package, may do so at a cost which is highly pertinent to their economic development.

The arguments that indicate the importance of the multinational enterprise in the diffusion of technology suffer from a major weakness. This is a lack of empirical backing. There is limited evidence to validate this type of reasoning. The suggestion that the global corporation is an exceptionally powerful means to spread technology is highly plausible. Data that indicate what effect may occur in terms of the speed, cost, type and location of transfers under the influence of the MPE, are distinctly lacking. Observers are aware that they have identified an important influence on the world-wide spread of technology. However, the transformation from plausible assertion to confident statement, awaits the results of further research. There is fragmentary evidence that the rate of the international diffusion of technology is increasing. It is believed that an important part of this quickening transfer is the multinational enterprise.[85] Specific examples which identify the global corporation as responsible, are scarce. One case study based on semi-conductors is, however, indicative. It finds that of the major innovations in semi-conductors in the 1960s, American subsidiaries were the first to produce about 1/3 of them in Britain, and about 1/5 of them in France.[86] The inference to be drawn is that the presence of these foreign affiliates hastened the usage of the innovations. Note, however, that this is only an inference, and furthermore that this presumes in favour of the MPE. The unique properties of the direct investment package make such a conclusion plausible, but strictly do not establish this at an empirical level.

The present study has attempted to add evidence to the arguments indicating a link between innovative activities and the multinational enterprise. The findings indicate that such a hypothesis is not denied. The underlying theory based on imperfect competition, as exemplified by proprietary knowledge, and a desire for market penetration based on foreign direct investment, apparently yields a prediction that is not at variance with the real world. The special properties of the package indicate how such companies may affect the spread of knowledge in a host economy. As users and producers, the global enterprise is likely to be the most powerful agent in the diffusion of technology. The evidence presented here suggests that such a presumption may be well grounded.

Patents

11

Invention produces knowledge. Knowledge has a number of awkward properties which make it difficult to handle within conventional economic theory. Knowledge tends to have substantial external economies. Benefits may accrue over a wide area. Inventors' profits and royalties may be far outweighed by the benefit to society.[1] Knowledge is also difficult to transform into economic benefit.[2] An inventor has a considerable appropriation problem. Rivals may copy his invention. The costs of copying are likely to be very much lower than those of invention, so the originator is likely to be undersold by his rivals. If the invention is sold not as a product but as a piece of knowhow, or as pure knowledge, the seller is faced with a number of dilemmas: his commodity for sale is largely indivisible, the purchaser has no idea of its economic worth, and once sold the knowledge can never be returned to the seller. The seller of knowledge cannot usually sell a part of his idea to a buyer. In this sense knowledge is indivisible. The buyer cannot release a small portion of his idea. An idea is an entity which is normally not susceptible to fragmentation. Once split up it will not amount to the idea and therefore be largely worthless. The purchaser of knowledge is in an awkward position. He does not know the details of the item he is going to purchase and so cannot judge its economic worth. Without being able to assess the value of the knowledge his bid price has to be a hunch. Without firm information on the value of the idea, the price paid will not be guided by economic considerations. If the seller were to reveal his knowledge so that the buyer could make a more informed bid the result would be just the opposite. The buyer would have received his information free and so would revise his price to zero or some trivial sum. The seller could not then retrieve the information because it would have been absorbed by the acquirer. In this sense his property would be lost forever.

These awkward properties of knowledge make it difficult to handle within conventional economic theory. The marketing of knowledge is not the rational interplay of demand and supply factors, with buyers and sellers acting in an informed manner. Rather the picture is that of a game strategic situation, where bluff and counterbluff are demand and supply, and the price a matter of luck. Once knowledge has passed from the originator then marginal cost criterion would indicate that the price paid for the knowledge should be zero or close to zero. Unlike a normal economic good the acquisition of such knowledge does not diminish its stock. The marginal cost of the transfer of knowledge will therefore not be determined by production costs but merely by the costs involved with the distribution. These will typically be postage, paper and secretarial time, and will be small. This has resulted in the conclusion that the optimal price for the distribution of knowledge should be zero, or close to zero. This prescription, based on the proposition that knowledge is expensive to produce but cheap to copy is not adopted in practice because of the likely effects on the generation of new knowledge. Zero cost transfer of existing knowledge would be an optimum pricing policy in a static world where no further new knowledge would be forthcoming. In a dynamic world where new knowledge is generated and incorporated into the production process, a deliberate attempt is made to raise the incentive to invent. This is the major role of patents.

Patents counter a number of the awkward properties of knowledge. By conferring a legally enforceable period of monopoly upon the inventor, knowledge becomes a commodity capable of being marketed in the normal fashion. Rivals are debarred from infringement. Alternatively they may be licensed as producers. The ideas embodied in the patent are now in a sense recoverable. A rival cannot turn these to his economic advantage without risking legal action. The damage to the inventor of disclosing his idea is greatly reduced. As a result the incentive to generate new knowledge is raised. The originator is in a position to benefit through the sale of his commodity.

The general procedure to acquire a patent in the UK is outlined here and where this differs in major respect from practice elsewhere this will be indicated. It is important to have some idea of the process involved in order to appreciate the limitations of a patent. A patent does not confer an unconditional monopoly. There are a whole series of requirements which must be satisfied before a patent is granted. Even after a patent is acquired the holder is not free from obligation. He must comply with a number of conditions to avoid modification or revocation. The law defines and circumscribes patents and therefore has considerable influence on their economic importance.

The stages involved in acquiring a patent under the UK system are as follows:

Application

Application for a patent involves the submission of a specification. A provisional specification may be submitted to be followed by a complete specification within twelve months. This procedure is unique to the UK. Other countries do not allow this interim period during which the inventor may clarify the exact nature and coverage of his application. The date of application is important in establishing an inventor's claim to be first in the field. The 'priority' date is not the time when the idea is formulated into an invention but the date of first application for a patent. Thus it is no defence for an applicant to claim that he thought of the idea first. This is not the case in the United States, where rules and procedures are adopted to establish who is the first inventor in time, and not the first to establish priority by application.

Before applying, the inventor will normally have employed the services of a patent agent. This expert will advise his client on the requirements to be met to acquire a patent and will normally draft the application. An invention to be submitted for a patent must be tangible and useful. Thus a new scientific principle, even of major importance, may not be patentable. An abstract idea must be incorporated into a tangible produce or process to be eligible for a patent. An invention must be new, not be obvious and must not have been subject to prior publication claim or use. Furthermore any patent granted must be to the 'true and first' inventor or his assignee. These requirements will be explained below.

Examination

The Patent Office examiners conduct an official search. In the UK this occurs after the receipt of the complete specification. The search is intended to establish that the claim is within the scope of the relevant patent laws, that only one invention is covered, that the specification is clear and unambiguous, and that the invention has not appeared in an earlier publication or earlier specification. The last two areas of examination are called prior publication and prior claim. The examination does not attempt to establish the utility of an invention. No assessment is made of technological feasibility, and the novelty of an invention is not judged in terms of the size of the inventive step, but on the technical grounds of first publication. Novelty in this sense is no prior publication nor prior claim, not the degree of newness. In the UK the search is usually confined to British Patent Specifications which are not more than fifty years old. The coverage may widen to foreign specifications and technical literature where appropriate, but does not normally do so. The inventor's claim will be disallowed if a single document anticipates his idea. A large number of publications which aggregate to his idea will not cause refusal. If the application conforms to the examination requirements it is 'accepted'. Acceptance does not mean that a patent has been granted. It merely means that the application has not been rejected.

Practice varies between countries on the purpose and thoroughness of searches. Some countries have no search for novelty. France is an example. In this case submissions are examined to establish that they cover a single invention and that they comply to the required form. Some countries have an exhaustive search to establish novelty; West Germany and the USA are examples. In the USA searches include foreign patents and all relevant technical literature. The different approaches of various countries may be conveniently summarised by contrasting a registration and an examination system. A strict registration system does not involve a search to establish the novelty of an application. Instead it is assumed that a patent will be tested at law after it has been granted. This will be achieved as a result of objections. The vigilance of third parties, together with the checks and balances of the patent law it is assumed, will ensure that only valid patents survive. In contrast the approach adopted by an examination system has a different emphasis. Greater reliance is placed on the official search to establish validity. An application is subjected to a wide range of thorough screening processes. This normally ensures that if a patent is granted it will prove valid. However under both types of system the ultimate test of a patent is at law. The mere possession of a patent is no guarantee of its validity. This will depend on successful defence against the claims of objectors.

Publication

It is at this stage that the general public usually become aware that a patent may be granted for the invention concerned. A list of titles of applications are published in the *Official Journal* (*Patents*). These relate to provisional or complete specifications. Publication of the contents is confined to complete specifications and these are on sale at the Patent Office or at certain provincial libraries. They do not appear in the *Patent Journal.* Abridgements or summaries of all complete specifications are published as a divisional volume of the Patent Office. A number of countries do not give information about patent applications. The official journals or gazettes are confined to the reporting of patents that have been granted. The USA and West Germany are examples. These two countries adopt an examination system in vetting applications. Their system is not dependent on alerting public attention to the existence of patent applications. They express reliance in the thoroughness of their investigations by reporting only patents granted.

Oppositions

Following publication the granting of a patent may be resisted by interested parties. Opposition may occur before the patent has been granted or sealed. Opposition may also occur within a year after sealing. In the latter case it is known as 'belated opposition'. Actions to revoke a patent occur after the period for belated oppositions. As will be explained below revocation proceedings have wider grounds than those available to oppositions. Revocation proceedings are the final test through which a patent has to pass in order to establish validity. At the opposition stage, grounds include prior publication and prior claim already mentioned, obtaining, prior user, obviousness, insufficiency and 'not an invention'. Obtaining refers to the possibility that the invention may have been obtained from the original inventor. The law is concerned that the applicant or holder of a patent should be the 'first and true' inventor or his assignee. Prior user amounts to public use of the invention by the patentee or applicant or anyone else; secret use or private experiment is not included. Obviousness relates to the inventive step involved. There must be a step forward for there to be a defence against obviousness. Insufficiency relates to the quality of the complete specification. Disclosure of the contents of an invention must be sufficient. The specification must describe the invention in a full and fair manner. An opposition based on 'not an invention' would attempt to show that the patent or patent application does not come within a definition of invention. The definition has to be implied from what is patentable. This has to be inferred from the tests applied by the patent granting authorities, and from the courts and from case law.
exclusions applied by various countries. In the UK there is no unified definition of invention, and definition has to be implied from what is patentable. This has to be inferred from the tests applied by the patent granting authorities, and from the courts and from case law.

In the British system tests used to revoke a patent are wider in scope than those used to oppose an application. A very small percentage of patents are challenged at this stage where the complete range of tests is applied. As a result the full definition of invention implied by the law is rarely put into effect. This has led to the conclusion that the operative definition of invention does not in fact include inventiveness or utility.[3] A sharp distinction should be drawn between patentability and invention. Patentability is defined by the tests applied by the patent office in accepting patents. Invention is only fully tested when there is an action to revoke a patent. It is only at this final stage that the full rigour and range of tests are used and thus it is only here that the entire definition emerges.

Sealing

Within four months of acceptance the inventor must apply for his patent to be sealed. Sealing represents the official granting of a patent. Until an application is sealed there is no patent. In the vast majority of cases there are no objections and so an accepted application proceeds to sealing. In the USA, as already pointed out, the *Patent Gazette* gives information on patents granted and not patent applications. There is no time lag for oppositions. It is assumed that the search is a sufficient test and so the patent pending procedure is not adopted. The granting of a patent is not of course a guarantee of validity. The patent may still be challenged at any time during its life.

Renewal

The patent rights conferred are limited in the first instance to four years. The time period runs from the filing date of the complete specification at the Patent Office. After four years have expired the holder has to renew his patent annually. British patents remain valid and in force only if the renewal fee continues to be paid. This renewal fee rises in amount from £6 in the sixth year to £30 in the sixteenth year. The total payment of renewal fees amounts to £216 and the total including application, filing and sealing comes to £230.[4] The majority of countries adopt an annual renewal procedure. Not all of these, however, use a rising scale of fee. Major examples where a graduated renewal scheme is used are the UK, Switzerland, the Netherlands and Germany. In the USA there is neither a rising scale nor an annual renewal fee. Once a patent is granted and the official fees paid there is no further financial obligation.

Obligations and limitations

The major conditions to acquire a patent thus emerge as: application in the proper form involving appropriate timing and disclosure of sufficient information, the meeting of oppositions and the payment of fees. Once acquired the holder of a patent is not free from obligation.

Renewal fees must be paid. The patent must be 'worked'. It is a requirement of British patent law that the patent be worked within three years from the sealing date. The majority of countries require that a patent be worked. Non-working means that the item described by the specification is not produced for sale, or is not being worked to the fullest extent reasonably practical. The Comptroller of Patents has the power to ensure that the public interest does not suffer unduly from a patent monopoly. There are wide grounds by which the power of a patent holder may be limited. These are largely aimed at preventing abuse of monopoly power. A patent may be compulsorily licensed. The state may make use of the invention for its own purposes. Reference may be made to the Monopolies Commission, and a patent may be endorsed 'licence of right'. An interested party or a government department may petition the Comptroller that a compulsory licence or a compulsory licence of right be granted. A licence of right is normally a voluntary arrangement whereby the holder allows his patent to be endorsed in this way so that anybody who wants to take out a licence can do so as of right. The major advantages of a voluntary endorsement licence of right to the patent holder are a halving of renewal fees and a reduction in the likelihood of litigation on abuse of monopoly grounds. In specified circumstances this limitation of a patent holder's monopoly position may be compulsorily enforced upon him. This is the compulsory licence of right. The United States is a major exception to most of the above provisions. There is no requirement that a patent be worked and there is no system of renewal. In addition there is no general compulsory licence procedure. A patent may be compulsorily licensed, but this will only arise out of an Anti-Trust case.

Numerically and as proportion of patents sealed, the use of compulsory licences and licence of right provisions is small. It would be misleading, however, to conclude that these procedures are unimportant. Patents vary greatly in their quality and usefulness. One exceptional patent which is compulsorily licensed or endorsed licence of right may have great economic impact. Furthermore, the existence of the procedures may have the effect of forestalling any undue monopoly exploitations. The possibility of their use may be sufficient to induce responsible economic behaviour. The numbers of patents compulsorily licensed and endorsed licence of right therefore will not measure the full extent of the influence of the provisions.

Patents are a legal device to protect an inventor, but they only protect knowledge to the extent that it is embodied in a tangible item which is patentable. If it conforms with the requirements of the patent law then that knowledge incorporated in a product is protected. The greatest inventions may in fact involve the discovery of fundamental principles. Until these are incorporated into a product or process no legal protection is available except to the extent that they may relate to the law of trade secrets, trade marks and copyright. The patent law confines itself to tangible items on practical grounds. Surveillance of the use of an abstract principle would be virtually impossible, whereas use of a product or process is much easier to establish as a question of law. Furthermore, restriction on the use of a principle may dull the incentive to search for improvements. Patents are therefore a compromise. They protect the use of a thing rather than the knowledge involved. In this way the inventor has a marketable commodity but at the same time the knowledge may be used by others in the search for improvements. If this search is successful the law allows the discoverer of the improved use to take out a 'selection' patent. If patent protection were complete a rival would risk legal action if he experimented. As it is 'patents were never granted to prevent persons of ingenuity exercising their talents in a fair way'.[5] The law recognises the likelihood of technological change and the interdependence of knowledge. Knowledge is a product of invention and also an input for further invention. To constrain this input may be to stifle change.

Incentive to invent

Without a patent an inventor would have to protect his discovery by being the sole producer. Such a monopoly may be achieved by barriers to entry of rival producers. These barriers may include the complexity of the manufacturing process, the sheer size of the investment required before production is possible, the market power of the inventing firm, and secrecy of the process involved in the invention. In practice it is unlikely that the inventor will be lucky enough to have these factors operating in his favour. An invention is not necessarily complex. Secrecy may not be possible. The invention may be well within the technological knowledge of rivals. The inventor may be a lone individual with no economic power. He may not be in a position to exploit his ideas. In these circumstances his invention would be thrown on the wind once it became public knowledge. Any economic advantage would be annexed by rivals almost before the inventor could benefit. A patent removes the necessity of the fortuitous set of circumstances set out above applying before an inventor can benefit. The inventor need no longer be involved with the production and marketing of his discovery. Now he has a negotiable instrument. The law protects him from infringement by rivals and so he may sell his product, or license producers. The inventor may not be a good businessman. Without patent protection he would be forced to enter business to benefit from his ingenuity. Now he may sell or license his patent. In this way his abilities need not be taken up in running a business. Instead he may concentrate on exercising his mind to further discoveries.

By offering the inventor the possibility of a monopoly the potential return to invention is raised. This ought to raise the incentive to invent. Appropriation of the benefit of invention should be improved because rivals are expressly debarred from infringement. The basic theory lying behind the argument is thus demand orientated. It is assumed that men of ingenuity will respond if their potential rewards are greater. The emphasis is not on reducing the cost of invention, rather demand is seen as the key to the incentive to invent. The economic logic of the patent law is essentially that the price mechanism is inefficient at generating new knowledge. Special help is required so that an inventor may benefit from his brilliance. Rivals need to be discouraged from emulating his invention and appropriating the benefits for themselves. The fixed cost involved in bringing an invention to a marketable stage tends to mean that new products have increasing returns to scale. Rivals will almost always be able to undercut the originator because they do not have these fixed costs to carry. The economic logic of the patent law therefore turns on raising the potential returns to invention by mitigating the competitive powers of the market mechanism and by improving the ability of the inventor to appropriate the benefits of his ingenuity. By offering him a monopoly the destructive effect of rivals' reaction is largely eliminated.

A further strand in the economic logic of patents relates to the diffusion of knowledge. The granting of a patent involves disclosure of the principles of an invention. In jargon terms, modification of competition internalises the benefits of invention, raises the incentive to invent and accelerates the diffusion of knowledge. Patents are a piece of social engineering which deliberately support monopoly at the expense of competition on the grounds that the benefits to the community of improving the potential flow of new knowledge, outweigh the misallocation effects associated with deliberately creating market imperfections.

Effectiveness of patents

A patent is an exchange. An inventor receives a legally enforceable period of protection. In exchange for this he must disclose the principles of his discovery so that it becomes public knowledge and complies with the requirements of the patent law. He is induced to disclose by the prospect of a monopoly. Society will gain where the costs of monopoly are outweighed by the benefits of the discovery. The benefits to society show themselves as an increase in the stock of technological knowledge and a quickening of its diffusion. The discovery will however be no gain to society, in terms of assessing the effectiveness of patents, if it would have been made anyway. It is only those inventions which are induced by the patent system and which otherwise would not have occurred which may be included in the economic arithmetic.[6] This is important. If all discoveries arose spontaneously and were not influenced by the prospect of legal protection the case for patents would be considerably weakened. This statement however requires some sophistication. Even if all discoveries arose spontaneously and were unaffected by patent protection, the bias towards disclosure which the system gives may affect the rate of discovery. In a technological community it is not merely the act of discovery which is important but the rate at which discoveries are made. The timing of discoveries may be heavily influenced by the availability of knowledge embodied in patents, and so even if patents make no difference to the numbers of discoveries but only influence their timing this would be a sufficient economic case to justify the system. Thus the proposition that only those discoveries which are induced by the patent system are relevant in its assessment, needs modifying to take account of the effect on the rate of discovery. It is hoped of course that the patent system affects both the actual amount of discovery and its timing. Evidence on this is not however available. Judgment of what might happen in the absence of patents is clearly hazardous. Patents have a long historical standing and are deeply woven into the fabric of industrial nations. There have been many prestigious committees of investigation, but no major nation has dared to abandon the system. The continued existence of patents is not, of course, an unequivocal sign that they are beneficial to society, merely that their deficiencies are so difficult to assess that caution dictates no radical action.

The life of patents

Patents are intended to raise the supply of inventive output, but like any practical instrument of policy it is difficult to match the general provisions with detailed requirements. Patents exchange legal protection over a defined period for disclosure of the details of the invention. The period of protection is normally constant and not related to particular inventions, and disclosure must be adequate in terms of the requirements of the patent administrators. The period of protection is inevitably a compromise. Patentable inventions vary in importance from the trivial to the dramatically important, and yet with the majority of countries no distinction is made in the period of legal protection granted. West Germany is an exception. A short-term patent is granted for items showing novel design or construction. These are largely in the category of mechanical contrivances and are called *Gebrauchsmuster*. The life of these petty patents is three years as opposed to the eighteen-year period for a full patent.

Theoretically it would be possible to adjust the life of a patent to the quality of the invention concerned, but if this were undertaken adjustment is not necessarily the obvious one. An invention of major importance does not necessarily warrant a longer period of protection, nor does a minor invention necessarily imply a shorter period. The factors relevant to the decision are the importance of the invention, the speed at which it yields its advantages, and the complexity and length of the development stage. If a major invention yields its advantages quickly and has ready market acceptance, then a shorter than average period of patent protection is appropriate. The inventor is able to recoup his expenses fast and earn an adequate rate of return. In these circumstances a long period of protection would be harmful to society. The misallocation effects would soon begin to outweigh the benefits of the invention. It has been calculated that for a process innovation which reduces costs by approximately 10 per cent, the optimum life of a patent ranges between three and seven years for demand elasticity of 0.7 to 4.0.[7] If the process innovation has a less dramatic effect on costs and savings are in the region of 1 per cent and are realised slowly, then a longer period of patent protection is appropriate where elasticity of demand is less or equal to 1. In these circumstances an optimal patent life would range between fifteen and twenty years. Again, if an invention has a lengthy and complex development period before a marketable product is available a long period of protection may be appropriate. Clearly it would have to be a highly sophisticated patent administration to adjust the period of legal protection to the economic characteristics of inventions. The assessors would require considerable technical knowledge of the industries concerned, be blessed with economic foresight, and also in the event of an error of judgment have powers to vary the original terms. All this would be expensive and not necessarily worth while, for reasons outlined below.

It is plausible to assert that the actual life of a patent is only crucial to a relatively small number of inventions. The majority of patents succumb to economic obsolescence. The survival figures for patents indicate that only a small percentage continue in existence for their full term. For example, in countries where the holder has to renew his patent, typically only 50 per cent last more than six years and only 10 per cent survive to their final year.[8] The majority of patents thus appear to suffer from economic senescence. Developments in technology render them economically useless. For these patents the debate on the optimal period of protection is somewhat academic. The figures perhaps add weight to a general conclusion that a shorter period of legal protection may be appropriate as so few patents survive to their full term. However, these survival percentage figures must not be overused as an argument against the importance of the life of patents. The patents that do survive their full life may not be very important in percentage terms but nevertheless their economic impact may be large. There are such enormous quality differences in patents that numerical arguments are dangerous. Another reason why the period of protection may be important is the impetus it may give to rivals' technological effort. A long period of legal protection may induce inventive effort to sidestep a patent. If the life of a patent had been much shorter, the rival might have been content to wait for the expiry date. Patents and the period of protection may therefore have a direct influence on the character of commercial rivalry. Innovative competition may be stimulated by the desire to acquire patents and also as a response to the length of the life of existing patents.

These arguments throw the problem of the life of a patent into some relief. The balance of arguments probably support a shortening of the period of protection from the fifteen to eighteen year period which is typical in most systems. Important cost-saving inventions are capable of earning handsome returns even within a short period of protection. Minor improvements which may justify a longer period of protection, where elasticity of demand is low, may in fact succumb to economic obsolescence fairly quickly. In this case they will join the ranks of paper monopolies. In practice it may be the case that patent protection is largely unnecessary for the majority of inventions. It has been found that for seven major process innovations in the United States the imitation period defined as the period between first use and use by 60 per cent of the producers varied from one year to twenty years.[9] The majority of these innovations would have allowed the inventor at least four years before 60 per cent of the producers had adopted his process. This may well have been long enough for him to have benefited handsomely without legal protection.

The argument that imitation rates are in practice slow and therefore make legal protection largely unnecessary does however overlook two important points. These are the expectational effects and the optimism of inventors. It is the state of mind of inventors at the planning stage which is important. So long as individuals and companies believe that patents will give them economic protection this is all that matters. It is the expectational *ex ante* incentive effect of patents which is crucial. If they believe that imitation will be fast then they will seek patent protection. Without the prospect of patent protection to delay imitation, the inventive effort may not be forthcoming. The fact that imitation turns out to be slow does not make any difference. At the time of the decision to commit funds to inventive effort, patents may represent a form of insurance which inventors use to cover their activities. This is likely to be particularly important to the private individual who does not have the economic power to muster resources quickly to take advantage of any discoveries. In this instance, patents may give him the confidence and also the time necessary to become an entrepreneur. In addition the more important an inventor believes his idea to be, the more anxious will he be to secure patent protection. The rate of imitation is linked to the profitability of an innovation.[10] An optimistic inventor believing his idea to be highly commercial will therefore be anxious to secure a patent. In this way he will hope to damp the amount of market encroachment. Furthermore the prospect of a glittering economic prize may sustain the occasional genius in his development of a spectacular invention. Similarly a company may be induced to take a much higher level of risk in its R and D programme by the knowledge that there may be extremely high rewards to be achieved through patenting its discoveries. Again this is the expectational effect. It may be that for the majority of inventions, patents turn out to be of little value. But for the occasional discovery of major significance patents may be crucial. The lone inventor who is sustained in a life long effort, or the company that carries on despite prolonged frustration, these may be examples where the prospect of a patent provides a very real incentive. The occasional but sparkling discovery of this character may provide the major case for patents.

Disadvantages of patents

Any legal system which does not dovetail its rules to varying circumstances is bound to suffer from a number of disadvantages. The problem of reform is to minimise these and at the same time preserve the major rational. The central justification for patents is the incentive effect. This must remain but the side effects and by-products of the system must be kept under review so that they do not overwhelm the major purpose. The patent system has a number of major weaknesses. A patent is capable of being misused, especially if it is held by a wealthy company. It may be used as a means to suppress technological advance in a particular area. A company may build up a patent position whereby a large number of patents is acquired either through direct research and development or through acquisition of companies. The resultant position may be so complex and formidable that rivals are deterred. Particular patents may be of little value but the cumulative effect of a large number may add up to a formidable legal barrier to rivals already in the field or considering entry. As a result competitors may not attempt to innovate around the dominant company's advantage and innovative competition may therefore be frustrated. There are examples of this happening in a number of industries which include cellophane, plastics, radio, telecommunications, data processing equipment and electric lamps.[11] The dominant company may protect itself not by economic or innovative excellence but by the device of the patent position. In these circumstances the pace of technological change in such industries becomes dependent on the sole efforts of the major company. The resultant pace of change may be slower. This company might also take deliberate steps to slow down the pace of innovation. It may suppress its own inventions or block others. Innovations which are inconvenient in terms of accepted technology and which may involve a great upheaval in present production methods may be put to one side. Another company or individual which may succeed in acquiring a patent may be so hounded by the threat of litigation that any attempt to put the invention into production may be abandoned. The threat of litigation is real. Legal expenses can be extremely high. Ultimately a patent is only a protection if its holder is prepared to enforce it by taking legal action. The state does not take action on behalf of patent holders. The onus is on the individual to defend his rights. This can become something of a lottery. A patent is not an absolute right to legal protection. It is conditional on the holder being prepared to take legal action to defend his rights and may therefore be represented as merely 'a licence to sue'.[12] An individual or small company facing a large corporation would clearly be at a disadvantage. Without the depth of pocket of a large company, a patent may be infringed and no action follow. Litigation can be so expensive and the outcome so unpredictable that in these circumstances the practicalities of finance may overcome the niceties of justice.

Table 11.1 suggests that patenting tends to increase with firm size.[13] Interpretation of this tendency must be cautious. It may indicate increased innovative activity amongst large firms or a higher propensity to patent. In the present context, the greater use of patents by large companies may represent the advantage that sizeable concerns have in the acquisition and defence of patents.

A patent may offer the holder too much protection. For example from 1956 to mid-1960 Pfizer were able to sell tetracycline at a wholesale price of $30.60 per bottle of 100 capsules. Production costs ranged between $1.60 to $3.80 per bottle. When competitors ventured into the field encouraged by doubts about the validity of the patent, they sold the article for approximately $2.50 per bottle.[14] As already

Table 11.1   Size distribution of firms patenting and not patenting

Net assets £ million	Chemicals			Electrical engineering and electronics			Machine tools		
	Patenting	Not patenting	Total	Patenting	Not patenting	Total	Patenting	Not patenting	Total
<1.0	1	2	3	4	2	6	2	3	5
1–2.5	2	1	3	4	0	4	7	4	11
2.5–5.0	5	1	6	4	1	5	8	3	11
5.0–7.5	1	1	2	1	0	1	3	2	5
7.5–10.0	0	0	0	1	0	1	2	0	2
10.0–25.0	1	0	1	3	1	4	4	1	5
25.0–50.0	3	0	3	2	0	2	0	0	0
>50.0	3	0	3	3	0	3	0	0	0
Total	16	5	21	22	4	26	26	13	39

Source. D. J. Smyth, J. M. Samuels and T. Tzoannes, 'Patents, profitability, liquidity and firm size', *Applied Economics*, June 1972.

indicated, in the UK the Comptroller of Patents has the power to invoke the public interest to modify a patent monopoly. In practice this power is rarely used. The reason is fairly clear. For the incentive effect to be strong, patents must at least offer a promise of a period of monopoly so that an inventor can recoup his R and D costs and a reward which is large enough to tempt him to the effort. If this reward is frequently modified by intervention by the authorities acting in the public interest, the expectational effect will be severely modified. Clearly there ought to be provisions in the patent law to protect the public interest and to guard against abuse of monopoly, nevertheless if these are used too frequently the prospective value of a patent to an inventor may be reduced. The result may be a reduction in inventive effort. This is probably the economic explanation for the low usage of compulsory and licence of rights procedures. The effect may be that certain patents do provide their holders with too much protection. This may be tolerated by the authorities in order to preserve the general incentive effect of patents, and may have to be accepted by rivals because they are unable to invent around them.

When a patent is granted there is an exchange involving disclosure on the one hand and a promise of a legal monopoly on the other. The principles are clear; there should be sufficient information in the specification for a person well versed in the field to comprehend and put the discovery into practice. However, vetting of specifications is not in the hands of experts in the particular technology but a matter for the Patent Office. Here concern is for legal form and presentation. Highly expert technological knowledge cannot be expected. As a result an inventor may be in a powerful position. He may be able to disclose little and yet acquire a patent. From the inventor's point of view he is anxious to disclose as little as possible consistent with acquisition of a patent. A patent may subsequently be revoked on grounds of insufficient disclosure, but as so few cases are challenged at this late stage, the chances are low that this will happen. In terms of the effect on the rate of diffusion of knowledge, the nature of this legal game may be that not much is added to the pool of technological knowledge. An inventor may acquire a patent which involves very little disclosure. He may acquire a period of legal protection and still retain secrecy. If this happens a great deal, then part of the economic case for patents disappears. Patents are supposed to add to the stock of technological knowledge and speed up the rate of diffusion of knowhow. If this does not occur then the exchange may be viewed as onesided.

Evidence on the impact of patents on the diffusion of knowledge is mixed. Use of the Patent Office library is considerable. Readership is in excess of 120,000 per annum. Facilities exist for tracing published specifications. Requests number over 400 per month for use of this facility. However, information retrieval is not particularly discriminating and as a result duplication of research is a real possibility. At 1962 prices it has been estimated that wastage through duplicated research effort in generating information which already exists, amounted to approximately £6 million per annum or 0.9 per cent of total British research expenditure.[15] Clearly if information retrieval were improved this duplication could be reduced. Numbers of enquiries are relatively low in terms of patents granted. The use of abridgements by members of the general public is small, and enquiries relating to complete specifications few. This presumably means that interested parties do not find them very useful. The argument that patents therefore speed up the rate of diffusion has to be treated with caution. Competitors may await the appearance of the product or process before they set about appraisal. This is just what would have happened if there had been no patent procedure. If this practice is widespread, then the net impact on the flow of technological knowledge generated by patents may be low.

In applying for a patent, as has been explained earlier, no 'prior claim' is an important condition. An earlier claim for the same invention may destroy an application. In these circumstances the 'priority' date can be crucial. Priority is a matter of registration. The date is normally the working day when the Patent Office receives the provisional specification. If no provisional specification is submitted, then it is the date of the complete specification. Under British Patent Law priority goes to the earliest applicant. In this way the first inventor may suffer. He may lose this race to the Patent Office. There is a dilemma here. In his anxiety to establish priority, an inventor may submit a provisional application which reflects the early state of development of his invention. Later when the complete specification is submitted it may include new information which was not covered by the first application. In which case the new claims will have the priority date of the complete specification. This may have the effect of losing him the race against a rival who was in no sense the first inventor but who managed to establish an earlier priority date. In some industries the race to the Patent Office can literally be headlong. Pharmaceuticals and electronics are two examples where R and D rivalry can be so close that priority dates can be of great relevance. In circumstances of such close innovative rivalry it is important that the patent system should reward the true inventor. If this does not occur then the element of lottery may become so high as to dampen the incentive to invent. It may also encourage unscrupulous methods to acquire patents. Where acquisition of a patent becomes dependent on winning the race, this may stimulate industrial espionage. Legal action by an aggrieved party is always a possibility but not necessarily a satisfactory remedy. 'Obtaining' is difficult to prove and may involve protracted and costly litigation. There is a case for a shift in the emphasis in the British system so that the priority date becomes less important. As will be made clear later however this may increase the time taken to acquire a patent.

A further weakness of the patent system may be in its emphasis. A patent is designed to give the inventor legal protection. It may be however that it would be more appropriate to defend the innovator or developer of an idea. Development is much more costly than invention, and it may be this aspect of technological change which needs encouraging. The transformation process whereby an invention becomes a marketable good can be lengthy and extremely costly. The hovercraft is an example of a brilliant idea which has taken years and many millions of pounds to become a commercial proposition. Even with state subsidy, NRDC involvement and university research effort, this has by no means achieved full acceptance. There are still a host of technological problems to be solved before this innovation makes a major impact on the transport industry. With the hovercraft it was pretty clear that in its early stages special help would be required. With other less dramatic and technologically complex inventions it would not be so obvious. As a result development may be slow. Patent protection may not offer sufficient incentive for rapid development, and so the exploitation rate of technological ideas may be slow. Patents are supposed to foster both the routine improvement of technologies and also the occasional brilliant inventive step. They are perhaps better at supporting small improvements. The difficulties of making the idea marketable are probably minor. It is with a major breakthrough that commercialisation may be lengthy and costly. Here the distinction between invention and innovation may be crucial and patents may fail to give adequate protection.

In most advanced economies there is an indirect admission of the failure of the patent system. In the USA over 60 per cent of total research and development is financed by the government. In the UK the figure is similar. Of course, a part of this is for specific types of research, for example, defence. Even so government involvement is high. Effectively it is admitted that the patent system does not provide sufficient incentive to yield the desired level of effort. The major failure is in the area of basic research. The time span to results is long, the uncertainty level high and the output may not be a tangible product but rather a fundamental principle. In these circumstances the output will not be patentable. Even if it were, it is doubtful whether patents would evoke the desired level of effort. In practice the government intervenes and research institutes, cooperative research, direct subsidies and university research effort, are the result. Effectively therefore the discussion of patents is limited to that area of inventive activity where it is practical to expect patents to have some impact. This is likely to be where time and risk discounts are acceptable to companies and individuals. As the figures of government expenditure on research and development indicate, the patent system has a weak claim to universality. Research has to be reinforced by government monies.

There are some who argue that because the patent system protects invention rather than innovation it should be abolished. This is an extreme conclusion. There is a distinction between the two activities. In modern economic conditions it may be that development is becoming an increasingly costly and lengthy process. However this argument is easy to overstress. The law is concerned with what is patentable rather than what is an invention. As a result a considerable number of patents arise through the development process. Rarely does a single patent describe and encompass a product which is complete in its development. More usually there are a whole series of patents which trace the history of the technology of a particular product. In aggregate they amount to the knowhow in the field. An individual patent in this pool is really one small step demonstrating patentable ingenuity. The distinction that is usually drawn between invention and innovation is normally an oversimplification. There is rarely the flash of genius which is then developed into a marketable product so that there are two discrete and identifiable processes namely conception and commercialisation. The product is rarely complete in its technology. Further development is usually required. This may give rise to further patents. Such patents represent the process of technology building on technology,[16] where each patent relates to an aspect and not the whole of a product, and where the inventive step is really an innovative step representing an improvement of an original product. In this sense patents are part of the iterative process which is the development of knowledge of a particular technology, and not the simplistic invention-innovation pattern. The process of technology building on technology is a more realistic model of the role of patents. It recognises the complexity of the process of development and admits that the vast majority of patents relate to small developments in an existing technology. Most patents are now the result of company research and arise largely from development activity. The Patent Office is not concerned with invention. It merely has to apply the tests of patentability. Provisions do exist for improvement or 'selection' patents. These represent a new or better use, or the avoidance of a major disadvantage of the original patents. Furthermore patents may be extended. Extensions will however only apply to inventions which are classed as of great importance, and when the inventor can show that he has been inadequately remunerated and that this was not his fault. Thus where a great invention proves difficult to bring to commercial fruition it is possible to lengthen the period of protection. In this sense the law can be said to recognise development as a distinct activity and make provision for it. In numerical terms there have been fewer than ten applications in the United Kingdom between 1950 and 1967 for an extension. The qualitative importance of these few applications is of course extremely difficult to assess.

There is evidence which may suggest that patents are offering a decreasing stimulus to invent. Patents produced per unit expenditure on R and D seem to be declining over time.[17] Apparently in modern economic conditions patents are considered less desirable. This interpretation of the data is only one of many. There are several forces in action which may explain the figures. The efficiency of R and D may have declined. Output of invention may have decreased for a given expenditure on R and D. Alternatively research may now be more costly and complex, and so patents are secured only after a greater effort. Again those concerned with invention may be aiming for a larger step forward so that on a quality basis there may actually be an improvement in performance. The most plausible explanation, however, probably relates to a change in the composition of those primarily involved in the inventive process. Company research is becoming dominant. The lone individual's role is much less marked.[18] Furthermore there has probably been a character change in the type of company involved with research. With the reduction in the importance of the individual in patenting, this will almost automatically cause a rise in expenditure on research and development per patent acquired.

Individuals tend to have very low research and development expenditure. Companies, on the other hand, tend to spend much more. Their research is on an organised, budgeted and continuing basis. Once companies become the chief producers of patents the expenditure in relation to total patents is likely to rise. In addition the type of company primarily involved in research is probably changing. With the emergence of 'big firm, few firm' competition, associated with competitive oligopoly, the necessity to secure patent protection is probably decreasing. These large companies have the economic power to defend their discoveries, thus they may tend to acquire patents only in unusual circumstances. Their propensity to patent may be lower than the smaller company which has less power in the market place. In these circumstances the change in the type of company involved with R and D may help to explain the apparent decline in patents in relation to R and D expenditure. The evidence that patents appear to be offering a decreasing stimulus to invention must therefore be interpreted with caution. It may be the case, but the truth is much more likely to be a change in the character of those responsible for the majority of R and D.

A further disadvantage is the delay in the acquisition of patents. In the USA, for example, the average delay is 3.5 years. The delay in the UK is somewhat less, being approximately 2.5 years. In the UK the examination procedure relating to priority is less rigorous than in the USA. The first applicant acquires priority. In the USA a genuine attempt is made at the examination stage to establish who is the first inventor. This is not necessarily the first applicant. Such a rigorous examination inevitably involves delay. In the UK publication of specifications before the granting of a patent helps speed the process in the sense that information is available to the public prior to sealing. This helps remove some of the weight in the argument that the rate of diffusion of knowledge is impeded by the patent system. Nevertheless the administrative delays associated with all patent systems are a source of concern to applicants. There are some inventions which could easily succumb to economic obsolescence within the time period taken to acquire a patent. The faster becomes the rate of technological change the more will fall within this category.

A further argument may be advanced against the patent system. Non-price competition may be so prevalent that a legal incentive is not required to induce inventive activities. Businessmen may be so averse to price competition that economic rivalry takes the form of product or innovative competition. By differentiation and improvement of their products companies vie with each other for customers. Where this takes the form of innovative competition, companies attract business through technological novelty and excellence. Research and development becomes a normal business expense and there is a premium on inventive output. This type of competition may not be dependent on patents for its continuance. Commercial rivalry based on improved products may find its impetus from the technological base of the industry. The demand for improved performance by customers and developments achieved by suppliers, may effectively force companies to compete in this way. The knowhow embodied in a product becomes more important than its price. Customers may be prepared to pay such a premium for improved products, that recoupment of R and D expenses is fast. In these circumstances investment in research is profitable even though obsolescence may quickly overtake each individual inventive step. Patents would be unlikely to improve returns and would offer notional protection as soon as the industry has advanced to a new state of development. If an industry is new and the rate of change of technology so fast that R and D is unprofitable, then patent protection is unlikely to relieve the situation. Companies may continue to finance development in spite of current losses in the hope of long-term gain. The stakes here are survival for eventual profits. Under this situation the structure of the industry may become a crucial factor in sustaining innovative competition and not patents. If the firms are large and highly diversified, then current unprofitable R and D may be subsidised from other activities. The pressure to innovate may thus come not from the incentive effect of patents, but from the particular type of company involved. The computer industry is an example of the effects of fast technological change. In the 1950s and '60s improvements came so fast that it was virtually impossible to achieve a long enough run of production of a particular model to be profitable. Losses were common and the British industry had to be sustained by government aid to prevent its economic ruin.

Evidence of the importance of patents to innovative competition is difficult to assess. There are circumstances where patents are unnecessary to foster technological change. If companies are able to maintain secrecy, where entry barriers are high, where imitation lags slow, and where concentration is high, patenting will be largely unnecessary. Innovating companies will not need to defend their new knowhow with legally enforceable periods of priority in time. The economic circumstances of the industry will protect them. Patents may merely reinforce an existing situation and therefore be unnecessary. Concentration in an industry does appear to have some effect on the propensity to patent, but as pointed out in Chapter 4, on innovation, the effect of the market structure is difficult to separate from the influence of technological opportunity. Industries where innovative competition is typical do tend to make greater use of patents, but this does nothing to establish the importance of patents to this type of economic rivalry. Innovating industries have relatively high levels of R and D and as a result patents are an almost inevitable byproduct. The interesting causative question is, are patents merely a byproduct or are they a crucial factor in inducing innovative rivalry? Circumstances may be postulated where patents could be crucial. There are examples where efforts to invent around a major patent position have affected the technology of an industry. The radio and petroleum cracking industries are examples.[19] Substitute invention has been stimulated. Companies have responded by improving on a basic patent rather than by imitating. In other industries patents may well have frustrated technological change. The du Pont position in nylon may have had this effect. As a generalisation it is probably true to say that industries which are changing fast probably generate more patents than their more staid counterparts. But the use of patents probably reflects the type of competition and does not necessarily cause it. Where change is fast, patents succumb quickly to economic obsolescence. While a particular development has novelty, patents probably speed up recoupment, but they may not amount to a crucial factor causing the change. Individual patents are relatively cheap to acquire and there is always the possibility that they may prove extremely valuable. Patents can be represented as a means of reducing uncertainty levels in that there is always a chance that they may slow imitation. Companies probably take them out as a form of insurance, but in fact defend their commercial position not by relying on them but by continuing to develop further products to enhance their competitive power.

Patenting can be an expensive process. The fee to acquire a single patent is relatively modest, but to acquire adequate protection for a particular area of technology may require a large number of patents. For example, one company holds thirty-eight patents in ejector seat design, and over eighty have been awarded to its managing director. Unless a company is fortunate enough to hold a master patent, it may decide not to become involved.[20] To achieve adequate protection may require so many patents as to become a drain on company resources. A patent department within the company may be required. This will be yet another fixed cost to be carried and will thus favour the larger company. They may have to resort to patenting only for major inventions. This is a form of discrimination which reflects the economic effects of size. Figures which attempt to indicate the contribution to technology by size of firm, and which use patent numbers, should therefore be treated with caution.

A further disadvantage which must be set against the benefits is the cost of the patent system. For example over the period 1953–64 the average deficit of the Patent Office in the United Kingdom was £136,500. No consolidated information exists on costs to the whole economy. For this the accounting network would have to be cast very much wider than the Patent Office. It would include for example the costs of inventor's time and effort in the acquisition of the patents, patent agents' activities, the costs of litigation and all the other costs occasioned by patents in the economic activity of the economy. Without such information assessment of the value of patents is largely a matter of faith. The investigator has to weigh the advantages and disadvantages when neither is expressed in precise terms. Judgment is based on ordinal appraisal, and the final conclusion is expressed in cautious terms with a liberal dosage of probability terminology.

The International Convention for the Protection of Industrial Property

Before proceeding to discussion of the reform of patents it is important to pause and describe the International Patent Union. This has considerable bearing on national policies because it is a major practical constraint on the potential to reform patents. It also has considerable relevance to the multinational company. Eighty countries are signatories to the International Convention for the Protection of Industrial Property. The Convention effectively extends the scope of patents. It allows patents for the same invention to be held in member countries. Foreigners acquire the same rights to protection as the nationals of the countries concerned. It is not a unified and standardised world system where a recognised form of application to the Union headquarters immediately secures world coverage for a patent. Rather it is a more practical and *ad hoc* arrangement which gives limited and defined rights to member countries. The Union first came into being in 1883 and has gradually extended its influence. It is now administered by the World Intellectual Property Organisation (WIPO) at Geneva. This institution is the successor to the Bureaux Internationaux Réunis pour la Protection de la Propriété Intellectuelle (BIRPI) which used to undertake this task.

The five major articles of the Convention which regulates the operation of the International Union for the Protection of Industrial Property relate to: national treatment, the right of 'priority', the independence of patents, importation, and the abuse of monopoly.

'National treatment' essentially rejects reciprocity of treatment for individuals and countries. Article 2(1) states that 'Nationals of any country of the Union shall, as regards the protection of industrial property, enjoy in all other countries of the Union the advantages that their respective laws now grant'.[21] An individual patent holder in one country is subject to the laws of that country. Because he comes from another country does not permit him to claim the same treatment as he receives at home. This has meant that members which have no patent system in their own country are able to hold and enjoy the benefits of patents in other Union countries. In 1883 neither Switzerland nor the Netherlands had a patent system, yet they were amongst the founder members of the Union. If this 'national treatment' provision did not apply it would mean foreign holders of Union patents would receive different treatment from nationals. This would add to the complexity of enforcement of patents and may significantly affect the terms of competition. For example if a Union holder of a patent could claim favourable tax treatment equivalent to that prevailing in his home country, this could affect the local producer's ability to compete. Some of his economic advantage would derive from his nationality and not from the commercial efficiency of his patent. This benefit would not be available to home producers who might therefore be at a disadvantage.

The right of 'priority' allows an inventor to acquire a patent in all member countries. There is a time limit of twelve months imposed for the period of priority. An inventor must make application for patents within a year of filing in the country of origin. Without the Convention application for a patent in one country would amount to prior publication when application is subsequently made in another. Thus an inventor would be unable to acquire a patent in more than one country. As explained in Chapter 7, the International Convention is intended to reduce the geographical concentration effect. Without the Convention an inventor would be effectively limited to a single application. He would therefore tend to acquire a patent where it would be of the greatest value to him. Inevitably applications would be attracted to the world's industrial centres. This concentration of technological knowledge would presumably enhance the industrial advantage of such countries and raise a whole series of controversial nationalist issues.

The independence of patents means that a patent in one country is independent of all other patents for that invention in other countries. Thus invalidation in one country will not automatically cause invalidation of the same patent in other countries. Duration is related to the laws of the country issuing the patent and not to the practice of the patent law in the originating country. The Convention is not intended to extend the geographical scope of one patent but rather to permit an inventor to acquire patents for the same invention in member countries. Foreigners' patents are subject to exactly the same provisions as the nationals of a country. No category is created requiring different patent provisions, and the law of the country of origin is not applied. The Convention does not aim to establish a uniform world patent law, rather it is intended to allow inventors to acquire patents in member countries.

Article 5a(1) reads: 'importation by the patentee into the country where the patent has been granted of articles manufactured in any of the countries of the Union shall not entail forfeiture of the patent.'[22] This article covers the situation where the inventor from a member country acquires a patent in another member country and then imports the object. Such action will not entail forfeiture. Without this provision, for patent holders to benefit they would have to set up manufacture facilities in every Union country in which they hold a patent. This might run counter to international specialisation and the comparative cost doctrine. In addition it would greatly favour the company with sufficient resources to become involved in multinational operations.

National interests to avoid abuse of monopoly are protected. If exercise of the exclusive rights of the patent holder is abused, for example by failure to 'work', then compulsory licence procedures may be used. Where this is not sufficient to prevent the abuse, the patent may be forfeited or revoked. There are time limits before these procedures can be invoked. A compulsory licence may not be applied for on grounds of insufficient or failure to work before three years from the granting of the patent. Forfeiture or revocation can only follow two years after the granting of the first compulsory licence. Notice that the patent holder is not forced to work his invention in order to benefit from his patent. The Articles allow a time lapse before compulsory licence procedures may be instituted. Even when the patent is compulsorily licensed, the holder still benefits under the terms of the licensing arrangements. If revocation or forfeiture action is taken, then the minimum period before this can take place is five years.

The Union for the Protection of Industrial Property has obvious relevance to the multinational company. The Union complements and emphasises their international character. The 'working' provisions of the Convention are not onerous. These companies are already located throughout the world and are thus in a position to produce and market their inventions in member countries and also to benefit from widespread patent protection.

The Union is supposed to stimulate additional invention through widening patent protection. For individuals and ordinary companies this may not be a direct stimulus to inventive effort. An international scale of operations is so far beyond their immediate scope that any benefit that may flow from patents protected under the Convention is probably in the nature of a bonus, rather than a significant factor in the decision to invent. To the multinational company however the picture is different. International operation is normal. Their R and D effort is directed at world markets. The possibility of patent protection in these markets probably therefore has a positive impact on their incentive to invent. The possibility of worldwide patent coverage will be a normal parameter in the R and D decision process. The fact that multinational companies stand to benefit from the Convention more than smaller economic units, may be represented as a disadvantage of the system. It should be remembered however that the normal way to generate patents is through R and D. Multinationals may therefore respond to their locational advantages by being more research intensive than their national counterparts. If this is in fact the case, part of the explanation may lie with the International Convention.

The advantage of multinational companies is also enhanced by the 'independence' rule of the Convention. A patent that is invalidated in one country will not automatically suffer a similar fate in another. Consequently a company which has widespread patent coverage for a given invention will stand a better chance of acquiring at least one patent monopoly, than a company with a single patent. The independence rule therefore encourages widespread application. The multinational is well placed to do this.

One major fear that is linked with the Union is the ability of multinational companies to form International Patent Cartels. An International Patent Cartel is formed when multinational companies in the same or similar industries, exchange rights to use processes and technological information on mutually agreed terms. The existence of patents enables enforcement of the agreement by legal action. The Convention allows companies to acquire patents in many countries. A tight monopolistic arrangement may thus result with international coverage. Patents can be exchanged between companies on mutually advantageous terms. The terms of the licences which regulate the exchange of products and processes will include such items as the output, markets to be served, and price to be charged. By regulating competition in this way, companies can enhance their respective monopolies and at the same time create a cartel of great economic power. A major advantage of such cartels is the exchange of knowhow and technological developments between members. This may result in an enhanced rate of technological progress and avoid duplication of R and D. A major fear, however, is the unscrupulous exploitation of monopoly without regard to the interests of particular countries. The Union for Protection of Industrial Property without doubt improves the ability of companies to form cartels of this character. But it does not of itself cause their formation. Such cartels would probably be formed even if the Union did not exist. Multinational companies would still find it to their advantage to pool technological knowledge and allocate markets. Furthermore it is always open to national governments to mitigate the effects of these cartels. They can invoke compulsory licence powers and generally regulate the behaviour of companies. The real target for criticism may therefore be the timidity of governments in the use of these powers and not the institution which permits international patenting. This timidity probably arises from a fear that over-vigorous action may destroy technological exchanges between companies. But there is probably too much anxiety here. Information exchanges and pooling arrangements are likely to continue even with more vigorous government regulation.[2][3]

The major economic rationale of the Union is to eliminate the arbitrary influence on location of independent national patent systems. It is clear that in practice this is only partially achieved. The Convention has not established a uniform standardised international patent system where a single application to headquarters will secure protection. The system is very far removed from this ideal. Application is still required in each and every member country. This is an expensive and lengthy process. With limited time and funds available, the inventor will therefore only apply in those countries where he judges patent protection will be most worth while. As a result there will still tend to be a concentration effect. At best the International Convention will only have mitigated this. Until there is a true international system, patents will tend to be taken out in the industrialised wealthy countries, and knowhow will concentrate there. Whether it is in the realms of the practical to establish a true international patent system is debatable. It remains a criticism of the Union that it falls short of this end.

There are moves afoot to meet some of these criticisms. In June 1970 a Patent Cooperation Treaty (PCT) was signed in Washington. Thirty-five states were signatories. This treaty establishes what is known as an 'international application'. Filing of such an application by an inventor will have the same effect as if separate filings had been made in the countries where protection is desired. The application is subjected to a search to discover 'prior art' and a report issued. Once this has been done, the application is processed separately by individual countries each of which will then grant or refuse protection. This procedure has the major advantage that as a result of the international search report the applicant should be in a good position to judge whether the expense of proceeding in a number of individual countries is worth while. The international examination which is a preliminary to the national searches, should also help reduce the task for individual patent offices. Centralised administration of this PCT is operated through the World Intellectual Property Organisation (WIPO) at Geneva.

There are also moves afoot to create a European Patent. There is a Europatent Scheme which will be open to all European countries. The holder of a centrally ratified Europatent will effectively acquire nineteen or twenty separate patents. These will be regarded in each country as national patents, but national practice may have to be overruled on the length of life. A twenty-year span is envisaged as a common life for such a Europatent. Revocation criteria may be also standardised for these patents.[24] A further scheme beginning to move towards reality, is the Common Market Patent Convention. These proposed Community Patents will be open only to members of the EEC. A single European (Community) Patent will be effective in all member countries.[25] It seems unlikely however that the scheme will be operative until 1976. Thus the chances of an inventor being granted a single patent, at least for Europe, are improving. It is hoped that any success in this direction will strengthen the pressure for greater international cooperation and induce a more uniform treatment of intellectual property throughout the world.

Reforms

VARIABLE LIFE PATENTS

The disadvantages of patents lead to a series of suggestions for reform. Substantive ones include variable life and split period patents, the use of renewal fees, the establishment of a utilisation journal and alternative means of achieving the same ends with greater efficiency. As has already been pointed out, a patent is a rather blunt instrument to achieve a given end. Little attempt is made to adjust the degree of protection to particular circumstances. If an idea is patentable then the majority of countries make no distinction between the quality of invention. Trivial and path-breaking inventions receive equal treatment. The period of monopoly is the same and the full legal processes equally available to both. The variable life patent as it is normally recommended would attempt to be more discriminating. It would allow a longer period of protection for important discoveries and grant only a short monopoly for minor inventions. In this way it is hoped that emphasis would shift towards quality and towards larger inventive steps. Previous analysis has indicated that the period of legal monopoly granted by a patent may be relatively unimportant. Economic obsolescence weeds out the vast majority of patents, so that only approximately 10 per cent survive for their full term. Furthermore from the point of view of the economy, it was pointed out that a variable life patent should in certain specified circumstances discriminate against important discoveries, in that the more significant an invention is the shorter should be the period of protection. It was argued that recoupment of costs would be fast, so a long period of protection would not be necessary. The argument had the effect of challenging intuitive reasoning on the subject and putting the debate in perspective. In terms of reform of the patent system, this type of argument may amount to a strong case for a split period patent.

The economic logic of the argument that an important invention with relatively high elasticity of demand will allow fast recoupment and therefore should only have a short patent life is difficult to refute. But it must be remembered that the backcloth of this logic is *ex post*. Essentially it is concerned with the economic effects of a patent once it is granted. It is not concerned with *ex ante* or expectational arguments. The crucial function of patents is to raise the incentive to invent. Deliberately to reform the system to reflect *ex post* assessment of the importance of discoveries might have a catastrophic effect on expectations. If at the time that patents are granted a shorter period of protection is given to important discoveries, the incentive to seek significant inventions may be severely damped. The problem is to retain the incentive to invent and yet minimise the actual misallocation effects associated with monopoly. The split period patent may be a good compromise to achieve this. The overall period of patent protection would remain the same. No attempt would be made to adjust the life granted to the quality of the invention. However the term of the protection would be split into two periods. In the first half, the patentee would have an exclusive right, and in the second the patent would automatically be available for endorsement 'licence of right'. This system would preserve the incentive effect in that no attempt would be made to adjust the life of the patent, yet should it prove important, then the misallocation effects to the economy would be reduced by the licence of right provision in the second half of the term.

The split period patent would achieve a compromise between the incentive and misallocation effects. In practice it would reduce the absolute level of protection for important inventions. Rivals would be anxious to use the patent and therefore widespread endorsement 'licence of right' would occur. In this way the effects of a strong patent monopoly position would be reduced to the economy and yet the expectational qualities associated with patents would be preserved. The patent holder would be in a position to influence the terms of licensing and thus would be unlikely to view the licence of right period as equivalent to free competition. At the planning stage, when expectational effects are the most crucial, the split period patent would appear not very different from a conventional patent. In its practical operation however it may approximate to a shorter life for more important inventions. The more significant a given patent, the more anxious will rivals be to take advantage of the endorsement provisions. These will therefore be taken up much faster than for less significant patents. As a result a more competitive position will be established earlier with important inventions. It will be more competitive in the sense that a larger number will be using the process or offering the invention for sale. The terms of the licensing arrangement may constrain the type of rivalry which new entrants may adopt, but they are most unlikely to frustrate competition completely. There are so many ways in which companies can compete that it is virtually inevitable that the monopoly effects will be mitigated. The originating company will still benefit through licensing fees but the economy will also benefit through an improvement in the allocation of resources.

FEES

The relative smallness of patent fees would suggest that these are biased towards the pocket of the individual rather than the company. In fixing the level of fees the authorities face a practical problem. If patent fees are too high they may exclude the individual from achieving protection. If they are too low they may induce frivolous applications. A compromise must be reached whereby the individual is induced to seek patent protection and at the same time the company does not have an overwhelming advantage.

It may be tempting to introduce a discriminatory fee system. Under such an arrangement companies would be charged a higher rate for a patent than individuals. This is unlikely to be successful. A normal condition of work for an individual employed in a research and development team is that he will assign any inventions to the company. As a result a high proportion of patents are taken out in the names of individuals, but the royalties and rights are assigned to companies. Thus with a discriminatory fee system there would be an identification problem of considerable difficulty. The Patent Authorities would have to identify the lone inventor and differentiate him from the company employee. This might be an impractical exercise and not be worth the effort. Patent fees are only a proportion of total fees involved. Legal fees paid to patent agents are in most cases just as important or even more important. Modification of patent fees in favour of the individual would thus only make a relatively small difference to total expenses and consequently have only a marginal impact on the decision to apply for a patent. The advantage which companies have in the acquisition of patents is a fact of life. Patent fees are not meant to value an invention. They are merely intended to recoup the costs of running the Patent Office and no more. Valuation of a patent is done by the market after it is granted. This shows in the profits accruing to the inventor. Fees should not be a significant factor in the decision to apply for a patent. There may be a case for renewal fees once a patent is granted, but even this is dubious for reasons that will be indicated below.

The majority of countries adopt an annual renewal procedure; not all of these use a rising scale of fees. Major examples where a graduated renewal scheme is used are the UK, Switzerland, the Netherlands and Germany. In the USA a single payment secures a patent for its full legal term. No further payment is required to keep the patent in force. At first sight this no renewal system would appear somewhat deficient. It implies no official economic test of the value of patents, and provides no incentive for patents to lapse if proved worthless. The holder does not have to decide if the patent is worth the renewal fee and he is not faced by an automatic lapse if payment is not affected in time. Patents will therefore continue in existence because they are legally valid rather than economically useful. In the UK, where there is a graduated renewal scheme, the proportion of patents renewed for their whole life is surprisingly small. This would appear to support the case for such an arrangement. The payment of a progressively higher renewal fee apparently weeds out worthless patents. In practice this conclusion is unlikely to be sound. It is doubtful whether renewal fees are a major factor in the decision to retain patents. The renewal decision is complex and subject to a whole range of influences which may be unrelated to the amount of the fee. This is certainly the view of the United States Senate Committee which examined the issue in 1958.[26]

Some of the factors which will affect the decision to renew include the inventor's optimism, the timing of revenue flows, developments in complementary technology, the identity of the patent holder, the motive for patent holding and the rate of technological obsolescence. A highly optimistic inventor is likely to renew his patent even though it may be worth less to him than the annual fee. He may take the view that the idea will eventually break through to market acceptance. It may therefore be that revenues will only flow late in the life of the patent. Earning power may be linked to developments in complementary technologies, which may prove intransigent. For example numerically controlled machine tools are depended upon successfully coupling mechanical and computer technologies via sensor devices. If these devices are not sufficiently developed their application will be hindered. The identity of the patent holder may be important. Companies may be less concerned to keep patents than individuals. They may have sufficient economic power to be monopolists of the idea without a patent. Alternatively companies may be more anxious to keep patents than individuals for a variety of motives. They may wish to 'road block' rivals by establishing what is known as a patent position. They may acquire a large number of patents in a particular field. This may effectively debar other companies from the technology. This 'territory marking' is certainly a well-known technique. By acquiring and maintaining a maze of patents a company may establish a monopoly position which is difficult to break. Each individual patent in such a position may be almost worthless, but the aggregate effect of a large number may represent a lucrative monopoly. An associated technique known as patent diplomacy may have a similar effect. By exchange of patents between companies, monopoly positions may be established. In this situation individual patents become the currency of company negotiations and may be held as bargaining counters and not for current revenue earning power.

Technological obsolescence ought to have a predictable effect on the renewal of patents. Once an invention has been overtaken by further advance presumably the associated patent will be allowed to lapse. However, the arguments above indicate that renewal may not necessarily be an expression of the economic or technical utility of a patent. Even if it were possible to disentangle the effects of technological change from all the other influences affecting patent renewal, it would not necessarily indicate the expected pattern. A quickening of the pace of technological change would not necessarily lead to a decline in the percentage of surviving patents. Survival is related to the quality of the inventive step involved. If patents typically represent a small step forward then even in a time of slow change, the obsolescence rate may be high. Alternatively if patents represent a considerable inventive step, then a fast rate of change may lead to a lower fall-out rate. Inventors may take the view that with a fast rate of advance proceeding, only substantial discoveries are worth patenting. Their propensity to patent may therefore be lower but the survival rate higher. Thus technological change clearly has a bearing on the economic value of patents, but it is not obvious how this will affect the percentage of renewals. The American system of a single fee and no renewal fee would appear superior. It has the major administrative advantages of cheapness and simplicity. In effect the British system of a rising annual renewal fee is a progressive tax on patents. If the arguments are accepted that this tax does not amount to a test of the economic worth of the patents, then the logical justification for the British system evaporates, and the case for reform is made.

UTILISATION JOURNAL

Worthwhile inventions may be neglected because they are costly and difficult to make commercial, because publicity or information retrieval is inadequate, or because a patent may be held by men of small economic means. Individuals who do not have the resources to put their patented inventions into production can always license them. Official publicity could help to make a market for them. At the moment this does happen but only in a limited way. The *Department of Trade and Industry Journal* publishes in a single issue, patents which are endorsed 'licence of right'. The impact of such publicity, however, must be limited, and there is a case for improving this facility. A utilisation journal with an international circulation giving details of patents available for licensing agreements could help to increase the diffusion of knowledge and aid the making of a market. By improved publicity, duplication of research effort may be reduced and some benefit flow to patent holders who otherwise would go unrewarded. The advantages of such a journal could be considerable and would not involve a great deal of extra work. The information already exists. It merely requires improved dissemination.[27]

ALTERNATIVE SYSTEMS

The reader should remember that it is fairly easy to catalogue the disadvantages of patents, but less easy to list the advantages. Failures tend to show themselves in overt ways. A particular company may have a patent monopoly and legal action may reveal gross exploitation. Successes on the other hand may go unheralded. Intangibles like expectations, incentives and the flow of knowledge are difficult to assess and do not show themselves in obvious ways. Thus the investigator may incline his judgment towards the shortcomings. Add to this the complexity of the whole system and the enormous aggregation problems involved, and it is hardly surprising that committees of investigation are extremely cautious and confine their recommendations to detailed provisions of the system, rather than alternative means of achieving the same ends.[28] Their caution is reinforced by knowledge that the patent system of most of the major countries of the world is in fact interwoven by international agreements like the International Convention for the Protection of Industrial Property. It is thus unrealistic to assume that investigating committees have a free hand to reform and change the patent system. Their action is constrained by the practical and the realistic. A radical departure from accepted procedure might well have international repercussions. Discussions of alternative means to the patent system therefore tend to be hypothetical and used as vehicles to highlight deficiencies.

If it was possible to start from a 'green field' situation perhaps cheaper, more efficient and more direct means could be devised to encourage invention. Suggestions include a prize system, direct government subsidy, and finally no system at all. A prize system would award cash to deserving inventions based on their utility to the economy. Significant inventions would be granted monetary rewards. The possibility of such a prize would provide the incentive effect. The misallocation effects associated with patents would not be present because there would be no monopoly. A company or an individual would have to rely on technological lead to recoup expenses and earn a return. There would be no legally enforceable period of protection. But there would be the possibility of a prize. Such a system might be cheaper. It would operate in an *ex post* fashion; assessment of inventions would be based on performance and not on potential. Administration would presumably be cheaper because only successful inventions would be considered. Under a patent system the vast majority of inventions do not survive for their full term. A high proportion of these presumably therefore would not be eligible for a cash grant under a prize system. The expenses associated with administering these failures would consequently be saved. The award system could also be more flexible in its operation. Greater emphasis could be placed on innovations. Recognition could be given both to inventors and to those who bring inventions to commercial fruition. It is here that the award system may have considerable advantages.

There are drawbacks however with such a system. It may be even more capricious than patent procedure. It is often difficult to trace the inventor. The sources of the idea may have been very widespread.[29] It is probably susceptible to greater levels of corruption and its administrators would probably tend to be less than open handed in their awards.[30] The patent system has the advantage of being impersonal. The exigencies of the market determine how a patent holder will fare. With an award system the inventor becomes dependent on those administering and deciding the handouts. The personalities and composition of the investigating committees become relevant. Corruption and bribery may thus ease the path of a particular award. In this sense the decision may be capricious and corrupt. In addition it will be difficult for the authorities to resist the temptation to treat the award budget as a cost. There is thus likely to be pressure to limit munificence to the minimum. If this is the case, the incentive to invent may be reduced and thus risk bearing suffer under an award system.

Direct government subsidy as alternative to the patent system would appear to have some advantages. Governments can identify national need and apply economic resources accordingly. There should be a more rational and planned application of funds to technological problems. In the cost-benefit arithmetic used to assess the merits of invention encouragement systems, the emphasis would presumably swing away from private towards public benefits. All these points hold some attraction. Research may become more centralised and less duplication occur. Social goods may receive greater emphasis. Two major influences may however suffer. This is the incentive to invent of the private individual, and the efficiency of expenditure on R and D. Direct government subsidy of R and D may have an adverse effect on efficiency in research. The pressure to achieve results by companies may be reduced because the money is earmarked for research and will not come from companies' pockets. Opportunity cost considerations of the alternative use of funds may become less relevant. The funds are specifically allocated for research and thus the range of alternatives is reduced, and presumably the sharpness of the financial appraisal. The incentive effect provided for the private individual may disappear. Motivation for company research may also be affected. This will largely depend on assessment of imitation rates and the type of competition operating. As has already been argued, there may be circumstances under which company research will not be affected by patents. This is unlikely to be the case with private individuals. To eliminate the incentive effect to private individuals by abolishing patents and relying on government subsidy may result in a decline in inventive output. The private individual is still responsible for a significant proportion of inventions[31] and thus the abolition of patents may be a high cost decision. It is instructive to note that even in the USSR where the state is much more involved with the organisation of production, it has been found necessary to preserve an incentive to invent. Certificates of authorship are granted. These provide cash awards on a sliding scale according to the importance of invention. Most major nations have a significant proportion of R and D financed directly or indirectly by government. These funds are used not as a means of replacing patents but rather as a supplement. This is probably a wise approach in view of the lack of direct evidence on the efficiency of alternative methods, and the practical difficulties associated with radical change. Governments are unlikely to abolish the patent without clearcut and unequivocal evidence of the superiority of alternative systems. At the moment the tendency is to reform the patent system. This involves identifying those areas which would appear to be inefficient and taking appropriate action. In these terms the alternative means to the patent system are not genuine alternatives but rather potential supplements. In the current state of knowledge this is a proper approach.

The last major alternative, the abolition of the patent system, can be dealt with promptly. To make this a practical possibility, the evidence against the system would have to be damning. For example, if it could be demonstrated that patents had no effect on the incentive to invent and the diffusion of knowledge, an irresistible case would be made. At a less demanding level, which would apply if the move were not so radical, it would be adequate to show that the costs outweighed the benefits to an economy. In view of the upheaval involved, and the international repercussions, this would probably not be enough to motivate the will. It may be the case that the balance sheet of the patent system indicates a deficit, but nevertheless it may still survive. The emotional picture of the lone inventor changing the direction of technology with a single patent is immensely appealing. It probably has little to do with reality but it may be enough to sway the decision making machinery. The author has an open mind on the case for and against patents. The evidence is so difficult to assess that pragmatic acceptance of what history has conferred may not be inappropriate. Society always has an option to change, but experimentation in this area may be irresponsible. Alteration rather than abolition may be the limit of the practical.

Conclusion

Patents are supposed to counter the inefficiency of the price mechanism in the generation and exchange of new knowledge. They should transform knowledge which is embodied in a product or process into a saleable commodity. They are supposed to raise the incentive to invent and thus the level of risk taking by offering the possibility of a period of monopoly. They should also speed the diffusion of technological knowledge because disclosure is involved in the acquisition of patents. In practice patents may only be partly successful in meeting these requirements. Disclosure may be insufficient, economic conditions may discriminate against the lone inventor in spite of patent protection, and only certain sorts of inventions may benefit from patents. The disadvantages of patents which include the ability of companies to blockade entry via patent positions, the social and economic costs associated with monopoly, the fear of costly litigation, administrative costs and the possibility that under competitive oligopoly, innovative competition may proceed even in the absence of patents, all these tend to add perspective to an assessment of the system. Strictly, patents should evoke inventions which would not otherwise have occurred and should also speed up the rate of technological change. Whether these aims are actually achieved is not known. It may be that in the last resort the patent system survives because evidence for change is so difficult to assess. Certainly ignorance on the effects of patents is almost complete. As a piece of social engineering they have a long history and are deeply entrenched into the ethos of industrial nations. This does not protect them from criticism or investigation but does tend to engender caution in reform.

Summary

Knowledge has a number of awkward properties which make it difficult to handle within conventional economic theory. There tends to be a substantial element of external economics. It is difficult to market in a conventional manner. The costs of copying are generally much lower than those involved in its original production. An inventor is therefore likely to face a considerable appropriation problem. The prescription that the optimal price for the distribution of knowledge should be zero, or close to zero, is not adopted in practice because of the likely effects on the incentive to invent. Patents are a deliberate attempt to improve the incentive to invent. A legally enforceable period of monopoly is conferred on a patent holder. This permits knowledge to be marketed to the advantage of the inventor. The knowledge may be embodied in a product or process, which is marketed in the normal way. Alternatively, other producers may be licensed, or the patent may be sold. Rivals are legally debarred and thus disclosure does not destroy the owner's proprietary interest.

A patent does not confer an unconditional monopoly. The law defines and circumscribes the rights of a holder and thus has considerable bearing on the economic importance of patents. The stages in acquiring and retaining a UK patent are Application, Examination, Publication, Opposition, Sealing and Renewal. A patent involves a bargain between the inventor and the state. In exchange for adequate disclosure of the principles involved, a sixteen-year period of protection is granted where there is the required degree of novelty and no valid opposition. A sharp distinction should be drawn between patentability and invention. Patentability is determined by the tests applied during the acquisition process. In the UK invention is only fully tested in an action for revocation. The majority of patents are not put to this test.

The Comptroller of Patents has wide power to limit a patent monopoly. These include compulsory licensing and licence of right procedures. In the United States there is no general compulsory licence system and patents do not require renewal. In the UK the use of licence of right and compulsory licences is small. This should not mislead the observer into the belief that these procedures are unimportant.

The theory behind patents is demand orientated. The potential reward to the inventor should be raised by a legally enforceable period of priority in time. Patents will only be effective as a piece of social engineering if they induce inventions which would otherwise not have occurred, or speed up the rate of discovery. Judgment on the effectiveness of patents is limited by lack of evidence and inevitably must be cautious.

The period of protection granted by a patent does not normally vary with the importance of the invention. If adjustment were made in the period of protection according to the importance of the invention, the adjustment should not necessarily be the obvious one. There are powerful arguments suggesting that in defined circumstances, important inventions should have a shorter life than normal. For the majority of patents, however, discussion of their life is somewhat academic. Most do not survive for their full term. But expectation effects and the optimism of inventors should not be overlooked. The occasional brilliant invention which is fostered by the prospect of a patent monopoly, may provide the major justification for the system.

Patents have a number of disadvantages. Companies may establish patent positions based not on innovative excellence, but on the sheer numbers and legal complexity of the patents they hold. This may slow the pace of technological change in the industries concerned. Litigation to defend patents can be so expensive that the individual and the small company may be at a disadvantage. Patents may confer too much protection on the holder, and excessive profits may result. Patents may be acquired which involve little genuine disclosure of technological knowledge and as a result diffusion of knowhow may not be improved. Where there is close innovative rivalry the 'priority' date may be crucial. In such a race to the patent office the true and first inventor may suffer. Patents may not give adequate protection to development. It is here that the distinction between invention and innovation may be crucial. Where the process of transforming an idea to a marketable reality is extremely costly, patent protection may be misdirected. However, it is possible to overstate the arguments here. Patents do recognise development in the sense that a high proportion arise out of the process of technology building on technology. There are also provisions to include improvements via 'selection' patents and under certain restrictive circumstances extensions may be granted. There is indirect evidence that patents are now offering a decreasing stimulus to invention. A more plausible explanation of the evidence is a change in the character of those responsible for most inventions. There are considerable delays involved in the acquisition of patents. In industries which compete by technological rivalry, patents may be unnecessary. Patenting can be expensive, both to the individual inventor and to the nation.

The International Patent Union allows patents for the same invention to be held in member countries. It is not a unified and standardised world patent system, where a single application secures global coverage. The International Patent Union is intended to reduce the geographical concentration effect which would inevitably follow if inventors were restricted to a single application. The system has obvious relevance to the multinational company. It may provide a direct incentive encouraging R and D, and it may also facilitate the operations of patent cartels. The International Patent Union can in practice only mitigate the tendency for technological knowledge to concentrate in the most advanced countries. The time consuming and expensive process of multiple application in the eighty member countries, means that inventors will still tend to apply where they consider it worth while. There are moves afoot which may improve this position.

The disadvantages of patents suggest a number of reforms. These include a variable life or split period patent, the use of renewal fees, a utilisation journal, and alternative means to achieve the same ends with greater efficiency. The split period patent has the major advantage that it may not radically impair expectations. The use of renewal fees is of doubtful economic benefit. A utilisation journal may improve the diffusion of knowledge. Alternatives to the patent system appear to have some attraction, but in the current state of knowledge a cautious approach is proper. Alteration and modification, rather than radical change, may be the limit of the practical.

Conclusions

12

Invention, innovation and diffusion are stages in the process of technological change. Invention is best treated as that subset of technical innovations which are patentable. The origination involved typically takes the form of technology building on technology. Innovation covers all the activities in bringing a new product or process to the market. Research and development is involved. This tends to be time consuming and expensive. It is also risky. Involvement reflects managerial attitudes and the competitive environment. Successful innovation has a considerable impact on the economic performance of companies. Large firms are not necessarily the most propitious in terms of research spending or output. The size of companies, the market form, and diversification are probably secondary influences on research intensity. Technological and commercial opportunity, and the number of independent centres of creative initiative may well be more important to innovative output.

Innovation is a management intensive activity. A number of 'ground rules' are indicated to avoid the more obvious routes to failure. These stress the importance of user needs and marketing, and the involvement of senior personnel with particular schemes. The choice of projects by companies can be explained reasonably well by profit maximisation models. The choice of projects seems to be influenced by the degree of technological ambition involved, and the priority given to them. Management would appear to achieve development times which are somewhat leisurely.

Innovations spread by diffusion. Major determinants of the speed of this process are expected profitability of use, the relative size of the investment involved, the proportion of adopters and the industry concerned. The economic characteristics of innovations would appear more important to diffusion than the particular circumstances of companies that become eventual users.

Arguments which have their roots in the product cycle thesis, suggest that market penetration may be a powerful motive in overseas location of manufacturing capacity. Companies anxious to defend their innovations may capture a high proportion of premium earning capacity and deter market pre-emption by others, if they establish subsidiaries abroad. Alternatively, by having a widespread network of affiliates, chances of early involvement in the innovations of others may be improved. A pattern of location is predicted which would suggest that global corporations are predominantly engaged in technological activities.

Six hundred and thirteen of the world's largest manufacturing companies are classified by their involvement in research intensive activities and their multinational status. Within the particular definitions used in this study, it is not shown that international companies predominate in technological activities. An outward investment pull is however suggested by contrasts in the cell frequencies revealed by the classification procedure. Companies in research intensive activities are typically highly multinational in character and those in more prosaic lines of business are not. The Japanese companies would appear to be a notable exception to this pattern. Shortcomings in the data and classification procedures make caution necessary in interpretation. Nevertheless it is suggested that market capture may be important in outward direct investment and thus in the diffusion of technology.

The unique properties of the direct investment package summarised by commercial and technological independence, structural alignment, and the multiplier effects, suggest that the multinational enterprise is a most effective agent in the diffusion of technology between countries. The tendency to favour research intensive activities relative to other companies which are merely national in status, strengthens the argument considerably. The case is transformed from a tentative suggestion to a more confident assertion. As users and creators of technology, multinational companies are likely to be the most important mechanism of transfer when diffusion between countries is under scrutiny.

Patents are a deliberate attempt to raise the incentive to invent, by conferring a legally enforceable period of priority in time. Appropriation should be improved by deterring the encroachment of rivals. The occasional brilliant invention which is encouraged by the prospect of a patent monopoly may provide the major justification for the system. Patents do recognise development in the sense that a high proportion arise out of the process of technology building on technology. There are very real disadvantages in any patent system. Alteration and modification rather than radical change may however be the limit of the practical in any reforms.

Appendix 1

Classification of research intensive activities

Activities classed as research intensive are aircraft, electrical engineering (including instruments), chemicals (including pharmaceuticals and petroleum). Not all activities within these headings are included. Details based on the Standard International Trade Classification are as follows:[1]

Group

331	Petroleum, crude and partly refined for further refining (excluding natural gasolene)
332	Petroleum products
512	Organic chemicals
513	Inorganic chemicals, elements, oxides and halogen salts
514	Other inorganic chemicals
515	Radioactive and associated materials
521	Mineral tar and crude chemicals from coal, petroleum and natural gas
531	Synthetic dyestuffs, natural indigo and colour lakes
533	Pigments, paints, varnishes and related materials
541	Medicinal and pharmaceutical products
561	Fertilisers, manufactured
571	Explosives and pyrotechnic products
581	Plastic materials, regenerated cellulose and artificial resins
599	Chemical material and products N.e.s.
711.4	Aircraft engines (including jet propulsion engines)
711.7	Nuclear reactors
714.2	Calculating machines, accounting machines and similar machines incorporating a calculating device (including electronic computers)
714.3	Statistical machines, e.g. calculating from punched cards or tape
714.91	To include Xerox copying machines

[1] *Standard International Trade Classification*, revised, United Nations, 1961, Series M, no. 34.

718.22   Type making and setting machinery
722   Electric power machinery and switchgear
723   Equipment for distributing electricity
724   Telecommunications apparatus
726   Electric apparatus for medical purposes and radiological
         apparatus
729   Other electrical machinery and apparatus
734   Aircraft
861   Scientific, medical, optical, measuring and controlling
         instruments and apparatus
862   Photographic and cinematographic supplies
891.1   Phonographs (gramophones), tape recorders and other sound
         recorders and reproducers
899.6   Orthopaedic appliances, hearing aids, artificial parts of the
         body and fracture appliances
899.97   Vacuum flasks, etc.
951.0   Firearms of war, and ammunition

Classification of the world's largest manufacturing companies by their multinational status and their research intensity

MPE 2 = a company with an international location policy
MPE 1 = a lower level of involvement in foreign production
        than MPE 2
Not MPE = a company which is national in outlook
RI = Research Intensive
NRI = Not Research Intensive
(Both RI and NRI are defined in terms of activities undertaken, not research and development expenditure.)

AMERICAN COMPANIES

General Motors	MPE 2	NRI
Standard Oil	MPE 2	RI
Ford Motor	MPE 2	NRI
General Electric	MPE 2	RI
International Business Machines	MPE 2	RI
Mobil Oil	MPE 2	RI
Chrysler	MPE 2	NRI
Texaco	MPE 2	RI
International Tel & Tel	MPE 2	RI
Western Electric	Not MPE	RI
Gulf Oil	MPE 2	RI
Standard Oil of California	MPE 2	RI
US Steel	Not MPE	NRI
Westinghouse Elec.	MPE 2	RI
Standard Oil (Ind)	MPE 2	RI
EI du Pont de Nemours	MPE 2	RI
RCA	MPE 2	RI
Goodyear Tire & Rubber	MPE 2	NRI
Ling-Temco-Vought	Not MPE	RI

Procter & Gamble	MPE 2	NRI
Atlantic Richfield	MPE 2	RI
Continental Oil	MPE 2	RI
Boeing	Not MPE	RI
Union Carbide	MPE 2	RI
International Harvester	MPE 2	NRI
Swift	MPE 2	NRI
Eastman Kodak	MPE 2	RI
Bethlehem Steel	Not MPE	NRI
Kraft Co.	MPE 2	NRI
Lockheed Aircraft	MPE 2	RI
Tenneco	Not MPE	NRI
Greyhound	Not MPE	NRI
Firestone Tire and Rubber	MPE 2	NRI
Litton Industries	MPE 2	RI
Occidental Petroleum	MPE 2	RI
Phillips-Petroleum	MPE 2	RI
General Foods	MPE 2	NRI
North American Rockwell	MPE 2	RI
Caterpillar Tractor	MPE 2	NRI
Singer	MPE 2	NRI
Monsanto	MPE 2	RI
Continental Can	MPE 2	NRI
Borden	MPE 2	NRI
McDonnell Douglas	Not MPE	RI
Dow Chemicals	MPE 2	RI
W. R. Grace	MPE 2	NRI
United Aircraft	Not MPE	RI
Rapid-American	Not MPE	NRI
Union Oil of California	MPE 2	RI
International Paper	MPE 1	NRI
Xerox	MPE 2	RI
Honeywell	MPE 2	RI
Sun Oil	MPE 2	RI
American Can	MPE 2	NRI
General Dynamics	MPE 1	RI
Minnesota Min. & Mfg	MPE 2	RI
Beatrice Foods	MPE 2	NRI
R. J. Reynolds Inds	MPE 1	NRI
Cities Service	MPE 2	RI
Boise Cascade	MPE 2	NRI
Ralston Purina	MPE 2	NRI
Sperry Rand	MPE 2	RI
Coka-Cola	MPE 2	NRI

Burlington Industries	MPE 2	NRI
Armco Steel	Not MPE	NRI
Consolidated Foods	MPE 2	NRI
Uniroyal	MPE 2	NRI
American Brands	MPE 2	NRI
Ashland Oil	MPE 2	RI
Bendix	MPE 2	RI
Textroen	MPE 1	RI
US Plywood-Champion Papers	Not MPE	NRI
Gulf & Western Industries	MPE 2	NRI
TRW	MPE 2	RI
National Steel	Not MPE	NRI
Owens-Illinois	MPE 2	NRI
CPC International	Not MPE	NRI
National Cash Register	MPE 2	RI
United Brands	Not MPE	NRI
Georgia-Pacific	Not MPE	NRI
Aluminium Co. of America	MPE 2	NRI
American Home Products	MPE 2	RI
American Standard	MPE 2	NRI
US Industries	Not MPE	NRI
Standard Oil (Ohio)	MPE 1	RI
Republic Steel	Not MPE	NRI
FMC	MPE 2	RI
Amerada Hess	MPE 2	RI
Warner-Lambert	MPE 2	RI
Getty Oil	MPE 2	RI
Allied Chemical	MPE 2	RI
Colgate Palmolive	MPE 2	NRI
Raytheon	MPE 2	RI
Genesco	MPE 1	NRI
B. F. Goodrich	MPE 2	RI
Weyerhaeuser	MPE 2	NRI
American Cynamid	MPE 2	RI
Signal Companies	MPE 2	RI
Whirlpool	MPE 1	NRI
Inland Steel	Not MPE	NRI
Columbia Broadcasting	MPE 2	NRI
PPG Industries	MPE 2	RI
Celanese	Not MPE	RI
American Motors	MPE 1	NRI
Pepsico	MPE 2	NRI
Philip Morris	MPE 2	NRI
Deere	MPE 2	NRI

Marathon Oil	MPE 2	RI
Borg Warner	MPE 2	NRI
Carnation	MPE 2	NRI
Olin	MPE 2	RI
Johnson & Johnson	MPE 2	RI
General Mills	MPE 2	NRI
Teledyne	Not MPE	RI
Reynolds Metals	MPE 2	NRI
Nabisco	MPE 2	NRI
Bristol-Myars	MPE 2	RI
Combustion Engineering	MPE 1	RI
Standard Brands	MPE 2	NRI
Mead	Not MPE	NRI
Kenecott Copper	MPE 2	NRI
Norton Simon	Not MPE	NRI
Eaton	Not MPE	NRI
Campbells Soup	MPE 2	NRI
Iowa Beef Processors	Not MPE	NRI
General Tire & Rubber	MPE 2	RI
H. J. Heinz	MPE 2	NRI
Crown Zellerbach	MPE 2	NRI
Babcock & Wilcox	Not MPE	RI
Martin Mariette	MPE 2	RI
Pfizer	MPE 2	RI
Anaconda	MPE 2	NRI
Kimberley-Clark	MPE 2	NRI
Burroughs	MPE 2	RI
Motorola	MPE 2	RI
N. L. Industries	MPE 2	RI
St Regis Paper	MPE 2	NRI
Kaiser Aluminium & Chemical	MPE 2	RI
Anheuser-Bush	Not MPE	NRI
Lykes-Youngstown	Not MPE	NRI
SCM	MPE 2	NRI
Avon Products	MPE 2	NRI
J. P. Stevens	MPE 1	NRI
Allis-Chalmers	MPE 2	RI
Interco	Not MPE	NRI
White Motor	MPE 1	NRI
Squibb	MPE 2	RI
Merck	MPE 2	RI
Hercules	MPE 2	RI
Dart Industries	MPE 2	RI
Studebaker-Worthington	Not MPE	NRI

Dresser Industries	MPE 2	RI
Ingersoll Rand	MPE 2	NRI
Grumman	Not MPE	RI
Crane	MPE 2	NRI
Otis Elevator	MPE 2	NRI
Illinois Central Industries	Not MPE	NRI
Texas Instruments	MPE 2	RI
American Metal Climax	MPE 2	NRI
American Broadcasting	Not MPE	NRI
Del Monte	Not MPE	NRI
Central Soya	Not MPE	NRI
Scott Paper	MPE 2	NRI
Whittaker	MPE 1	NRI
Clark Equipment	MPE 2	NRI
AMF	Not MPE	NRI
United Merchants & Manufacturers	MPE 2	NRI
Gillette	MPE 2	NRI
Eli Lilly	MPE 2	RI
Evans Products	MPE 1	NRI
Pet	Not MPE	NRI
National Distillers & Chemicals	MPE 1	NRI
Phelps Dodge	MPE 2	NRI
Jim Walker	Not MPE	NRI
Walter Kidde	MPE 2	NRI
GAF	MPE 2	RI
Pillsbury	MPE 1	NRI
White Consolidated Industries	Not MPE	NRI
Pullman	MPE 2	NRI
Avco	Not MPE	RI
Johns-Manville	MPE 2	NRI
Quaker-Oats	MPE 2	NRI
Kellogg	MPE 2	NRI
McGraw Edison	Not MPE	RI
Archer Daniels Midland	Not MPE	NRI
American Smelting & Refining	MPE 2	NRI
Emerson Electric	MPE 2	RI
Sterling Drug	MPE 2	RI
Colt Industries	Not MPE	RI
Carrier	MPE 2	RI
Dana	Not MPE	NRI
Magnavox	MPE 1	RI
Amstar	Not MPE	NRI
Anderson Clayton	MPE 2	NRI
Zenith Radio	Not MPE	RI

Time Inc.	MPE 2	NRI
Northrop	MPE 2	RI
Corning Glass Works	MPE 2	NRI
Kerr-McGee	MPE 2	RI
Alco-Standard	MPE 1	RI
North American Philips	Not MPE	RI
Koppers	MPE 2	RI
Essex International	Not MPE	RI
Liggett & Myers	MPE 1	NRI
Ethyl	MPE 1	RI
Diamond Shamrock	MPE 2	RI
Control Data	MPE 2	RI
Diamond International	MPE 2	NRI
Northwest Industries	Not MPE	NRI
Armstrong Cork	MPE 2	NRI
Sherwin Williams	MPE 2	RI
US Gypsum	MPE 2	NRI
Budd	Not MPE	NRI
Loews	Not MPE	NRI
City Investing	Not MPE	NRI
Owens-Corning Fibreglass	MPE 2	NRI
Libby-Owens-Ford	Not MPE	NRI
Wheeling-Pittsburgh Steel	Not MPE	NRI
Container Corporation of America	Not MPE	NRI
Joseph E. Seagram & Sons	MPE 1	NRI
Polaroid	MPE 2	RI
Jos. Schlitz Brewing	Not MPE	NRI
Times Mirror	Not MPE	NRI
Union Camp	MPE 1	NRI
International Minerals & Chemical	MPE 2	RI
Paccar	Not MPE	NRI
Brunswick	MPE 2	RI
Lear Siegler	MPE 1	RI
Rohm & Haas	MPE 2	RI
Foster Wheeler	MPE 2	RI
Brown Group	Not MPE	NRI
Castle & Cooke	MPE 2	NRI
Cluett, Peabody	MPE 1	NRI
Stauffer Chemical	MPE 2	RI
Cummins Engine	MPE 2	NRI
Allegheny Ludlum Industries	Not MPE	NRI
Fruehauf	MPE 2	NRI
Kayser-Roth	MPE 1	NRI
Scovill Manufacturing	MPE 1	NRI

Kaiser Steel	MPE 2	NRI
Universal Leaf Tobacco	Not MPE	NRI
Abbott Laboratories	MPE 2	RI
National Gypsum	Not MPE	NRI
A. O. Smith	MPE 2	NRI
Chromalloy American	Not MPE	NRI
Crown Cork & Seal	MPE 2	NRI
USM	MPE 2	NRI
Indian Head	Not MPE	NRI
Eltra	MPE 2	NRI
M. Lowenstein & Sons	Not MPE	NRI
Universal Oil Products	MPE 2	RI
Airco	MPE 2	RI
Ward Foods	MPE 1	NRI
Upjohn	MPE 1	RI
Schering-Plough	MPE 2	RI
National Can	MPE 2	NRI
Sunbeam	MPE 2	NRI
International Multi Foods	MPE 1	NRI
Westvaco	MPE 1	NRI
Di Giorgio	MPE 2	NRI
Cerro	MPE 2	NRI
Flintkote	MPE 1	NRI
Addressograph Multigraph	MPE 2	RI
Timken	MPE 2	RI
Richardson-Merrell	MPE 2	RI
Admiral	MPE 2	RI
Pennwalt	MPE 2	RI
Levi-Strauss	Not MPE	NRI
McGraw-Hill	MPE 1	NRI
Hoover	MPE 2	NRI
Coastal States Gas Producing	Not MPE	RI
Hershey Foods	MPE 1	NRI
Revlon	MPE 2	RI
Tecumseh Products	MPE 2	NRI
Crowell Collier & Macmillan	Not MPE	NRI
Kelsey-Hayes	MPE 1	NRI
Bemis	MPE 2	NRI
Libby, McNeill & Libby	MPE 2	NRI
Hewlett-Packard	MPE 2	NRI
Lone Star Industries	MPE 1	NRI
Heublein	MPE 2	NRI
Warner Communications	MPE 2	NRI
Hart & Schaffner & Marx	Not MPE	NRI

Hammermill Paper	Not MPE	NRI
American Beef Packers	Not MPE	NRI
Allied Mills	MPE 2	NRI
Mattel	Not MPE	NRI
ATO	Not MPE	NRI
Smith & Kline & French	MPE 2	RI
Chicago Bridge & Iron	MPE 2	NRI
Great Northern Nekoosa	Not MPE	NRI
Sybron	MPE 2	RI
West Point-Pepperell	Not MPE	NRI
Mohasco Industries	Not MPE	NRI
Potlatch Forests	Not MPE	NRI
Outboard Marine	MPE 2	NRI
Fuqua Industries	Not MPE	NRI
Interlake	Not MPE	NRI
Harris-Intertype	MPE 1	RI
Fedders	Not MPE	NRI
Purex	MPE 2	NRI
General Cable	MPE 1	NRI
Norton	MPE 2	NRI
Cambell Taggart	Not MPE	NRI
Morton-Norwich Products	MPE 2	RI
Gould	MPE 1	RI
R. R. Donnelley & Sons	Not MPE	NRI
Rex Chainbelt	MPE 2	RI
Cyclops	Not MPE	NRI
US Smelting Refining & Mining	MPE 2	NRI
National Service Industries	Not MPE	NRI
Rohr Industries	Not MPE	RI
Fairmont Foods	Not MPE	NRI
Revere Copper & Brass	MPE 2	NRI
A. E. Staley Manufacturing	MPE 1	NRI
ACF Industries	Not MPE	NRI
Certain-Teed Products	Not MPE	NRI
I-T-E Imperial	MPE 2	RI
Hygrade Food Projects	MPE 2	NRI
American Bakeries	Not MPE	NRI
General American Transportation	Not MPE	NRI
General Host	Not MPE	NRI
Bell & Howell	MPE 2	RI
Inmont	MPE 2	NRI
MCA	MPE 2	NRI
Champion Spark Plug	MPE 2	NRI
Springs Mills	Not MPE	NRI

US Shoes	Not MPE	NRI
Cannon Mills	Not MPE	NRI
Kane Miller	Not MPE	NRI
Miles Laboratories	MPE 2	RI
Saxon Industries	MPE 1	NRI
Cone Mills	Not MPE	NRI
Harsco	MPE 2	NRI
Reliance Electric	MPE 2	RI
Simmons	MPE 2	NRI
Anchor Hocking	Not MPE	NRI
Dan River	Not MPE	NRI
Dayco	MPE 1	NRI
Pabst Brewing	Not MPE	NRI
Carborundum	MPE 2	RI
Air Products & Chemicals	MPE 2	RI
ESB	MPE 2	RI
Pitney-Bowes	MPE 2	NRI
Missouri Beef Packers	Not MPE	NRI
Stanley Works	MPE 2	NRI
Chesebrough Ponds	MPE 2	RI
Jonathan Logan	MPE 2	NRI
Joy Manufacturing	MPE 2	RI
NVF	Not MPE	NRI
Avnet	MPE 1	RI
Kendall	MPE 2	NRI

JAPANESE COMPANIES

Nippon Steel	Not MPE	NRI
Hitachi	Not MPE	RI
Toyota Motor	MPE 2	NRI
Mitsubishi Heavy Industries	MPE 2	NRI
Nissan Motors	MPE 2	NRI
Matsushita Electric Industrial	MPE 2	RI
Tokyo Shibaura Electric	MPE 2	RI
Nippon Kokan	Not MPE	NRI
Sumitomo Metal Industries	Not MPE	NRI
Kobe Steel	Not MPE	NRI
Mitsubishi Electric	Not MPE	RI
Taiyo Fishery	MPE 2	NRI
Ishikawajima-Harima Heavy Industries	MPE 1	NRI
Kawasaki Steel	Not MPE	NRI
Mitsubishi Chemical Industries	Not MPE	RI
Honda Motors	MPE 1	NRI

Toray Industries	MPE 2	RI
Nippon Electric	MPE 1	RI
Kawasaki Heavy Industries	MPE 1	RI
Asahi Chemical Industry	Not MPE	RI
Kanebo	Not MPE	NRI
Toyo Kogyo	Not MPE	NRI
Nippon Mining	Not MPE	RI
Unitika	Not MPE	RI
Toyoba	Not MPE	NRI
Sanyo Electric	MPE 1	RI
Komatsu	MPE 2	NRI
Hitachi Shipbuilding and Engineering	Not MPE	NRI
Kubota	MPE 1	NRI
Teijin	MPE 1	NRI
Kirin Brewery	Not MPE	NRI
Toa Nenryo Kogyo	Not MPE	NRI
Showa Denko	Not MPE	RI
Furukawa Electric	MPE 1	RI
Ube Industries	Not MPE	RI
Sony Corpn.	MPE 1	RI
Takeda Chemical Industries	MPE 2	RI
Sumitomo Electric Industries	Not MPE	RI
Fujitsu	Not MPE	RI
Mitsubishi Oil	Not MPE	RI
Snow Brand Milk Products	Not MPE	NRI
Bridgestone Tire	MPE 1	NRI
Mitsui Shipbuilding and Engineering	Not MPE	NRI
Fuji Electric	Not MPE	RI
Suzuki Motors	Not MPE	NRI
Mitsui Mining and Smelting	Not MPE	NRI
Asahi Glass	Not MPE	RI
Nishin Steel	Not MPE	NRI
Ajinomoto	MPE 1	RI
Mitsui Toatsu Chemicals	Not MPE	RI
Sharp Corpn.	Not MPE	RI
Mitsubishi Metal Mining	Not MPE	NRI
Meiji Milk Products	Not MPE	NRI
Honshu Paper Manufacturing	Not MPE	NRI
Morinaga-Milk Industry	Not MPE	NRI
Fuji Phote Film	MPE 2	RI
Hino Motors	MPE 1	NRI
Kuraray	Not MPE	RI
Jujo Paper Manufacturing	Not MPE	NRI
Nisshin Flour Milling	Not MPE	NRI

Fuji Heavy Industries	Not MPE	NRI
Sumitomo Shipbuilding and Machinery	Not MPE	NRI
Nippon Suisan	MPE 1	NRI
Nippon Denso	Not MPE	RI
Shiseido	MPE 1	NRI
Dainippon Ink and Chemicals	Not MPE	RI
Toppan Printing	MPE 2	NRI
Daishowa Paper Manufacturing	MPE 1	NRI
Sumitomo Metal Mining	Not MPE	NRI
Oji Paper	Not MPE	NRI

UK COMPANIES

Royal Dutch/Shell Group	MPE 2	RI
Unilever	MPE 2	NRI
British Petroleum	MPE 2	RI
ICI	MPE 2	RI
British Leyland Motor	MPE 2	NRI
Dunlop Pirelli Union	MPE 2	NRI
British American Tobacco	MPE 2	NRI
General Electric	MPE 2	RI
Courtaulds	MPE 2	NRI
Associated British Foods	MPE 2	NRI
GKN	MPE 2	NRI
Reed International	MPE 2	NRI
Imperial Tobacco Group	Not MPE	NRI
Hawker-Siddley Group	MPE 2	RI
Rio Tinto Zinc	MPE 2	NRI
British Insulated Callender's Cables	MPE 2	RI
Ranks Hovis McDougall	MPE 1	NRI
Tube Investments	MPE 2	NRI
Thorn Electrical Industries	MPE 2	RI
Tate & Lyle	MPE 2	NRI
Unigate	MPE 1	NRI
Consolidated Tin Smelters	MPE 1	NRI
Union International	MPE 2	NRI
Joseph Lucas (Industries)	MPE 2	RI
Allied Breweries	MPE 1	NRI
Coats Patons	MPE 2	NRI
Cadbury Schweppes	MPE 2	NRI
Distillers	MPE 2	NRI
Burmah Oil	MPE 2	RI
Bowater	MPE 2	NRI
Plessey	MPE 2	RI

Metal Box	MPE 2	NRI
Brooke Bond Liebig	MPE 2	NRI
British Oxygen	MPE 2	RI
Bass Charrington	Not MPE	NRI
EMI	MPE 2	RI
Beecham Group	MPE 2	RI
Ready Mixed Concrete	MPE 1	NRI
Spillers	MPE 1	NRI
Consolidated Gold Fields	MPE 2	NRI
J. Lyons	MPE 1	NRI
Reckitt & Colman	MPE 1	NRI
Lonrho	MPE 2	NRI
Vickers	MPE 2	RI
Delta Metal	MPE 2	NRI
Associated Portland Cement	MPE 2	NRI
Glaxo	MPE 2	RI
English Calico	MPE 2	NRI
British Aircraft	Not MPE	RI
Rank Organisation	MPE 2	RI
Johnson Matthey	MPE 2	RI
Tarmac	MPE 2	NRI
Carrington Viyella	MPE 2	NRI
International Computers (holdings)	MPE 2	RI
FMC	Not MPE	NRI
Arthur Guinness	MPE 1	NRI
Dickinson Robinson Group	MPE 1	NRI
Whitbread	MPE 1	NRI
Pilkington Bros.	MPE 2	NRI
Rowntree Mackintosh	MPE 1	NRI
Turner & Newall	MPE 2	NRI
Babcock & Wilcox	MPE 2	RI
Albright & Wilson	MPE 2	RI
Courage	Not MPE	NRI
Watney Mann	Not MPE	NRI

GERMAN COMPANIES

Volkswagenwerk	MPE 2	NRI
Siemens	MPE 2	RI
Farbwerke Hoechst	MPE 2	RI
Daimler-Benz	MPE 2	NRI
BASF	MPE 2	RI
August Thyssen-Hütte	MPE 2	NRI
AEG Telefunken	MPE 2	RI

Bayer	MPE 2	RI
Gutehoffnungshütte	Not MPE	NRI
Krupp-Konzern	MPE 2	NRI
Mannesmann	MPE 2	NRI
Robert Bosch	MPE 2	RI
Rheinstahl	Not MPE	NRI
Hoesch	MPE 1	NRI
Metallgesellschaft	MPE 2	NRI
Henkel	MPE 1	RI
Gelsenberg	MPE 2	RI
KHD	MPE 1	NRI
Buderus'sche Eisenwerke	Not MPE	NRI
Feldmühle-Dynamit Nobel	MPE 2	RI
Agfa-Gaveart Group	MPE 2	RI
Klöckner Werke	Not MPE	NRI
BMW	Not MPE	NRI
Degussa	MPE 1	RI
VIAG	MPE 2	RI
Varta	MPE 2	RI
Preussag	MPE 2	NRI
Continental Gummi-Werke	MPE 1	NRI
Deutsche Babcock & Wilcox	MPE 2	NRI
Reemtsma Cigarettenfabriken	MPE 2	NRI
Veba-Chemie	MPE 2	RI
Chemische Werke Hüls	MPE 2	RI
Demag	MPE 2	NRI
Stahlwerke Röchling-Burbach	MPE 1	NRI
Freudenberg	Not MPE	NRI
Stahlwerke Südwestfalen	MPE 1	NRI
Schering	MPE 2	RI
Grundig-Werke	MPE 2	RI
Messerschmitt-Bölkow-Blohm	Not MPE	RI
Boehringer Ingelheim	Not MPE	RI
Norddeutsche Affinerie	MPE 1	RI

FRENCH COMPANIES

Pechiney Ugine Kuhlmann	MPE 2	RI
Cie Francaise des Petroles	MPE 2	RI
Rhône-Poulenc	MPE 2	RI
Saint-Gobain-Pont-à-Mousson	MPE 2	NRI
Citroen	MPE 2	NRI
Cie Générale d'Électricité	MPE 2	RI
Peugeot	MPE 2	NRI

Michelin	MPE 2	NRI
Thomson-Brandt	MPE 2	RI
Usinor	Not MPE	NRI
Wendelor-Sidelor	Not MPE	NRI
Boussois Souchon Neuvesel	MPE 2	NRI
Vallourec	Not MPE	NRI
Creusot-Loire	Not MPE	NRI
Schneider	Not MPE	NRI
Librairie Hachette	Not MPE	NRI
Le Nickel	MPE 1	NRI
L'Air Liquide	MPE 2	RI
Enterprise Minière et Chimique	Not MPE	RI
Centrale Roussel Nobel	MPE 2	RI
Agache-Willot	MPE 2	NRI
Cie Financière Lesieur	MPE 2	NRI
Gervais Danone Group	MPE 2	NRI
Dassault (Avions Marcel)	MPE 2	RI
L'Oreal	MPE 2	NRI
Perrier Group	Not MPE	NRI

CANADIAN COMPANIES

Alcan Aluminium	MPE 2	NRI
Massey-Furguson	MPE 2	NRI
Canada-Packers	MPE 1	NRI
International Nickel	MPE 2	NRI
MacMillan Bloedel	MPE 1	NRI
Steel Co. of Canada	MPE 1	NRI
Distillers Corp.-Seagrams	MPE 1	NRI
Domtar	Not MPE	NRI
Noranda Mines	MPE 1	NRI
Moore	MPE 1	NRI
Dominion Foundaries & Steel	Not MPE	NRI
Burns Foods	Not MPE	NRI
Hiram Walker-Gooderham and Worts	MPE 2	NRI
Consolidated-Bathurst	MPE 1	NRI
John Labatt	Not MPE	NRI
Imasco	Not MPE	NRI

SWEDISH COMPANIES

Volvo	MPE 2	NRI
SKF	MPE 2	NRI
Saab-Scania	MPE 2	NRI

Asea	MPE 2	RI
LM Ericsson Telephone	MPE 2	RI
Gränges	MPE 1	NRI
Svenska Tandsticks	MPE 2	NRI
Stora Kopparbergs Bergslags	MPE 2	NRI
Atlas Copco	MPE 2	NRI
Sandvik Group	MPE 2	NRI
Alfa-Laval	MPE 2	NRI
Svenska Cellulosa	MPE 2	NRI
Electrolux	MPE 2	RI

BELGIAN COMPANIES

Petrol Fina	MPE 2	RI
Solway	MPE 2	RI
Cockerill	MPE 2	NRI
Metallurgie Hoboken-Overpelt	MPE 2	NRI
Société Industrielle Belge des Pétrolés	MPE 2	RI

DUTCH COMPANIES

Royal Dutch/Shell Group	MPE 2	RI
Unilever	MPE 2	NRI
Philips' Gloeilampenfabrieken	MPE 2	RI
Akzo	MPE 2	RI
Schlumberger	MPE 2	RI
Hoogovens	Not MPE	NRI
VMF	MPE 2	NRI

ITALIAN COMPANIES

Montedison	MPE 2	RI
Fiat	MPE 2	NRI
Dunlop Pirelli Union	MPE 2	NRI
Olivetti	MPE 2	RI
Scia Viscosa	MPE 2	RI

SWISS COMPANIES

Nestle	MPE 2	NRI
Ciba-Geigy	MPE 2	RI
Brown Boveri	MPE 2	RI
Hoffmann-Laroche	MPE 2	RI
Sandoz	MPE 2	RI

Sulzer	MPE 2	NRI
Alusuisse (Swiss Aluminium)	MPE 2	NRI
Holderbank Financière Glarus	MPE 1	NRI

OTHERS

BHP	MPE 2	NRI
Dunlop Australia	Not MPE	NRI
ARBED	MPE 2	NRI
De Beers Consolidated Mines	MPE 1	NRI
Seat	Not MPE	NRI
Premier Milling	Not MPE	NRI
Altos Homos de Vizcuya	Not MPE	NRI

References

CHAPTER 1 INTRODUCTION

1. K. Arrow, 'The economic implications of learning by doing', *Review of Economic Studies*, June 1962.
2. R. M. Cyert and J. G. March, 'Organisational factors in the theory of oligopoly', *Quarterly Journal of Economics*, February 1956.
3. W. Beckerman and Associates, *The British Economy in 1975*, Cambridge University Press, 1965.
4. F. V. Mayer, D. C. Corner and J. E. S. Parker, *Problems of a Mature Economy*, Macmillan, 1970.
5. For a survey of an extensive literature, see A. Sen, *Growth Economics*, Penguin, 1970.
6. J. Schmookler, *Invention and Economic Growth*, Harvard University Press, 1966.

CHAPTER 2 THE COMPETITIVE ENVIRONMENT

1. J. M. Samuels and D. J. Smythe, 'Profits, variability of profits and firm size', *Economica*, May 1968. A. Singh and G. Whittington, *Growth Profitability & Valuation*, Cambridge University Press, 1968.
2. F. M. Scherer, *Industrial Market Structure and Economic Performance*, Rand McNally, 1970, p. 342.
3. D. C. Mueller and J. E. Tilton, 'Research and development costs as a barrier to entry', *Canadian Journal of Economics*, November 1969.
4. Two notable exceptions are E. Penrose, *The Theory of the Growth of the Firm*, Blackwell, 1959, and R. Marris, *The Economic Theory of Managerial Capitalism*, Macmillan, 1964.
5. See J. M. Clark, 'Towards a concept of workable competition', *American Economic Review*, June 1940; J. M. Clark, *Competition as a Dynamic Process*, Washington Brookings Institution, 1971; Scherer, *op. cit.*
6. C. Freeman, 'The plastics industry: a comparative study of research and development', *National Institute Economic Review*, November 1963; R. Vernon, 'International investments and international trade in the product cycle', *Quarterly Journal of Economics*, May 1966; L. T. Wells, 'Test of a product cycle model of international trade: U.S. exports of consumer durables', *Quarterly Journal of Economics*, February 1969; S. Hirsch, *Location of Industry and International Competitiveness*, Oxford, Clarendon Press, 1967.
7. Mueller and Tilton, *op. cit.*

8. Figures quoted in G. Wills, R. Wilson, N. Manning and R. Hildebrandt, *Technological Forecasting*, Penguin Books, Pelican Library of Business and Management, 1972.

9. G. F. Ray, 'The diffusion of new technology', *National Institute Economic Review*, May 1969.

10. For other versions see T. S. Robertson, *Innovative Behaviour and Communication*, Holt, Rinehart & Winston, 1971.

11. See for example the judgment given by the Restrictive Practices Court on 12 July 1963 and 27 November 1966 relating to the National Sulphuric Acid Association.

12. OECD, *Gaps in Technology, Plastics*, Paris, 1969.

13. Robertson, *op. cit.*

14. Robertson, *op. cit.*

15. M. Gort, *Diversification and Integration in American Industry*, Princeton University Press, 1962; K. D. George, *Industrial Organisation*, Allen & Unwin, 1971.

CHAPTER 3 INVENTION

1. F. M. Scherer, *Industrial Market Structure and Economic Performance*, Rand McNally, 1971, p. 350.

2. J. Schumpeter, *Business Cycles*, McGraw-Hill, 1939.

3. J. Langrish, M. Gibbons, W. G. Evans and F. R. Jevons, *Wealth from Knowledge*, Macmillan, 1972, p. 7.

4. J. Schmookler, *Invention and Economic Growth*, Harvard University Press, 1966.

5. V. Ruttan, 'Usher and Schumpeter, on Invention, Innovation and Technological Change', *Quarterly Journal of Economics*, November 1959.

6. A. P. Usher, *A History of Mechanical Invention*, Harvard University Press, 1954.

7. S. C. Gilfillan, *The Sociology of Invention*, University of Chicago Press, 1935, p. 10.

8. *Statistics of Science and Technology*, HMSO, 1970.

9. W. H. Gruber and D. G. Marquis, eds, *Factors in the Transfer of Technology*, MIT Press, 1969.

10. *Technology in Retrospect and Critical Events in Science (Traces)*, A report to the National Science Foundation prepared by Illinois Institute of Technology Research Institute, vol. 1, 1968.

11. Naval Research Advisory Committee, *Basic Research in the Navy*, vol. 1, June 1959.

12. R. S. Isenson, 'Project Hindsight: an empirical study of the sources of ideas utilised in operational weapon system', in Gruber and Marquis, eds, (*op. cit.*).

13. D. J. de Solla Price, in Gruber and Marquis, eds, *op. cit.*
14. J. Langrish, M. Gibbons, W. G. Evans and F. R. Jevons, *Wealth from Knowledge*, Macmillan, 1972, p. xii.
15. Langrish, *et. al., op. cit.*
16. D. A. Schon, *Technology and Change*, Pergamon, 1967.
17. Langrish, *et al., op. cit.*
18. J. Jewkes, D. Sawers, R. Stillerman, *The Sources of Invention*, 2nd edn, Macmillan, 1969, p. 200.
19. H. S. Hatfield, *The Inventor and his World.*
20. Jewkes, *et al., op. cit.*
21. W. F. Mueller, 'The origins of basic invention underlying du Pont's major product and process innovations, 1920-1950', in *The Rate and Direction of Inventive Activity*, Princeton University Press, 1962.
22. Langrish, *et al., op. cit.*
23. K. Pavitt, 'The multi-national enterprise and the transfer of Technology', in J. H. Dunning, ed., *The Multi-National Enterprise*, Allen & Unwin, 1971, p. 64.
24. Gruber and Marquis, eds, *op. cit.*
25. *Ibid.*, p. 12.
26. Jewkes *et al., op. cit.*
27. Schmookler, *Invention and Economic Growth.*
28. J. Schmookler, 'Inventors, past and present', *Review of Economics and Statistics*, August 1957.
29. *Report by the Science Policy Research Unit to the Committee of Inquiry on Small Firms*, Cmnd 4811, HMSO 1971.
30. Jewkes *et al., op. cit.*
31. *Ibid.*, p. 73.
32. Jewkes *et al., op. cit.*
33. D. Hamberg, 'Invention in the industrial research laboratory', *Journal of Political Economy*, April 1963.
34. Mueller, *op. cit.*
35. Schon, *op. cit.*
36. Jewkes *et al., op. cit.*, p. 92.
37. *Ibid.*
38. Scherer, *op. cit.*
39. Schmookler, *Invention and Economic Growth.*
40. *The Rate and Direction of Inventive Activity*, p. 224.
41. Schmookler, *Invention and Economic Growth*, p. 93.
42. R. R. Nelson, M. J. Peck and E. D. Kalachek, *Technology, Economic Growth and Public Policy*, Brookings Institution, 1967, p. 28.
43. Schmookler, *Invention and Economic Growth*, p. 184.
44. *The Rate and Direction of Inventive Activity.*

45. Jewkes *et al., The Sources of Invention*, 2nd edn., p. 210.
46. *Ibid.*
47. C. Freeman, 'Research and development in electronic capital goods', *National Institute Economic Review*, 1965; for a reply see J. Jewkes *et al., Sources of Invention*, 2nd edn., pp. 208-9.
48. Jewkes *et al., op. cit.*, p. 184.

CHAPTER 4 INNOVATION

1. F. M. Scherer, *Industrial Market Structure and Economic Performance*, Rand McNally, 1971.
2. See, for example, R. Vernon, 'International investment and international trade in the product cycle', *Quarterly Journal of Economics*, May 1966.
3. E. Mansfield, 'The rate of return from industrial R and D', *American Economic Review*, May 1965.
4. See Chapter 10 on Patents.
5. R. B. Hill, 'Improving returns from R and D investment', in E. M. Hugh-Jones ed., *Economics and Technical Change*, Blackwell, 1969, p. 34.
6. E. Mansfield, J. Rapoport, J. Schnee, S. Wagner and M. Hamburger, *Research and Innovation in the Modern Corporation*, Norton, 1971.
7. *Ibid.*
8. Scherer, *op. cit.*, ch. 15.
9. *The Rate and Direction of Inventive Activity*, Princeton University Press, 1962; see also E. Mansfield, *The Economics of Technological Change*, Norton, 1968.
10. Mansfield *et al., op. cit.*
11. See also W. O. Baker, 'The Dynamism of Technology', in E. Ginzberg, ed., *Technology and Social Change*, Columbia University Press, 1964.
12. Constructed by the Center for Integrative Studies, State University of New York, at Bingingham.
13. J. Langrish, M. Gibbons, W. G. Evans and F. R. Jevons, *Wealth from Knowledge, Studies of Innovation in Industry*, Macmillan, 1972.
14. B. Dixon, 'Death of a nice idea', *New Scientist*, 18 May 1972; also *The Futurist*, vol. 6, 1972.
15. E. Mansfield, *Industrial Research and Technological Innovation*, Norton, 1968.
16. Mansfield *et al., op. cit.*
17. A. Gerstenfeld, *Effective Management of Research and Development*, Addison-Wesley Publishing Company, 1970.
18. *Ibid.*

19. *Ibid.*
20. Langrish *et al., op. cit.*
21. Figures quoted in T. S. Robertson, *Innovative Behaviour and Communication*, Holt Rinehart & Winston, 1971.
22. Mansfield, *Industrial Research and Technological Innovation*.
23. Mansfield *et al., op. cit.*
24. Z. Griliches, 'Research costs and social returns: hybrid corn and related innovations', *Journal of Political Economy*, October 1958.
25. J. Enos, 'Invention and innovation in the petroleum refining industry', in *The Rate and Direction of Inventive Activity*, Princeton University Press, 1962.
26. Mansfield, *Industrial Research and Technological Innovation*.
27. Gerstenfeld, *op. cit.*
28. Mansfield *et al., op. cit.*
29. C. Freeman, 'Research and development in electronic capital goods', *National Institute Economic Review*, November 1965.
30. F. M. Scherer, 'Corporate inventive output: profits and growth', *Journal of Political Economy,* April 1965, and W. S. Comanor and F. M. Scherer, 'Patent statistics as a measure of technical change', *Journal of Political Economy*, 1968.
31. *Aspects of Spin-Off*, Centre for the Study of Industrial Innovation, October 1971.
32. Langrish *et al., op. cit.*
33. *Ibid.*
34. E. Mansfield, 'Entry, Gibrat's Law, innovation and the growth of firms', *American Economic Review*, December 1962.
35. A. Singh and G. Whittington, with H. T. Burley, *Growth, Profitability and Valuation*, Cambridge University Press, 1968.
36. A. Singh, *Takeovers: their Relevance to the Stock Market and the Theory of the Firm*, Cambridge University Press, 1971.
37. Singh and Whittington, *op. cit.*
38. E. Mansfield, 'The size of the firm, market structure and innovation', *Journal of Political Economy*, December 1963.
39. H. Villard, 'Competition, oligopoly and research', *Journal of Political Economy*, December 1958.
40. Scherer, *Journal of Political Economy*, April 1965.
41. J. Markham, 'Market structure, business conduct and innovation', *American Economic Review, Papers and Proceedings*, May 1965.
42. Mansfield, 'The size of firm, market structure and innovation', *loc. cit.*, Mansfield, *Industrial Research and Technological Innovation*.
43. E. Mansfield, 'Industrial research and development expenditure: determinants, prospects and relation to size of firm and inventive output', *Journal of Political Economy*, August 1964.

44. J. M. Blair, *Economic Concentration*, Harcourt, Brace, Jovanovich, 1972.
45. R. R. Nelson, 'The simple economics of basic scientific research', *Journal of Political Economy*, June 1959.
46. F. M. Scherer, 'Firm size, market structure, opportunity and output of patented inventions', *American Economic Review*, December 1965.
47. H. G. Grabowski, 'The determinants of industrial research and development: a study of the chemical, drug and petroleum industries', *Journal of Political Economy*, March/April 1968.
48. H. Villard, 'Competition, oligopoly and research', *Journal of Political Economy*, December 1958.
49. Scherer, 'Firm size . . . patented inventions', *Am. Econ. Rev.*, Dec., 1965.
50. D. J. Smyth, J. M. Samuels and T. Tzoannos, 'Patents, profitability, liquidity and firm size', *Applied Economics*, June 1972.
51. *Ibid.*
52. Scherer, 'Corporate inventive output . . .', *J. Pol. Econ.*, June 1965.
53. J. R. Minasian, *The Economics of Research and Development in the Rate and Direction of Inventive Activity*, New York, NBER, 1962.
54. H. G. Grabowski, *op. cit.*; Smyth *et al., op. cit.*
55. M. H. Cooper and J. E. S. Parker, 'Profitability ratios and foreign owned subsidiaries', *Business Ratios*, Autumn 1967.
56. J. H. Dunning, 'The role of American investment in the British Economy', *Political and Economic Planning*, 1969.
57. A. Phillips, 'Concentration, scale and technological change in selected manufacturing industries, 1899-1939', *Journal of Industrial Economics*, 1956.
58. G. J. Stigler, 'Industrial organisation and economic progress', in L. D. White, ed., *The State of the Social Sciences*, University of Chicago Press, 1956.
59. D. Schon, 'Innovation by invasion', *International Science and Technology*, March 1964.
60. See Scherer, *Industrial Market Structure and Economic Performance.*
61. F. M. Scherer, 'Market structure and the employment of scientists and engineers', *American Economic Review*, June 1967.
62. W. S. Comanor, 'Market structure, product differentiation and industrial research', *Quarterly Journal of Economics*, November 1967; Scherer, Dec. 1965 and 1970, 'Firm Size . . .' *Am. Econ. Rev.*
63. Scherer as n. 62; Comanor, *op. cit.*

64. Scherer, 'Firm size . . .', *Am. Econ. Rev.*, Dec. 1965.
65. D. C. Mueller, 'A life cycle theory of the firm', *Journal of Industrial Economics*, July 1972.
66. D. Hamberg, 'Invention and the Industrial Research Laboratory', *Journal of Political Economy*, 1963.
67. Scherer, *Industrial Market Structure and Economic Performance.*

CHAPTER 5 MANAGEMENT AND INNOVATION

1. J. Langrish, M. Gibbons, W. G. Evans and F. R. Jevons, *Wealth from Knowledge*, Macmillan, 1972, p. 69.
2. *Ibid.*
3. *Ibid.*
4. *Success and Failure in Industrial Innovation, Report on Project SAPPHO*, Science Policy Research Unit, University of Sussex, Centre for the Study of Industrial Innovation, 1972.
5. D. A. Schon, 'Champions for radical new inventions', *Harvard Business Review*, March-April, 1963.
6. *On the Shelf, A survey of industrial R and D projects abandoned for non-technical reasons*, Centre for the Study of Industrial Innovation, July 1971.
7. Langrish *et al., op. cit.*, p. 49.
8. E. Mansfield, J. Rapoport, J. Schnee, S. Wagner, M. Hamburger, *Research and Innovation in the Modern Corporation*, Norton, 1971.
9. *Ibid.*
10. *Ibid.*
11. *Ibid.*, ch. 3.
12. Langrish *et al.*
13. Mansfield *et al.*
14. E. Mansfield, *Industrial Research and Technological Innovation*, Norton, 1968.
15. Hypotheses of this character are to be found in R. Nelson, N. Peck, and E. Kalachek, *Technology, Economic Growth and Public Policy*, Brookings Institution, 1967; *The Rate and Direction of Inventive Activity*, Princeton U.P., 1962; F. M. Scherer, *Industrial Market Structure and Economic Performance*, Rand McNally, 1970; J. Jewkes, D. Sawers and R. Stillerman, *The Sources of Invention*, 2nd edn., Macmillan, 1969; Mansfield, *Industrial Research and Technological Innovation*, and Mansfield *et al.*, *Research and Innovation in the Modern Corporation*.
16. Mansfield *et al.*, ch. 4.
17. M. Peck and F. M. Scherer, *The Weapons Acquisition Process*,

University Press, 1962; D. Novick, *Lead Time in Modern Weapons*, Rand Corporation, 1957; A. Yorke Saville, 'Mining machine industry', *Iron and Coal Trades Review*, 19 Sept. 1958; Mansfield *et al., op. cit.*

18. Mansfield *et al., op. cit.*, chs. 6 and 7.
19. *Ibid.*, ch. 7.
20. *Ibid.*, ch. 7.
21. E. Mansfield *et al., op. cit.*
22. *Ibid.*
23. *Ibid.*

CHAPTER 6 THE DIFFUSION OF INNOVATION: THE NATIONAL COMPANY

1. E. Mansfield, J. Rapoport, J. Schnee, S. Wagner, M. Hamburger, *Research and Innovation in the Modern Corporation*, W. W. Norton, 1971, p. 186.
2. W. H. Gruber and D. G. Marquis, eds, *Factors in the Transfer of Technology*, M.I.T. Press, 1969, p. 255.
3. E. F. Denison, *Why Growth Rates Differ*, Brookings Institution, Washington, 1967, p. 288.
4. T. S. Robertson, *Innovative Behaviour and Communication*, Holt Rinehart & Winston, 1971.
5. E. M. Rogers, *Diffusion of Innovations*, New York Free Press, 1962.
6. J. S. Coleman, E. Katz and H. Menzel, *Medical Innovations: A Diffusion Study*, Bobbs-Merrill Inc, 1966.
7. E. Mansfield, 'Technical change and the rate of imitation', *Econometrica* **29**, Oct. 1961.
8. OECD, *Gaps in Technology, Analytical Report*, Paris, 1970.
9. Mansfield *et al., op. cit.*
10. Robertson, *op. cit.*
11. *Ibid.*
12. Rogers, *op. cit.*
13. *Ibid.*
14. C. F. Carter and B. R. Williams, 'The characteristics of technically progressive firms', *Journal of Industrial Economics*, March 1959.
15. W. E. G. Salter, *Productivity and Technical Change*, Cambridge University Press, 1960; J. Downie, *The Competitive Process*, Duckworth, 1958.
16. Salter, *op. cit.*
17. E. Mansfield, *Industrial Research and Technological Innovation*, Norton, 1968.
18. R. G. Lipsey and P. O. Steiner, *Economics*, Harper, 1966.

19. E. Mansfield, 'Technical change . . .', *Econometrica*, Oct. 1961.
20. E. Mansfield, *Economics of Technological Change*, Norton, 1968.
21. M. Frankel, 'Obsolescence and technical change in a maturing economy', *American Economic Review*, 1955.
22. *New Scientist*, 15 April 1971.
23. Mansfield, *Industrial Research and Technological Innovation*, p. 137.
24. 'Diffusion of a Major Manufacturing Innovation', in Mansfield *et al., op. cit.*
25. Mansfield *et al., op. cit.*
26. *Ibid.*
27. See, for example, G. J. Stigler, *Capital and Rates of Return in Manufacturing Industries*, Princeton University Press, 1963. P. E. Hart, *Studies in Profit, Business Savings and Investment in the United Kingdom*, vol. 2, Allen & Unwin, 1968; A. Singh and G. Whittington with H. T. Burley, *Growth, Profitability & Valuation*, Cambridge University Press, 1968.
28. Mansfield *et al., op. cit.*
29. 'Project selection, commercial risks, and the allocation to small business of Federal Research and Development contracts', in Mansfield *et al., op. cit.*
30. Z. Griliches, 'Hybrid corn and the economics of innovation', *Science*, 29 July 1960, p. 275.
31. Comment by N. Rosenberg on the findings of Z. Griliches in N. Rosenberg, ed., *Economics of Technological Change*, Penguin, 1971, p. 209.
32. G. F. Ray, 'The diffusion of new technology', *National Institute Economic Review*, June 1969.
33. Griliches, *op. cit.*
34. Mansfield, *Industrial Research and Technological Innovation*; Mansfield *et al., op. cit.*; Ray, *op. cit.*
35. E. Mansfield, 'The speed of response of firms to new techniques', *Quarterly Journal of Economics*, May 1963.
36. Mansfield, *Industrial Research and Technological Innovation.*
37. See D. C. McClelland in W. H. Gruber and D. G. Marquis, eds., *Factors in the Transfer of Technology*, M.I.T. Press, 1969.
38. *Ibid.*
39. Mansfield *et al., op. cit.*
40. Mansfield, 'The speed of response . . .', *Q. J. Econ*, May 1963.
41. Mansfield, *Industrial Research and Technological Innovation.*
42. Robertson, *op. cit.*
43. Mansfield, *Industrial Research and Technological Innovation.*
44. *Ibid.*
45. *Ibid.*, pp. 190-1.

CHAPTER 7 DIFFUSION AND THE MULTINATIONAL ENTERPRISE:
I TECHNOLOGY

1. C. P. Kindleberger, *American Business Abroad*, Yale University Press, 1969.
2. J. H. Dunning, 'The multi-national enterprise', *Lloyd's Bank Review*, July 1970.
3. R. E. Caves, 'International corporations: the industrial economics of foreign investment', *Economica*, Feb. 1971; J. H. Dunning, ed., *The Multi-National Enterprise*, Allen & Unwin, 1971.
4. Dunning, *Lloyd's Bank Review*, July 1970.
5. Dunning, ed., *op. cit.*
6. S. Rolfe, 'The international corporation in perspective', in *The Multi-National Corporation in the World Economy*, Praeger, 1970.
7. C. P. Kindleberger, *The International Corporation*, MIT Press, 1970.
8. J. C. McManus, 'The theory of the international firm', in G. Paquet, ed., *The Multinational Firm and the Nation State*, Collier-Macmillan, 1972.
9. C. P. Kindleberger, *American Business Abroad*, Yale University Press, 1969.
10. A. Silbertson, 'Economies of scale in theory and practice', *Economic Journal*, Supplement, April 1972.
11. Kindleberger, *op. cit.*
12. D. T. Brash, *American Investment in Australian Industry*, Harvard University Press, 1965.
13. Dunning, ed., *op. cit.*
14. M. Pavitt in *ibid.*
15. A. D. Chandler, *Strategy and Structure*, Doubleday, 1961.
16. Kindleberger, *op. cit.*
17. D. Robertson, 'The multi-national enterprise: trade flows and trade policy', in J. H. Dunning ed., *International Investment*, Penguin, 1972, p. 336.
18. Kindleberger, *op. cit.*
19. Dunning, ed., The Multinational Enterprise.
20. R. Vernon, 'International investment and international trade in the product cycle', *Quarterly Journal of Economics*, **80**, 1966.
21. W. Gruber, D. Mehta and R. Vernon, 'The R. and D. factor in international trade and international investment of United States industries', *Journal of Political Economy*, Feb. 1967; D. B. Keesing, 'Impact of R and D on U.S. trade', *Journal of Political Economy*, February 1967; OECD, *Gaps in Technology, Analytical Report*, Paris 1970.
22. OECD, *Gaps in Technology*.

23. Robertson, *op. cit.*
24. *Gaps in Technology.*
25. E. Penrose, *The Economics of the International Patent System*, Johns Hopkins Press, 1951.

CHAPTER 8 DIFFUSION AND THE MULTINATIONAL ENTERPRISE: II METHODOLOGY AND STATISTICS

1. OECD, *Gaps in Technology*, Table 9, Payments for technology are defined as payments for patents, licences and technology.
2. OECD, *Conditions for Success in Technological Innovation*, Paris, 1971.
3. *Ibid.*
4. *Fortune Magazine* only extended its list of non-USA companies to 300 in 1972.
5. OECD, *The Industrial Policy of Japan*, Paris, 1972.
6. *Fortune Magazine*, May and August 1972, published by Time Inc.
7. Published by Moodies Services Ltd, 1972.
8. Edited by Lionel F. Gray and J. J. Love; Sampson Low, Marston & Co., 1973.
9. Extel Statistical Services Ltd, London.
10. Extel-Nomura Japanese Service, discontinued 1971.
11. *1971 Diamond Japan Business Directory of 853 Companies*, Diamond Lead Co. Business Information Company, Tokyo, 1971.
12. *The Times 1000*, published by the Times Newspaper, 1972.
13. *A Directory of Parent, Associate and Subsidiary Companies*, compiled and published by O. W. Roskill and Co. (Reports) Ltd.
14. In particular Nomura Services, London.
15. J. H. Dunning and R. D. Pearce, 'The world's largest enterprises: a statistical profile', *Business Ratios*, Issue Three.
16. C. Freeman, *Development Effort in Western Europe, North America and the Soviet Union*, Paris, OECD, 1965.
17. Examples include Distillers Corporation, Seagrams and the Moore Corporation.
18. Examples include T. J. Lipton, and Akzona, in America.
19. F. V. Meyer, D. C. Corner and J. E. S. Parker, *Problems of a Mature Economy*, Macmillan 1970.
20. A. Sandles and C. Smith, 'The Japanese challenge comes very close to home', *The Financial Times*, 1 March 1973.
21. OECD, *The Industrial Policy of Japan*, Paris, 1972.

CHAPTER 9 DIFFUSION AND THE MULTINATIONAL ENTERPRISE: III INTERPRETATION

1. N. Kaldor, *The Causes of the Slow Rate of Growth of the United Kingdom*, Cambridge University Press, 1966.

2. Meyer *et al., op. cit.*
3. A. Lamfalusy, *Investment and Growth in Mature Economies: the case of Belgium*, Macmillan, 1961.
4. C. F. Pratten, 'The reason for the slow economic progress of the British economy', *Oxford Economic Papers*, July 1972.
5. J. H. Dunning, 'The Multi-National Enterprise', *Lloyds Bank Review*, July 1970.
6. J. H. Dunning, 'The role of American investment in the British economy', *Political and Economic Planning*, 1969.
7. S. Hymer and R. Rowthorne in C. P. Kindleberger, ed., *The International Corporation*, MIT Press, 1970.
8. R. Rowthorne, *International Big Business, 1957-67*, Cambridge University Press, 1970.
9. *Ibid.*
10. Figures quoted in J. H. Dunning and R. D. Pearce, 'The world's largest enterprises, a statistical profile', *Business Ratios*, Issue Three.
11. *Ibid.*
12. OECD, *Gaps in Technology, Analytical Report*, Paris, 1970; J. J. Servan Schreiber, *The American Challenge*, Hamish Hamilton, 1968.
13. C. Freeman, 'The plastics industry: a comparative study of research and innovation', *NIESR*, Nov. 1963.
14. *Gaps in Technology, op. cit.*
15. *Ibid.*
16. D. Robertson, 'The multi-national enterprise: trade flows and trade policy', in J. H. Dunning ed., *International Investment*, Penguin, 1972.
17. H. Villard, 'Competition, oligopoly and research', *Journal of Political Economy*, December 1958.
18. S. Hymer, 'The efficiency (contradictions) of multi-national corporations', in G. Paquet, ed., *The Multi-National Firm and the Nation State*, Collier Macmillan, 1970, p. 56.
19. For those who are interested, detailed tables relating to individual countries are available from the Economics Department, University of Exeter.

CHAPTER 10 DIFFUSION AND THE MULTINATIONAL ENTERPRISE: IV THE DIRECT INVESTMENT PACKAGE

1. W. B. Reddaway with S. J. Potter and C. T. Taylor, *The effects of UK direct investment overseas — Final Report*, Cambridge University Press, 1968.
2. G. C. Hufbauer and F. M. Adler, *Overseas Manufacturing Investment and the Balance of Payments*, US Treasury Department, 1968.

3. H. B. Lary, 'Imports of Manufactures from Less Developed Countries', NBER, 1968; H. K. May, *The Effects of United States and other Foreign Investment in Latin America*. A report for the Council of Latin America, New York, January 1970; S. G. Mousouris, 'Manufactured products and export markets: dichotomy of markets for Greek manufacturers', in L. T. Wells, ed., *The Product Life Cycle and International Trade*, Harvard University Press, 1970.

4. R. Vernon, ed., 'The Technology Factor in International Trade', NBER, 1970; L. T. Wells, ed., *The Product Life Cycle and International Trade*, Harvard University Press, 1972.

5. E. Mansfield, 'The multinational firm and technological change' in J. H. Dunning, ed., *Economic Analysis and the Multinational Enterprise*, Allen & Unwin, 1973.

6. W. Gruber, D. Mehta and R. Vernon, 'The R and D factor in international trade and international investment of US industries', *Journal of Political Economy*, February 1967; and R. B. Stobaugh in L. T. Wells, ed., *op. cit.*

7. See, for example, D. L. Spencer and A. Woroniak, eds., *The Transfer of Technology to Developing Nations*, Washington DC, 1966; J. Baranson, *Industrial Technologies for Developing Economies*, Praeger, 1969; K. Berrill, ed., *Economic Development With Special Reference to East Asia*, Macmillan, 1964; V. S. Balasubramanyan, *The International Transfer of Technology to India*, Praeger, 1973.

8. F. T. Knickerbocker, *Oligopolistic Reaction and the Multi-national Enterprise*, Harvard Business School, 1973.

9. J. H. Dunning, ed., *International Investment*, Penguin, 1970.

10. The Reddaway Report, *op. cit.*

11. J. H. Dunning, 'The Determinants of International Production', *Oxford Economic Papers*, November 1973; and *University of Reading Discussion Papers in International Investment and Business Studies*, No. 4, February 1973.

12. See Table 8.2, Chapter 8 also 'Conditions for success' in *Technological Innovation*, OECD., Paris, 1971.

13. C. P. Kindleberger, *American Business Abroad*, Yale University Press, 1969; E. Mansfield, 'The multinational firm and technological change' in J. H. Dunning, ed., *Economic Analysis and the Multinational Enterprise*, Allen & Unwin, 1973.

14. E. Mansfield, in J. H. Dunning, ed., *op. cit.*; M. Pavitt, in J. H. Dunning, ed., *The Multinational Enterprise*, Allen & Unwin, 1971; J. H. Dunning, 'The role of American investment in the British economy', *Political & Economic Planning*, 1969.

15. J. H. Dunning, *P.E.P.*, 1969, *op. cit.*; J. H. Dunning, US

subsidiaries in Britain and their UK competitors', *Business Ratios*, Autumn 1966.

16. J. H. Dunning, *Business Ratios*, 1966, *op. cit.*

17. M. H. Cooper and J. E. S. Parker, 'Profitability ratios and foreign-owned subsidiaries', *Business Ratios*, Autumn 1967.

18. J. H. Dunning, 'United States industry in Britain'. An Economist Advisory Business Research Study and Financial Times Paper, No. 1, 1973.

19. J. H. Dunning, *P.E.P.*, 1969, *op. cit.* and *Business Ratios*, 1966, *op. cit.*

20. See Chapter 7.

21. J. H. Dunning, 'Multinational Enterprises & International Capital Formation', S.U.E.R.F. Colloquium on Financial and Monetary Aspects of Developing Multinational Enterprises, Nottingham, 10—13 April, 1973.

22. M. H. Cooper and J. E. S. Parker, 'measurement and interpretation of profitability in the pharmaceutical industry', *Oxford Economic Papers*, November 1968.

23. J. H. Dunning, *Business Ratios*, 1966, *op. cit.*

24. S. Hirsch, 'The Multinational corporation: how different are they?' in G. Berstin ed., *The Growth of the large Multinational Enterprise*, Rennes, 1973; J. H. Dunning, *Oxford Economic Papers*, November 1973, *op. cit.* ·

25. H. P. Gray, *The Economics of Business Investment Abroad*, Macmillan, 1972; F. T. Knickerbocker, *op. cit.*

26. J. W. Vaupel, 'Characteristics and motivations of the US corporations which manufacture abroad', Paper presented to meeting of participating members of the Atlantic Institute. Paris, June 1971.

27. J. H. Dunning, *P.E.P.*, *op. cit.*

28. D. T. Brash, *American Investment in Australian Industry*, Australian National University Press, 1966.

29. D. J. C. Forsyth, 'US investment in Scotland', *Praeger Special Studies in International Economics and Development*, 1972.

30. Y. Aharoni, *The Foreign Investment Decision Process*, Harvard University Press, 1966; J. Baranson, *Industrial Technologies for Developing Economies*, Praeger, 1973; V. N. Balasubramanyan, *op. cit.*

31. J. J. Servan Schreiber, *The American Challenge*, Hamish Hamilton, 1968; J. H. Dunning, *P.E.P.*, 1969, *op. cit.*

32. J. H. Dunning, *Oxford Economic Papers*, 1973, *op. cit.*

33. The Reddaway Report, *op. cit.*

34. R. B. Stobaugh, 'The neotechnology account of international trade: The case of petrochemicals', in L. T. Wells, ed., *The Product Life Cycle and International Trade*, Harvard University Press, 1972.

35. R. Vernon, ed., *The Technology Factor in International Trade, op. cit.;* L. T. Wells, ed., *op. cit.*
36. J. H. Dunning, 'European and US Trade Patterns. US Foreign Investment and the Technological Gap', International Economic Association Conference, University of Western Ontario, Toronto, Aug.–Sep. 1969.
37. J. W. Vaupel, *op. cit.*; J. H. Dunning and R. D. Pearce, 'The world's largest companies: a statistical profile', *Business Ratios*, Vol. 3, 1971.
38. J. W. Vaupel, *op. cit.*
39. See Chapter 8.
40. *Gaps in Technology:* Analytical and individual industry reports, OECD, Paris. 1970.
41. *Gaps in Technology, op. cit.*; W. H. Wortzel, *The Multinational Enterprise and the Pharmaceutical Industry*, Basic Books, New York, 1973; C. Layton with C. Harlow and C. De. Houghton, *Ten Innovations; an international study on technological development and the use of qualified scientists and engineers in ten industries*, Allen & Unwin, 1972; A. J. Harman, *The International Computer Industry: Innovation and Comparative Advantage*, Harvard University Press, 1971; G. C. Hufbauer, *Synthetic Materials and the Theory of International Trade*, Duckworth, 1965.
42. J. H. Dunning, ed., *The Multi-national Enterprise*, Allen & Unwin, 1970; S. E. Rolfe and W. Damm, *The Multinational Corporation and the World Economy; Direct Investment in Perspective*, Praeger, 1970.
43. S. H. Hymer, 'The International Operations of National Firms: A Study of Direct Investment', unpublished doctoral dissertation, MIT, 1960; C. P. Kindleberger, *American Business Abroad*, Yale University Press, 1969; J. H. Dunning, 'US foreign investment and the technological gap', fn. 1, p. 383, in C. P. Kindleberger and A. Schonfield, eds., *North American and Western European Economic Policies*, Macmillan, 1971; D. Robertson, 'The multi-national enterprise: trade flows and trade policy', in J. H. Dunning, ed., *International Investment,* Penguin, 1972; E. Mansfield, 'The multinational firm and technological change' in J. H. Dunning, ed., *Economic Analysis and the Multinational Enterprise*, Allen & Unwin, 1973.
44. J. H. Dunning, 'US foreign investment and the technological gap' in C. P. Kindleberger and A. Schonfield, eds, *North American and Western European Economic Policies*, Macmillan, 1971.
45. J. W. Vaupel, *op. cit.*; S. Hirsch, *op. cit.*
46. For a survey see: J. H. Dunning, 'The determinants of international production', *Oxford Economic Papers*, November 1973.

47. E. Mansfield, 'Technical change and the rate of imitation', *Econometrica*, October 1961; C. Freeman, 'The plastics industry: A comparative study of research and innovation', *Nat. Inst. Econ. Soc. Rev.*, November 1963.
48. J. H. Dunning, ed., *The Multinational Enterprise*, Allen & Unwin, 1971.
49. J. H. Dunning, *Business Ratios* 1966, *op. cit.*
50. J. H. Dunning, ed., *The Multinational Enterprise*, Allen & Unwin, 1971.
51. M. H. Cooper and J. E. S. Parker, *Oxford Economic Papers, op. cit.*
52. M. H. Cooper and J. E. S. Parker, *Business Ratios*, Autumn 1967.
53. J. R. Meyer and M. Kuh, *The Investment Decision*, Harvard University Press, 1957; T. Barna, 'Investment and growth policies in British industrial firms, *Nat. Inst. Econ. Soc. Rev.*, Cambridge University Press, 1962; J. E. S. Parker, *Profitability and Growth of British Industrial Firms*, Manchester School, May 1974; R. Marris, 'Incomes policy and the rate of profit in industry', *Proceedings of the Manchester Statistical Society*, December 1964; A. Singh and G. Whittington, *Growth Profitability and Valuation*, Cambridge University Press, 1968; E. Filippi and G. Zanetti, 'Exogenous and endogenous factors in the growth of firms', in R. Marris and A. Wood, eds., *The Corporate Economy*, Macmillan, 1971.
54. E. Filippi and G. Zanetti, *op. cit.*
55. An example is to be found in the Public Accounts Committee of the House of Commons calculations of profitability in the pharmaceutical industry in the UK in 1964. It is clear from these that the investigators completely overlooked the subsidiary structure typical in the industry.
56. J. E. S. Parker, Manchester School, 1964; A. Singh and G. Whittington, Cambridge University Press, 1968, *op. cit.*
57. M. H. Cooper and J. E. S. Parker, *Business Ratios*, Autumn 1967.
58. *Gaps in Technology, op. cit.*
59. C. Freeman, 'The plastics industry: A comparative study of research and innovation', *Nat. Inst. Econ. Soc. Rev.*, November 1963.
60. H. P. Gray, *The Economics of Business Investment Abroad*, Macmillan, 1972.
61. See 1963 report of the Stanford Research Institute referred to in J. H. Dunning, ed., *International Investment*, Penguin, 1972.
62. E. Mansfield, in J. H. Dunning, ed., 1973. *op. cit.*
63. *Gaps in Technology:* Analytical report, *op. cit.*
64. D. Robertson, 'The multi-national enterprise: Trade flows and trade policy', in J. H. Dunning, ed., *International Investment*, Penguin, 1972.

65. J. Enos, *Petroleum Progress and Profits,* Boston MIT Press, 1962; J. Enos, *Invention and Innovation in the Petroleum Refining Industry in the Rate and Direction of Inventive Activity*, Princeton University Press, 1962.

66. J. H. Dunning and C. J. Thomas, *British Industry; Change and Development in the Twentieth Century*, Hutchinson University Library, 1961.

67. R. Stobaugh, 'The international transfer of technology in the establishment of the petrochemical industry in developing countries', United Nations Institute for Training & Research 1971; and 'Where in the world should we put that plant?', *Harvard Business Review*, Jan—Feb. 1969.

68. J. Maisonrouge, *Computers and International Trade in Technology and International Trade*, by R. Cooper, ed., National Academy of Engineering, 1971.

69. J. Maisonrouge, *op. cit.*

70. M. H. Cooper, *Prices and Profits in the Pharmaceutical Industry*, Pergamon Press, 1966; *Gaps in Technology:* Pharmaceuticals, OECD, Paris, 1969.

71. M. H. Cooper and J. E. S. Parker, *Business Ratios*, Autumn 1967; M. H. Cooper and A. J. Culyer, *The Pharmaceutical Industry*, Dun & Bradstreet and Economists Advisory Group, 1973.

72. The lists are published in E. Mansfield, *Industrial Research and Technological Innovation*, Norton, 1968; E. Mansfield, J. Rapoport, J. S. Schnee, S. Wagner and M. Hamburger, *Research and Innovation in the Modern Corporation*, Norton, 1971.

73. E. Mansfield and J. H. Dunning, ed., *Economic Analysis and the Multi-national Enterprise, op. cit.*

74. J. H. Dunning, 'US Foreign Investment and the Technology Gap', in C. P. Kindleberger and A. Schonfield, eds., *North American and Western European Economic Policies*, Macmillan, 1971.

75. J. H. Dunning, *op. cit.*

76. D. Brach, *op. cit.*

77. A. E. Sofarian, *Foreign Ownership of Canadian Industry*, McGraw-Hill, 1966.

78. S. Rolfe and K. Damm, *The Multinational Corporation in the World Economy*, Praeger, 1970.

79. Based on an interpretation of the evidence presented by J. H. Dunning in C. P. Kindleberger and A. Schonfield, eds., *op. cit.*

80. *Gaps in Technology:* Analytical report, *op. cit.*

81. J. H. Dunning in *International Investment*, Penguin, *op. cit.*

82. D. J. C. Forsyth, *US Investment in Scotland, op. cit.*

83. B. Bonin, 'The multinational firm as a vehicle for the international

transmission of technology', in G. Paquet, ed., *The Multinational Firm and the Nation State*, Collier-Macmillan, 1972.
84. T. Ozawa, 'Japan's technology now challenges the West', *Columbia Journal of World Business*, March–April 1972.
85. *Gaps in Technology: Analytical Report.* OECD, Paris, 1970; R. Cooper, *Technology and US Trade: A Historical Review in Technology and International Trade*, National Academy of Engineering, 1971.
86. J. Tilton, *International Diffusion of Technology: The Case of Semiconductors*, Brookings Institution, 1971.

CHAPTER 11 PATENTS

1. Z. Griliches, 'Hybrid corn: an exploration in the economics of technological change', *Econometrica,* 25, Oct. 1967; K. Grossfield, 'National aspects of innovation', in E. M. Hugh-Jones, ed., *Economics of Technical Change*, Blackwell, 1969.
2. K. Arrow, 'Economic welfare and the allocation of resources for invention', in *The Rate and Direction of Inventive Activity*, Princeton University Press, 1962; also reproduced in N. Rosenberg, ed., *The Economics of Technological Change*, Penguin, 1971.
3. K. Boehm, in collaboration with A. Silberston, *The British Patent System, 1, Administration*, Cambridge University Press, 1967.
4. *Ibid.*, p. 93.
5. See A. E. Kahn, in J. P. Miller ed., *Competition Cartels and their Regulations*, North-Holland Publishing Co., 1962.
6. *Ibid.*
7. W. D. Nordhaus, *Invention, Growth and Welfare: a theoretical treatment of technological change*, MIT Press, 1969.
8. P. J. Federico, *Renewal Fees and other Patent Fees in Foreign Countries, Study of Sub-Committee on Patents, Trade Marks and Copyrights*, U.S. Government Printing Office, 1958.
9. F. M. Scherer, *Industrial Market Structure and Economic Performance*, Rand McNally, 1970. Figures estimated from E. Mansfield, *Industrial Research and Technological Progress*, Norton, 1968.
10. Mansfield, *Industrial Research and Technological Innovation.*
11. Scherer, *op. cit.*
12. M. H. Cooper, 'Patents and innovation', in G. Teeling-Smith, ed., *Innovation and the Balance of Payments: the experience in the Pharmaceutical Industry*, Office of Health Economics, 1967.
13. See also F. M. Scherer, 'Firm size, market structure, opportunity and output of patented inventions', *American Economic Review*, 1965.

14. H. Steele, 'Monopoly and competition in the ethical drugs market', *Journal of Law and Economics*, October 1962, and 'Patent restrictions and price competition in the ethical drugs industry', *Journal of Industrial Economics*, July 1964.
15. J. Martyn, *Literature Searching by Research Scientists*, ASLIB, 1964.
16. J. Langrish, M. Gibbons, W. G. Evans and F. R. Jevons, *Wealth from Knowledge*, Macmillan, 1972.
17. J. Schmookler, *Invention and Economic Growth*, Harvard University Press, 1966.
18. *Ibid.*
19. See Scherer, Rand McNally, 1970.
20. Langrish *et al., op. cit.*
21. *The International Convention, further revising the Paris Convention for the Protection of Industrial Property, of the 20th March 1883*, Cmnd 4431, HMSO, Sept. 1970.
22. *Ibid.*
23. E. Penrose, *The Economics of the International Patent System*, Johns Hopkins Press, 1951.
24. See A. Hope, 'Office moves for the European patent', *New Scientist*, 18 May 1972.
25. *Patents in the Common Market, Preliminary Draft of the Convention for the European Community Patent*, HMSO, 1972.
26. *Renewal Fees and other Patents Fees in Foreign Countries, Study of Sub-committee on Patents, Trademarks and Copyrights*, U.S. Government Printing Office, 1958.
27. K. Boehm, *The British Patent System*, Cambridge University Press, 1967.
28. See, for example, the *Final Report of the Departmental Committee on the Patents and Designs Acts*. Cmnd 7206, HMSO, 1947, and the Banks committee report, Cmnd 4407, HMSO, 1970.
29. Langrish *et al., op. cit.*
30. Scherer, *Industrial Market Structure and Economic Performance*.
31. J. Jewkes, D. Sawers and R. Stillerman, *The Sources of Invention*, 2nd edn., Macmillan, 1969.

Index

Advanced passenger train, 55
Advertising, 8
Agriculture, 50, 102
Aid programmes, 125
Aircraft aerospace, 53, 58, 72, 73, 77,
    130, 146, 147, 148, 172
American companies, 132, 133, 140,
    141, 142, 143, 144, 151, 154,
    155, 159, 168, 174, 177, 178,
    179, 180, 181, 182, 191, 192,
    209, 210, 211, 212, 213 and
    Appendix 2
  in Europe, 132, 135, 136, 147, 182,
    205
Atomic energy, 22, 24, 102, 112
  bomb, 43, 45

Belgium, 142, 143, 154, 155, 174, 177
Brewing, 49, 108, 113, 146
Building, 8

Canada, 142, 143, 146, 151, 154, 155,
    174, 178
Carruthers, 24
Chain saw, 112
Chemicals, 24, 27, 47, 52, 54, 58, 60,
    62, 66, 67, 76, 77, 78, 83, 86,
    90, 130, 132, 147, 204, 209,
    212
City Business Library, Moorgate, 145,
    146
Census of Population, 77
Census of Production, 51
Coal, 49, 59, 73, 108, 213
Cockerell, C., 25
Competition, 2, 6, 7, 8, 9, 51
  Environment, 6–18, 74
  Innovative competition, 8, 9, 10, 12,
    18, 54, 62, 63, 205
  Market form, 62–78
  Perfect, 7, 63
  Phases of, 10, 11, 12, 13, 14, 16
  Strength of, 1
  Workable, 9
Computers, 3, 8, 53, 102, 191, 210
Concorde, 52, 55, 99
Conglomerates, 6
Contract research, 46, 79

Coupling, 4, 19, 21, 22
Cumulative synthesis, 19, 20

Developing countries or less developed
    countries (LDC), 186–7
Development, 39, 40, 41, 42, 45, 50,
    86, 89, 91, 92
  Gaps, 101, 179
  Stages of 95, *See also* R & D
Diamond Japan Business Directory, 145,
    146
Diesel locomotives, 121–3
Differentiation, 7, 8, 11, 53, 77, 131,
    132
Diffusion, 4, 11, 16, 26, 99–123
  intra-firm, 4, 120–3
    defined, 99, 185
  and the multinational enterprise,
    Ch. 7–10
Direct foreign investment, 168, 172,
    178, 188
Diversification, 6, 17, 18, 53, 57,
    61–62, 72, 79, 190
  conglomerates, 6
du Pont, 25, 29

E.E.C., 126
Electrical engineering, 77, 86, 130, 132,
    147, 148
Electronics, 8, 53, 54, 66, 73, 86, 90,
    130, 146, 147, 148, 191
Exporting, 133
Exports, 2, 129, 134, 149, 168, 178,
    213, 214
Extel-Nomura Statistical Cards of
    Japanese companies, 145
Extel Statistical Services, 145, 146

Fleming, Sir Alexander, 24
Food, 53, 54, 73, 132, 146
Footwear, 8, 53, 72, 73
Fork-lift truck, 109, 110
Fortune (magazine), 47, 50, 66, 126,
    140, 143, 144, 145, 146, 151,
    169, 173
France, 142, 143, 154, 155, 161, 163,
    172, 174
Furniture, 8, 53, 72, 73

Germany, 142, 143, 154, 155, 161, 163, 174, 178, 227, and Appendix 2
Government research, 5

Hybrid corn, 116
Hymer, S., 124

Innovation, 4, 7, 8, 9, 19, Ch. 4, 81, 99, 100, 101, 102, Ch. 12
  and the multinational enterprise, Ch. 7–10
  and the size of companies, 56–61
Interdependence, 128, 196, 197
Interrelatedness, 110, 111
Invention, 4, 19–38, 39, 41, 42, 43, 50, 57, 71, 124
  defined, 4, 19
  the individual inventor defined, 28
Iron and steel, 12, 49, 56, 59, 60, 73, 108, 113, 130, 172, 212
Italy, 142, 143, 154, 155, 174, 203

Jane's Major Companies of Europe, 145, 146
Japan, 141, 142, 143, 145, 154, 155, 160, 162, 163, 165–9, 170, 172, 174, 180, 191, 192, 257

Kindleberger, C. P., 124

Lead time, 17, 53
Learning by doing, 1
Licences and licensing, 133, 141, 178, 208, 213, 215, 223, 241, 245
Location, *See* Multinational Companies Ch. 7–10

Machine tools, 66, 73, 76, 108, 114–16
Management, 1, 2, 44, 49, 50, 51, 52, 64, 67, 75, 81–98, 101, 105, 119–20
Market capture, 129, 130–4, 167–8, 170, 172, 173
  escape and capture mechanisms, 177–84
Mature economies, 168, 176–84, 185
Mature products, 11, 12, 13, 16, 135, 186
M-form, 6, 131
Monopoly, 7, 12, 13, 40, 49, 62, 63, 64, 68, 69, 70, 71, 72, 74, 75, 225, 226, 231
Moodies, 47, 145, 146, 211

Motor vehicles, 58, 72, 73, 130, 132, 147, 148, 180, 191, 210
Multinational companies, 4, 6, 7, 11, 18, 40, 72, 99, Ch. 7–10
  Classification, 149–52, Appendix 2
  MCE, 126
  MOE, 126
  MPE, 125
  MTE, 125

Nationality of companies, defined, 140
Netherlands, 142, 143, 151, 154, 155, 174, 178, Appendix 2
Non-price rivalry, 8, 10, 65, 177
North Sea oil, 135–6
Nylon, 24, 238

Obsolescence
  technical, 12, 15, 16
  economic, 12, 16, 17
O.E.C.D., 130
Oligopoly, 7, 65, 66, 68, 69, 70, 71, 72, 79, 183
Organisational slack, 1

Package, the direct investment, Ch. 10
Patents, 17, 19, 24, 27, 29, 31, 32, 33, 34, 40, 49, 50, 54, 60, 62, 63, 66, 67, 105, 108, 183, Ch. 11
  International, 131, 136–8, 141, 143, 239–44, 254
Petro-chemicals, 190
Petroleum & petroleum refining, 43, 50, 54, 56, 58, 59, 60, 62, 90, 130, 135, 136, 147, 148, 209, 212, 238
Pharmaceuticals, 8, 12, 47, 52, 53, 58, 62, 67, 73, 90, 91, 92, 102, 130, 132, 146, 172, 191, 210
Photography, 45
Pilkington, A., 24, 133, 211
Plastics, 8, 15, 73, 102, 182, 191, 209
Portfolio investment, 188
Pricing, 8, 9, 13, 14, 15, 39, 64, 65, 167, 177
  average cost, 13, 14
  cost plus, 13, 14
  M.C., 13, 14
  intercompany, 127
Product-champion, 30, 37, 83, 85
Product cycle, 9, 10, 11, 12, 13, 14, 16, 18, 129, 130, 132, 167, 190, 193, 194–5

QSE, 144, 147
Queen's Award for Industry, 48, 56, 82, 88

R & D, 5, 8, 10, 17, 21, 22, 25, 26, 28, 45, 46, 50−72, 76, 77, 78, 79, 81, 85, 86−94
   mature economies, 177−84
   and the multinational enterprise, Ch. 7−10
   research exchange rate, 147−8
   research intensity defined, 146−9, Appendix 1
   and patents, Ch. 11
Railroad, 49, 108, 113
Risk, 39, 40, 79, 81, 111, 131
   Market risk, 46, 48−9, 54, 56
   Risk-shifting, 57, 205
   Technical risk, 45−7, 51, 52−4, 56
Robinson Crusoe, 1, 2

Scale economies, 1, 6, 12, 14, 59, 60, 73, 127, 128, 129
   external, 178
   M.E.S., 128
Schmookler, J., 31, 32, 33, 34, 35, 37
Schumpeter, J., 19
Scientific instruments, 58, 72, 73, 83, 147, 148, 191
Shipbuilding, 72, 73, 210
Silicones, 22, 24
SITC, 148, Appendix 1
Size Bias, 169−70
Slippage factor, 47
Small companies, 70, 72, 78, 117
Space research, 55
Specialisation, 1, 2, 101, 102
   Intra-company, 127, 128, 129
Spin off, 55
Stock Exchange Year books, 145, 146
Subsidiaries, Ch. 7−10

List of properties, 189−90
Sweden, 142, 143, 154, 155, 174, 178
Switzerland, 142, 143, 144, 154, 155, 174, 178

Tariffs, 127, 129, 130, 131, 133, 134, 136, 138, 150, 172, 173
Technological change, 1, 2, 4, 8, 9, 10, 17, 21, 64, 100, 101, 112
   Embodied, 1, 2
   Environment, 54−6, 76
   Disembodied, 1
   Push & pull, 10, 54−6, 59, 76, 77, 79
   and the multinational enterprise, Ch. 7−10
   & patents, Ch. 11
Technological multiplier, 3, 188, 215
Technology
   building on technology, 19, 22, 23, 24, 25, 34, 36, 37, 256
   defined, 23, 99
   and the multinational enterprise, Ch. 7
   ranking, 143
   gaps, 101, 207, 213, 214
Textiles, 72, 73, 75, 76, 102, 130
Thalidomide, 111
The Times 1000, 145
Time/cost trade off, 44, 68, 71, 77, 89, 93−8
Tobacco, 130, 191
Transistors, 24, Appendix 1

UK, 142, 143, 154, 155, 161, 163, 172, 174, 177, 178

Valuation ratio, 57

Wankel, 30
   engine, 110, 111
Who Owns Whom, 145